Of No ECCENTRIC WHIM

Of No ECCENTRIC WHIM

*A Memoir About
California Dreamin'*

Cary B. Lerman

Of No Eccentric Whim: California Dreamin' by Cary B. Lerman
Published by Night Vision Press

Copyright © 2021 by Cary B. Lerman

All rights reserved. No part of this publication may be reproduced, distributed, or transmitted in any form or by any means, including photocopying, recording, or other electronic or mechanical methods, without the prior written permission of the publisher, except in the case of brief quotations embodied in critical reviews and certain other noncommercial uses permitted by copyright law

Printed in the United States of America

Preassigned Control Number (PCN) 9781737768500.
Library of Congress Control Number: 2021920041

Cary B. Lerman
Of No Eccentric Whim: California Dreamin'

Cover jacket and interior design by Colleen Sheehan

ISBN 978-1-7377685-0-0 (hardcover)
ISBN: 978-1-7377685-1-7 (ebook)

First Edition

10 9 8 7 6 5 4 3 2 1

Contents

Preface xi

1. Beginnings 1
2. Albany Park 7
3. A Milkman's Story 17
4. There Must Be a Horse 23
5. The Ant Farm 33
6. The Car 39
7. Venturing Out 43
8. Not Strictly By the Book 51
9. The Catch 57
10. Use Your Sechel 61
11. Not My Favorite Beach 67
12. California Dreamin' 71
13. Bar Mitzvah 79
14. Role Models 83
15. Not in Kansas Anymore 89
16. The Alchemist 97
17. A Lawyer's Office 101
18. There's Something About Mary 105
19. Fixing it? 111
20. The Luckiest Kid in the World 115
21. Leaving Lane Tech 119
22. Snyder Sanctum 123
23. Life Classes 131
24. The Outer Circle 137

25. Second Year...............................143
26. Fakin' It...................................149
27. Leaving the Fog Behind................157
28. Not My Finest Hour.....................163
29. Taking Myself Seriously................167
30. Camp Winadu............................177
31. Who's That Girl?.........................187
32. A Blur of Bliss............................193
33. An Offer I Can Refuse.................. 203
34. Meeting the Families...................211
35. It Never Rains in Southern California.....229
36. The Dorm Is My Shelter...............239
37. Orientation Day.........................243
38. What Was I Missing?...................251
39. The Draft and the Dentist.............259
40. You Don't Need a Weatherman.........263
41. Pink Slips.................................271
42. Finding Wisdom in Unexpected Places... 277
43. A Perfect Diamond.....................283
44. A Summer in Beverly Hills............287
45. A Student Becomes an Advocate........293
46. The Wilhelm Wundt Affair............303
47. Keep on Moving Forward............. 307
48. Decision Time...........................311
49. A Surprise at Graduation..............319
50. The Wedding............................325

Postscript.......................................333

FOR HALLIE

"My mother thanks you, my father thanks you. My sister thanks you. And I thank you."

Yankee Doodle Dandy (1942)

"The past is never dead. It's not even past."
WILLIAM FAULKNER

"Memory is the diary we all carry about with us."
OSCAR WILDE

Preface

It started in college but has continued throughout my life. I have been drawn not just to difficult questions, but to those that can have no definitive answers. Is there such a thing as fate or is it all cosmic chance? How did I arrive on August 8, 1972, standing next to my car with my new wife, Hallie, about to start a new life in Washington D.C. in a year-long attorney position with the Department of Transportation? Was it the result of a set of unpredictable circumstances, which could have gone in a totally different direction but for events outside of my control? I think of the first time I saw Hallie, which was at a lecture at the University of Illinois in November 1968. What if the lecturer for that evening, Yitzhak Leor, from the Israel Consulate in Chicago, had declined the invitation or had asked for another date to speak? What if I had never gone to hear his talk? Or, if in December 1968, I had brought my Chevy in for repair at Sears Roebuck on a different day and never met Hallie coming out of a bookstore? Or if the mechanic had talked to me for an additional five minutes, causing her to leave the bookstore before I got there? Or if, in February 1969, I never went to the Illini Union when she just happened to be buying chocolate? Would I still have married her? Would I have married someone else, and, if so, what if that person had strong ties to Chicago? And, if that someone else had gone to Los Angeles with me from the beginning in September 1969, when I started law school, would I have done as well as I did if she were in constant need of my time, energy and attention? Would this someone else have insisted that I get my first job in Chicago rather than in D.C.? Was I standing on the curb on Belmeade Drive in Champaign on August 8, 1972, because of the chance alignment of random events? Quite possibly. And, if so, is that answer comforting or unnerving? Was the song "If" sung at my wedding a metaphor for something larger, more significant than the musings of newlyweds?

I think of the hidden ripples that have affected my life. I go back to November 21, 1968, when Yitzhak Leor came to the University of Illinois for his talk on Israel. I can picture Yitzhak talking to his supervisor weeks earlier. Chicago was his first overseas post. He was just given the assignment to go to Champaign-Urbana to talk with a group of undergraduates about Israel. "How do I get there?" he might have asked. "Just take the morning Illinois Central train on November 21, about a three-hour trip, and return the next day." I imagine Yitzhak slumping his shoulders forward, first suggesting someone else, then offering a different date, and finally agreeing but dreading having to spend two days traveling to a remote campus for an hour-long talk to a group of students. This assignment was not prestigious or high on his list. There were many eminent universities in the Chicago area. Why the University of Illinois? But he eventually agreed, the weather cooperated with a mean temperature of 35 degrees and no precipitation, the event was heavily advertised in the *Daily Illini*, and it drew a good crowd – one that included two strangers, Hallie Tager and Cary Lerman, who just happened to notice one another across the room. But for his willingness to speak on that night, I might never have seen, then dated and ultimately married Hallie. Without going to the speech, I still would have seen Hallie on December 3, 1968, in front of a bookstore, but, without the fleeting awareness of seeing me at the lecture, she would not have stopped to talk with me. There would have been no connection. No dating. No relationship. No wedding. No children. No family. At least, not the family I have today. No life as I know it today. I would not be the person I am molded by the specific circumstances of my life if Yitzhak Leor had not given that talk on November 21.

Does Yitzhak have any inkling of the personal ripple effect his appearance had on my life? On Hallie's life? On the lives of others? Or course not. He is as unaware of the ripples he left behind as each of us is about the effects we have unwittingly had on the lives of others. He went on to have a successful career in Israel's Foreign Affairs Ministry and eventually became the Israeli Ambassador to Switzerland and to Japan. He probably cannot even recall speaking at the University of Illinois. Yet on that forgettable night in November, he set in motion for me a series of lurches and stops, swerves and darts, acts and reactions from one encounter to another, gaining new experiences that thrust me forward to the next set of unpredictable circumstances. Did he add just one more random, cosmically-unimportant ripple to the confluence of prior, *ad infinitum* contingent series of causes and effects? Or was his ripple part of a greater plan, conceived by a powerful stone thrower, a prescient force that dropped the first stone, producing the seemingly unwitting ripples that have shaped my life? I choose to believe I walk in the ripples of the first stone thrower.

Chapter 1

BEGINNINGS

I was born lucky. It was January 26, 1948, a clear, dry cold day that dipped to 9 degrees, at Walter Reese Hospital on the South Side of Chicago in a neighborhood called South Lawndale. Except for a quick trip back to the hospital to treat bronchitis, I was a healthy and by all accounts an adored baby. My parents were warm, loving, constant supports in my life.

Following tradition, I was given both a secular name and a Hebrew name. I was named Cary Bruce because my mother needed names with the initials C and B to mimic the name of her grandfather, whom I never met. His name was Chaim Baruch, which means "blessed life." My mother was afraid that if she named me Charles, people would call me "Charlie." She associated the name "Charlie" with the expression "good time Charlie," and she had more serious aspirations for me. So I became Cary, which I believe was inspired by Cary Grant, then a leading actor. Since Cary Grant's birth name was Archibald Leach, I have been forever indebted to the Paramount Pictures executives who made him change his first name to Cary. I have no idea where Bruce came from, but, since my mom needed a name starting with a "B," it was a lot better than Brutus. My Hebrew name was the same as my great grandfather's, and I became Chaim Baruch. I am sure the name was my mother's prayer that I might enjoy a blessed life.

Louis Lerman, my father, was also lucky. Why? Because my mom agreed to marry him. He adored her his whole life. He was born in Brooklyn, never graduated high school, and moved with his entire family to Chicago. He had an older brother and two older sisters, and none of them graduated high school. After a small number of dates, he married my mother on November 5, 1942, just months after he reported for active duty in the United States Army Air Corps on September 5. He was on leave, and they got married on the spur of the moment. He was soon off to fight for Uncle Sam against the Japanese, and was stationed for almost two years during World War II in New Guinea as a tank turret repairman. (A vague rumor, never talked about and never confirmed, would occasionally swirl around our family that, while in Australia during the war, my father had an affair with a teacher. A friend once told me he saw my identical twin in Paris. I never learned if it were a doppelgänger or an unknown half-brother with an Australian accent!)

My mother did not think of herself as lucky. Shirley Shapiro was a vivacious beauty who turned my father's head upon first meeting him, just as she did so many others. Smart, fun-loving, headstrong, an irrepressible flirt and very popular, she had dreams. She often saw herself as a lounge singer, offering irresistible, romantic ballads to a crowd begging her never to stop. She never said so, but I always thought she dreamed of herself as a Susie Diamond sort of figure (played by Michelle Pfeiffer), the center of attention, sashaying along the top of a piano, as in the movie *The Fabulous Baker Brothers*. She graduated high school but that was as far as she went with formal schooling. Her future was shaped by the war and her marriage.

Like so many others who saw uncertainty and felt anxiety in 1942, she agreed to marry my father against the backdrop of the war. She was swept up in the fervor of the times, and, she would later say, "settled," with all the dismal connotations of the word, for an ill-timed, ill-conceived marriage to a man who was darn good-looking and decent, but not her Lancelot. She wanted Lancelot. She never achieved her dreams.

After the war, my father returned without an education, without money, without skills and without direction. He had a natural, untrained ability as a graphic artist, and he talked about taking advantage of the GI Bill of Rights to go back to school. But he had a family to support, including my sister, Barbara, who had been conceived when he was home on leave from training. When he returned from the war, Barbara pointed at him and asked, "Who that man?" He went into business with my mother's father, Louis Shapiro, selling cameras and developing film. It was a good time to enter the photography field. They could have made a killing. There was one problem: they knew nothing about running a business. Despite the potential, there could never be a good time to go into partnership with my grandfather: a dreamer, a Communist sympathizer, a poet (or so he thought), a dancer, and a lover of life – but not work. Bohemian to the core, romanticist and idealist all describe him. Businessman does not. I cannot think of a more powerful oxymoron than "my grandfather, the businessman." And, of course, the business soon failed.

My father was a gambler. He loved to gamble. He gambled on the outcome of baseball, basketball, and football games. He gambled at the horse races. He played poker. One day he came home from work late. My mother: "Lou, where's your paycheck? You haven't given it to me." Lou: "I don't have it." "What do you mean, you don't have it?" "I lost it at the track, but I will make it up to you next week." As reported to us so many times by family members, my mom said, "Damn straight you will. If you ever lose your paycheck by gambling again, don't bother coming home. I won't let you in." He knew she meant it, and it never happened again. Instead, each week, he handed his paycheck over to her, and she gave him an allowance, which he used for cigarettes and his horse racing bets. We learned early that gambling was not an acceptable avocation at the Lerman household. To this day, it holds no allure for me, and Las Vegas is that much poorer for it.

When I was born, South Lawndale was already undergoing a "change" (my parents' euphemism for the "wrong" people moving in) from a predominantly Jewish neighborhood to a Black neighborhood. My parents did what most of the Jews did: they moved. They were not seeking a diverse neighborhood. In fact, the more homogenous the better, so long as that homogeneity was Jewish. So we moved to a third floor walkup apartment on Wabansia and Spaulding. On the floor below, my father's brother, Al, moved in with his wife, Norma, and their three kids, my first cousins, Bruce, Cheryl, and Paula.

I have only a few memories from that early period. My elementary school was Harriet Beecher Stowe, only a short walk from my apartment. I did not learn anything about the author, Harriet Beecher Stowe, whose epic novel *Uncle Tom's Cabin* helped to fuel the abolitionist movement. But I did learn that the school's mascot was a wolf, a magnificent, misunderstood animal, which survives on the seemingly inconsistent traits of social cohesion and aloofness. I recall walking down Wabansia to the school by myself, the deep crush I had on Peggy Gerber in kindergarten, and my best friend Melvin (whom my parents called, with no offense intended, by the now cringe-worthy moniker, "my little colored friend"), and trick or treating with my sister and parents. It was a relatively carefree early childhood.

When I was six, my parents decided it was time for me to learn an instrument. My mother selected the accordion, and signed me up for a package that consisted of a set number of lessons and, the decisive incentive, a record. Why the accordion? Lawrence Welk is to blame.

His show began to air on TV in 1951, and he popularized the instrument. Accordions were expensive, so my parents rented a child-sized one. My father took me to all the lessons, and my favorite part was when we would stop at a bakery afterwards, and he would buy me cookies. I was no child prodigy, resisted practice like any kid, and struggled with the instrument, which was clumsy in my small hands. I finished the set course, and, as promised, I cut a record. I still recall my aunts, uncles, cousins, and everyone gathering around the phonograph player to listen to my recording. I then heard a tinny, squeaking voice say, "My name is Cary Lerman. I am six years old. This is my first piece." The adults burst into uproarious laughter. I can still hear their voices, chortling "it is his first piece." I had no idea what was so funny, but I was embarrassed. I wanted to cry, but I held it in. There was no way I was going to continue with lessons. My musical career ended with the laughter of others.

I also remember the jumps. There was the nearby construction site where a new apartment building was being erected. It was an open pit. No fences, no ropes. Nothing to stop curious kids from jumping from the concrete retaining wall into the open space to explore the intricacies of rebar, pipes, broken concrete and dirt. If anything defined what it was to be an attractive nuisance, this was it. I was no more than seven when I went with my friends to this deliciously attractive mountain of rubble. I jumped from the retaining wall into the pit below, tripping and cutting my wrist on a broken, ceramic pipe. The blood kept gushing out as I found my way home and sought maternal comfort. I got maternal care, but not comfort: my mother shrieked, calling for my father to get us to the hospital. Five stitches later, and with a bandage that looked as if it were hiding a reattached hand, I was cured of any interest in construction sites.

But I was not done with my jumping. I vividly recall standing on the wall adjoining the steps to our apartment building and looking down on my younger first cousin, Bruce Lerman, then only five, and without giving it a thought, I jumped on him. He crumbled and moments later came up with a broken collar bone. The whole neighborhood came to see what was causing the uproar, and I sheepishly stood by, feeling as guilty as I should have felt. The odd thing is that to this day I do not recall anyone yelling at me, blaming me or punishing me. They did not have to. I knew I had done wrong, and my days of jumping were over.

Chapter 2

ALBANY PARK

When our neighborhood started to change again, we, of course, moved. My mother did not want my sister to attend the local high school serving the Wabansia neighborhood, and Albany Park on the Northwest side of Chicago seemed just right. Albany Park was everything an eight and a half year old could dream of – plenty of friends, an excellent public school only a block away, neighbors who knew and looked out for one another, fireflies to catch and mosquitos to kill in the summer, and the best hot dogs at Maury's Hot Dogs on Lawrence Avenue. The hot dogs were wrapped in paper along with hot French fries, which made the hot dog buns extra steamy and flavorful. And just around our corner, there was a local grocery store that sold every brand of candy and ice cream a kid could want.

By 1930, almost 50 percent of the 50,000 people living in Albany Park was Jewish, and by the time we arrived in 1956, it seemed as if the whole neighborhood were Jewish. Even the non-Jews were Jewish, if you know what I mean. It was a largely working-class neighborhood. When we moved in, the "affluent" Jews were also on the move, leaving Albany Park for the suburbs of Skokie and Lincolnwood. Still, it was not easy to land an apartment there. This was the mid-1950s, and apartments were in short supply. It was a seller's (or lessor's) market. My parents complied with the standard practice by paying a one-time "fee" to the owners of the building for the privilege of renting the space and agreeing to add improvements, such as tiling the entry way.

Our new apartment building, at 5014 N. Harding Avenue, was yellow-bricked with two apartments on each floor; it felt luxurious. Each apartment ran the full length of the building, front to back. One of the ground floor apartments was occupied by the Movers, who owned the building. To me, they were rich: they had to be rich to own such a large apartment building. Their wealth was confirmed to me when I learned that their car had power steering.

The apartment itself was (again) on the third floor, and had two small bedrooms, one very small bathroom, living and dining rooms and a kitchen, all in about 900 square feet. Although she was thirteen and I was nine, Barbara grudgingly shared a bedroom with me. The room had one window – but what a window it was. We had a wonderful fire escape right outside. On humid Chicago nights, which meant almost every night during the summer, there was even a slight breeze. For a short time, my mother's mother came to live with us, and I was moved to the pullout couch in the dining room so that she could share the bedroom with my sister. The dining room was basically a pass through from the living room, bathroom and my parent's bedroom to the kitchen, but I learned to sleep soundly. I don't think my grandmother quite appreciated the fire escape in the same way I did. When my folks had accumulated a few dollars, they splurged and bought an air conditioner. They put it in the window in their bedroom and on oppressive summer nights the four of us would just stand there, seeking refuge from the heat. Eventually, the fronts of our bodies were cold while our backs continued to perspire.

Our household was fairly harmonious, with the exception of verbal clashes between my mother and father, almost always about money – or the lack of it. These fights were invariably initiated by my mother, who complained about not having a house, a washer and dryer, better clothes, exciting vacations, or more options in life. She had a sharp tongue and would say things that must have wounded his masculine pride, as they questioned whether he was fulfilling his responsibility to provide for his family in the way she wanted. My father had little to say, which, in retrospect, was probably the best response, as any retort would have escalated the fight. F. Scott Fitzgerald wrote that "Family quarrels are bitter things. They don't go according to any rules. They're not like aches or wounds, they're more like splits in the skin that won't heal because there's not enough material." I took this lesson to heart and have tried to avoid, albeit not always successfully, the proverbially knockdown, drag-down verbal brawl within the family.

I have no memory of Barbara ever being reprimanded, but I would frequently not do what I was told, leading to predicable discipline, which was firm but never mean. There would be four phases to the discipline, which took on the repetitiveness of a ritual. The first phase would invariably be initiated by my mother. She was blessed with great tonsils, and she would yell. But one gets accustomed to most adversity, and I eventually developed a survivor's tolerance to her screaming. She would then move to the second phase. "Lou, he's not listening to me, and he is fresh. Do something." My father would yell at me, making sure that my mother heard his displeasure, which was not difficult in the small space. I was never sure if he were truly angry with me or if he just knew that he had better do as he was instructed by the true chief of the household. If I were in a contrary mood, I would yell back. Then came phase three. My father would give me a whack on the tukhus, the Yiddish word for butt. It hurt, but not physically. My ego was so wounded that I would start to cry, run into my room and slam the door. My bawling was loud enough that it could be heard throughout the apartment. Phase four restored emotional balance to the household. My dad would enter, not say a word, but give me a half dollar. It was a peace offering. I regretted my insolence, knew there were consequences for my behavior, but my honor was intact.

There is no bliss greater than a languid, culinary respite, says the practiced Epicurean. They would have boycotted our family meals. Yes, we always had them together at 5:00 pm, and certainly no later than 5:30 pm. The food was always plentiful, if basic. There were no food fights and no political arguments. My mother was the cook and my sister the dishwasher and dryer. My dad and I were the consumers. The division of labor was strictly patriarchal. But this was no different than other homes, and it was in keeping with the tradition of the times. Dinners consisted of a lot of beef or chicken – hamburgers with onions mixed in, meatloaf with a hard-boiled egg inside, lamb chops, fried chicken livers, spaghetti with Bolognese sauce, the occasional skirt steak broiled in our oven to a medium-grade leather, broiled chicken with a minimum of seasoning. Never any fish. Vegetables were boiled. It didn't matter what kind; they were boiled until they were as soft and droopy as a French model's eye lids. And we always had a starch. It ranged from mashed to baked potatoes or rice, usually from an Uncle Ben's box. Oh yes, there was also the obligatory green salad, which I mainly moved around my plate to give the appearance of it having been eaten.

Thursday nights, however, were different. Every Thursday after work my mother went to the beauty shop. She was not going to stand over a stove and risk rearranging her newly-paid for coiffeur with steam from hot pots. We alternated by week. It would be Kentucky Fried Chicken or Chop Suey. If it were Thursday, we knew it was one or the other. It was then that I learned to hone my eating skills. It was a matter of survival and outright, fierce competition with my sister. The bucket of fried chicken had white and dark meat, but I wanted only the breast and wings. But so did my sister. And there was a limited number of them. I perfected the art of the quick takedown. I was able to swallow a piece of chicken and reach into the bucket for the next piece faster than anyone could even identify which piece of chicken I was eating. My sister would yell about the unfairness but that only encouraged me. I learned to eat fast – really fast. I wasn't always sure what I was eating, but at least I was getting to it first and getting seconds. Sophia Loren said that "Spaghetti can be eaten most successfully if you inhale it like a vacuum cleaner." I applied this valuable insight to other foods. I let my Thursday night technique slop over to dinners on other evenings. I would invariably be finished with an empty plate, except for scattered pieces of salad, while my mom and dad were leisurely finishing, and my sister was fuming. She would protest, "Make him slow down," but I never did. If there had been room at my table for Oscar Wilde or Winston Churchill, each of whom appreciated how to truly enjoy the consumption of the finest fare, they would have left immediately and condemned me to Gehenna as soon as they saw me reach for that first piece of chicken.

In Korean culture, a traditional full breakfast is the preferred way to start the day, and it is a feast, including rice, *jiggae* (stew soup) or some other soup, such as *miyeok* (seaweed) soup, *kongnamul guk* (bean sprout soup) or *seogogi mu guk* (beef radish soup), some type of meat and a full array of *banchan* (small side dishes). This could include *galbi* (grilled short ribs), *kongnamul bab* (bean sprout rice), *oi naengguk* (cold cucumber soup), *moo saengchae* (spicy kimchi), *kaktugi* (radish kimchi), *saengseon jolim* (stewed fish), kelp, salted greens, mushrooms, bean sprouts, anchovies, seafood salad, and, to ensure a healthy meal and guarantee that no one will leave the table hungry, they might throw in a vegetable omelet, red and black beans, tofu with soy sauce, Korean cole slaw and fruit. But that was not the start of the day at 5014 N. Harding. To the annoyance of my sister, my mother made sure that each morning I ate my favorite breakfast before going to school. For years, each weekday, without exception, even when she was rushing to get to work, my mother made sure that I had a power breakfast of Aunt Jemima pancakes or waffles, dripping with Log Cabin syrup. Chocolate milk made with Bosco syrup was the everyday drink for me. I started each day loaded with carbohydrates and sugars. My body did not seem to mind. Back then, I was allergic to calories.

While we did not belong to a synagogue until my bar mitzvah, we were Jewish and decidedly so. We did not keep kosher and, in fact, we brought into our house shrimp and lobster (although for some reason, no crab) and we fought over barbequed pork ribs, a delicacy. Everyone has their own red line. In our house, I knew it was ham. No ham in our fridge. Then, one night I learned about an even brighter red line. We were having dinner in our kitchen (we never ate a meal in our dining room), and my mother was serving a new dish. My father was enjoying it with vigor. "Shirl, what is this dish? It's terrific." "It's called beef Stroganoff," my mother answered with a touch of pride in her voice. She seldom made something new. "What's in it?" he asked. "Oh, sirloin steak, spices, sour cream." There was a loud crash of utensils hitting the table top, and a loud voice shouted in disbelief, "What, you mixed meat with milk? How could you? Don't you ever, ever do that again!" That was my lesson in the laws of Kashrut, prohibiting "cooking the kid in the mother's milk," and I never forgot it or violated it. My father had made sure that the Temple (our home) would not be defiled by mixing milk and meat. Pork ribs and shrimp were fine. I learned early that each person has his inviolate principle, his own red line. It is real, it matters, and it must be respected.

My father's older brother Al and his family followed us by moving from their apartment on Wabansia to Albany Park. They took an apartment in a building two down from us on the same side of the street. Like my father, Al never finished high school. He worked as a bartender and had a rough edge. Although he talked tough, he was protective of his family and warm toward me. His wife, Norma, was close to my mom. My abiding memory of Norma was her evident missing front tooth. I never understood why she did not have it replaced. Maybe she thought of it as a kind of signature. It certainly gave her a unique look.

Rounding out my father's family were his sisters Celia and Marion, both natural strawberry blondes. Aunt Cele was a very kind, hard-working woman who, together with her husband, Ben, owned an apartment building in West Rogers Park. It was a small three-story walk-up with only one apartment on each floor, but they were large three bedroom, two bathroom homes. She was the only person on my father's side who owned property. She never had any children, but, insofar as the Lerman extended family was concerned, her place was the center for most family get-togethers. We celebrated the high holidays of Rosh Hashanah and Yom Kippur – I did not go to school (our elementary school closed on the high holidays for want of students and teachers) and my father did not go to work, but none of us went to synagogue. Instead, we watched television. Starting at eight or nine years old, I was glued to a new television series called *The Mickey Mouse Club*, and instantly fell in love with Karen Pendleton, one of the original club Mouseketeers. Instead of wearing a kippa on the High Holidays, I wore a Mickey Mouse hat, complete with ears.

Passover was different. Passovers were always at Aunt Cele's place. She kept kosher and prided herself on a spotless house that was cleaner than many hospital operating rooms. One could have eaten from the floor with the same assurance of sanitation as the table. Because she worked, we always celebrated the Passover Seder on a Saturday night. It did not matter what the Hebrew calendar said; in our family, the first night of Passover was Saturday. Period. In attendance were my paternal grandfather, Jacob; Aunt Cele; Uncle Ben; Uncle Al and Aunt Norma; their three kids, Bruce, Cheryl, and Paula; and Aunt Marion, then unmarried. And my mom and dad, me, and Barbara. In all, thirteen of us. Grandfather Jacob lived with Aunt Cele. He had been a fruit seller, and I remember only a very old man who had lost his wife, my grandmother, Bertha, before I was born. Most of my memories of him are of a lonely elderly man sitting on a stool in the kitchen, wearing a sleeveless tee shirt and pajama bottoms and saying nothing.

We gathered not just for a Passover meal, but to actually read the Haggadah. And not any Haggadah. We read the Maxwell House Coffee Haggadah, which we were able to get through in twenty minutes. The youngest children did say the Four Questions, we did have our cups of wine and grape juice, and my Uncle Ben did hide a piece of matzah as the Afikomen for the kids to find. But it is the dinner itself I recall most vividly. We had the mandatory gefilte fish, but Aunt Cele would never stoop to serving it from a jar. She made it by hand, grinding the carp, whitefish and pike before adding in the spices. I still recall the large, powerful hand grinder that looked to me like a medieval torture device. If I had one today, I would not need a gym membership to exercise my arm muscles. Of course, the horseradish was also hand-ground. She served the traditional chicken soup with matzah balls, and we would all exclaim in unison how wonderful it was. It was obligatory to compliment the chef on the chicken soup and matzah balls, a condition of being invited back the next year, but Aunt Cele really did deserve the praise. She went all out, year after year.

After dinner, the adults cleared the dining-room table to play pinochle or poker, and we kids went to the living room to fidget, tease and fight. As a child, I perceived it all as natural, warm and protective, having no reason to doubt it would last forever. The only ones left of that contingent are me and my sister, and two of my first cousins, Cheryl and Paula. They remained in Chicago, but I have lost touch with them. My cousin Bruce married, moved to Dallas, Texas, and had children, but tragically died from meningitis while on an airplane. He was 50 years old. Cheryl later became a Playboy Bunny and eventually a Bunny Mother in charge of scheduling work shifts and hiring, firing and training Bunnies at one of the Chicago area clubs. Later in life, long after I had left Chicago, her work gave me bragging rights. Paula reportedly married into a minor branch of an Italian mobster family: a form of upward mobility in Chicago at that time.

I was never told that family was important. I just knew it. Yes, I saw family members fight, feel slighted, say hurtful things, stop speaking to one another, become resentful of one another, and express their dislike directly in sharp terms, but I also knew that family was the bedrock of my personal security and identity. And while our four-person nuclear family was my core, my sense of family extended well beyond my household. It included aunts, uncles, cousins, grandparents and great-grandparents and even what my mother referred to as "kissing cousins," her group of high-school friends who were like sisters to her. The degree of consanguinity was unimportant. I was often unaware of who was an uncle or a great-uncle or which cousin was second- or third-degree, or who was a biological relative or one by marriage. We were all part of a closely-knit kin group that was the center of my life. I knew I was part of something greater than myself. It was within that ill-defined but unbreakable tribe that I intuitively knew I was valued and loved, and, if needed, would be protected. It was within my family that I received encouragement and reinforcement and felt my first accepted place in the world. Family traditions were not to be broken. Whether it was going to someone's house for Passover, to another's for Thanksgiving, and to yet another's for July 4th, or getting together for births, birthdays, or anniversaries, there was an invisible nuclear force at work to ensure we would not break these bonds. My mother's sister, Myrna, married at the "old" age of 26. Aunt Myrna had been living with my grandmother in

Los Angeles, and she was desperate to escape the cloistered, suffocating control of her mother. Her only way out was to marry. Some marry for love, others for security, companionship, children, status, wealth, convenience, or tradition; Aunt Myrna married for freedom. But she married someone she did not love or even like, and she traded one prison for another. When she and her husband, who had no affection for our extended family, moved her to Portland, there was a hue and cry – for he had broken the bond. The unspoken commandment was that family needed to stay together and celebrate and grieve together. I intuited the family as the indispensable social unit acting as an anchor that, ironically, gives us the freedom and safety to maneuver during turbulent times.

Chapter 3

A MILKMAN'S STORY

I was lucky because my father was a milkman, which had many perks as far as I was concerned. He worked as a driver for Bowman Dairy Company for as long as I can remember, right up to the day he died in 1968. He was a proud member of the Teamsters Union. He had a route in downtown Chicago and delivered to department stores and other commercial outlets. He worked hard, very hard. He would go to bed by 8:30 pm so he could get up at 3:00 am, drive to the dairy, load his truck with heavy crates of milk and other dairy supplies, and start deliveries no later than 5:50 am. He never complained. He finished his route around 2:30 in the afternoon, and was often home by 3:30, so he was there when I got home from school. But even better was that he would frequently stop at Burny Bros. Bakery on Randolph Street in downtown Chicago to pick up cream puffs, Napoleons, chocolate eclairs, and other delicacies. (We were always well-nourished in the sweets department. My mother's dessert of choice was the chocolate pistachio cake from Heinemann's Bakery, a caloric overload that literally weighed at least five pounds and was consumed by our family of four in thirty, non-stop minutes!) I still remember sitting at the kitchen table, only me and my dad, while he read the paper and drank coffee, and I shoved a cream puff into my mouth and then got to wipe off the cream bordering my lips with my tongue. There was no talking, unless it was about the Chicago White Sox, but there was no need of talk. It was perfect.

One of the stops on Dad's delivery route was a sporting goods store. I will never forget the day when he brought home a brand new hardball. Pure white leather with red stitching, complete with the Rawlings stamp. We would go to nearby Eugene Field Park, an oasis of greenery on sixteen acres, to play catch or, more often, he would hit the ball, and I would chase it. How I hated that moment when the pristine ball first hit the grass, and I knew, even before I picked it up, that it would forever be consecrated with green smudges on the smooth white leather. He bought me a baseball glove and showed me how to oil it to perfection. Once he brought home a catcher's mask and shin guards, which puzzles me to this day. I never played catcher and never wanted to. It was clear who I wanted to be and that was Luis Aparicio, shortstop of the White Sox and one of the best second base stealers in the league. If I couldn't be shortstop, I would settle for Nellie Fox at second base but without the chewing tobacco that protruded from his cheek like a golf ball. I used to walk around the apartment, glove and ball in hand, and practice catching the impossible catch and throwing to first base just in time, oblivious to everything and everyone around me. I was awakened from my delusion to the loud shout of my sister, "Mom. Make him stop." It was her favorite refrain when it came to something I was doing that annoyed her, which was often.

My most vivid memories of my father are tied to baseball. When I was 8, I joined a little league team, and my dad would take me to all the practices and the games. My first team was the Indians. I was mostly assigned the position of the sidelines, where I watched more of a game than played. But I was a great observer. When I was 11, I was ready for the big leagues. Or, as it was called then, the Mighty Mites. We were living in Albany Park, and our teams were named after local businesses that paid for our uniforms. In turn, their business name would be emblazoned on our jerseys. My team was the Lake City Cleaners, and we played teams with names like Rol-a-Way Bowling, Lesser Drugs, or Central Cigar. I usually played second base, and my stomach would be in knots the entire time I was on the field, fearing that a ground ball would come my way, and I would flub it. I usually did. And my ratio of hits to errors was underwhelming. I made many more errors than hits. In fact, I considered it a triumph when my bat made contact with the ball, regardless of whether I made it to first base. Even a foul ball was a success. My career as a baseball player never made it out of the batter's box.

It was not simply taking me to my games, or the baseball goodies he brought home or the precious moments of playing catch, but listening to the radio together as Bob Elson called the plays with more color and detail than pictures ever could. Very recently, I read an article about people without a visual memory. People who are unable to see an image in their mind's eye have a condition called *aphantasia*. I quickly realized that the article too was describing me. Until I read the article, I had no idea that people, in fact, most people, are able to recall visual images and some can do it with great clarity, bringing to mind images from decades ago. I now realize that my inability to visualize events gave me a heighten ability to extract "color" or vividness from verbal descriptions. During the summers, my father would carry his transistor radio from room to room, making sure not to lose a minute of play, and I would tow along. And he would take me to White Sox games, driving across town, bypassing the closer Wrigley Field of the Cubs, to get to Comiskey Park, where we would see the antics of Andy the Clown. Andy was a fixture at the Park, and an unofficial mascot of the White Sox. He would walk up and down the aisles, prominently displaying a white and red polka-dotted clown costume and large red nose that would light up as he barked out calls of "Goooo White Sox." I was a quiet kid, the opposite of Andy the Clown, who was a larger-than-life, boisterous, in-your-face presence. When he would walk anywhere near my seat, I would shrink to avoid detection, but I could never stop staring at him, wondering how anyone could have the confidence to treat strangers like friends.

Getting to the games could be as memorable as the play itself. My father drove to the park, but, not wanting to pay the steep parking fees at the stadium, he would often park on the streets. The park was in the Armour Square neighborhood in the near southwest side of Chicago. It was not the type of place where one felt safe strolling after dark, but why pay more for parking than you needed to? One late afternoon, as we were leaving the car, a boy of about twelve said in a street-wise voice, "Mista, watch your car for a quarter?" My father gave him a quarter, and we walked on. "Dad, he isn't going to watch our car. He took your quarter and is going to run away," I said, proud of my new-found intuitive sense: I knew a con when I saw one. "That is exactly what I expect him to do," my dad replied. "If I hadn't given him a quarter, he would have made sure that I would remember it when we returned to our car." As we watched the game, and I loaded up on chocolate-malt ice cream and salted peanuts in the shell, I wondered if he did the right thing. When we got to our car after the game and found it just as we left it, I knew who was smarter. Years later, I thought back on this lesson. I had borrowed a car from a friend in Israel. Parking on a dirt road in Safed, a beggar approached me for money. I was dismissive and walked away. When I returned, the car had been keyed, and I had no doubt about the culprit. It cost me hundreds of dollars to get it fixed. My father would not have made that mistake.

The best part of being the son of a milkman was when he let me come with him on his milk runs. The first time was when I was about eleven and on school vacation. It was the third week of December, and bitterly cold in Chicago with winds that made one's tears feel like they are going to freeze. During the winter months, my father would get up at 2:00 am to warm up his car, parked on the street, to make sure it would start when he had to drive it off around 3:30. He would shovel the snow around the wheels and add salt just to make sure he could get the car moving. I got up with him for the 3:30 am departure, barely aware that he had already been up once to get the car ready. We drove to the dairy to pick up his refrigerated truck. I had no idea how heavy the crates of milk, cheese, and other milk products were. I helped a bit, but he was no-nonsense as he quickly loaded his truck, knowing which items to put where for easy delivery, and we were soon on our way. I sat in the front passenger seat, which was more like a stool with a backing. I was riding high and not just physically. Each bump in the road, magnified by worn oil coil springs in the suspension lifted me in the air. Riverview Park, the largest amusement park in Chicago, bragged about having the area's best rollercoasters, but no ride in that park could compete with riding shotgun in a 1950s milk truck in the pitch dark. It only got better after he started his deliveries.

My father was a shy man, of few words and even fewer friends, at least that I knew of. He mostly stayed at home, except for work, ball games and his regular Friday night vigils to the harness races. On his milk run, however, I saw a different man. Everyone knew him, shouted "How'ya doing, Lou? What's doing? Any cards this week? Who you bettin' on this weekend? Is that your kid with you?" He quickly moved milk cartons around like they were empty egg cartons, handed out parlay cards that listed the college football team lineups for the weekend and the points for each team, took bets on behalf of undisclosed principals, stuffed cards in his shirt pocket, paid off bets, and moved on quickly to the next store to repeat it again. My mom knew about his side-line parlay card venture, but there was no risk of him losing money unless he kept the bet himself, which he only rarely did.

He would always park his truck in an alley behind a store. And he would leave a carton of cream cheese or eggs or butter on the driver's seat when he exited. "'What're ya doing that for?" I asked. "It is illegal to park here. But I have to park here. Nowhere else. If a cop comes by, he knows my truck, and he knows there's something for him on my seat. I never get a ticket. We all work together." Chicago worked, and my dad was one of the regular folks who made it work. We stopped for a quick lunch at the Walgreen's counter, finished the route and headed back to the dairy to return the truck. We were home by 2:30. I was exhausted, having done nothing but try to keep up with him, but it was a glorious day.

Chapter 4

THERE MUST BE A HORSE

Volta Elementary was only a block from home, and I started there in the fourth grade in the fall of 1956 with Mrs. Wender as my teacher. Kind but firm, she warmly welcomed me to my new school, and I finished the year like any other undistinguished, but relatively smart, Jewish kid.

I quickly made friends with other boys, all of whom lived within a few blocks of me and almost all of us were of the same socio-economic, working class. There was Tony Mackin, always a bit taller and stronger than the others, a natural leader. He lived a block away but, by going through some passageways next to the apartments across the street, I could get to his apartment building in a minute. The mysterious thing about him was his father, who seemed always to be in the basement of the apartment, standing in a dark and dank room, surrounded by messy, oily tools and parts. I had no idea what he was doing there or if he ever worked. I don't think he did. A couple blocks away was Carl Fink, smart, wiry, huge ears, about my size (average Jewish height), and always up for an adventure – provided someone else led. Marvin Mitofsky was part of our group and in many ways was an odd sort. He was about a year older than most of us, likely because he was held back in school. As a student, Marvin could not keep up with the rest of us, and his face had the shape and twists of a professional boxer. He was strong, very strong, and loyal. I was always very comfortable around Marvin, and I felt like I had my own personal body guard. Michael Berman lived about a block away, and I remember him only because his father drove an Oldsmobile, many cuts above the cars the rest of our fathers could afford.

Then there was Richard Eisenstadt. Rick lived in a solid brick, single-story house, not an apartment, about a mile away from me. His father was a pathologist, rich and had a season's subscription to the Chicago Symphony. I recall that they had a dining-room table that was actually used for their regular meals, which was a definite sign of status. Rick's family was in a class by itself, and he was what we aspired to become. The rest of us were from working-class homes, and our parents were unabashedly ambitious for us. Education was the key. As I think back on my Albany Park friends, the only one who became really "famous" was Steve Goodman, the folk-song writer and singer who penned the song made popular by Arlo Guthrie, "City of New Orleans." That song won a Grammy award for best country song in 1985. Steve was shy, avoided sports and was not part of any "in-group." But he was well-liked and friendly toward everyone. His claim to fame at the time of graduation from Volta was his position as captain of the playground patrol, whose job it was to ensure that kids maintained order, lined up quietly and quickly and played safely on the field. His eighth grade law and order focus shows how the past is not necessarily prologue. I would never have predicted that the writer of some of the most iconic folk songs of our time, like "You Never Even Called Me by My Name," "A Dying Cub Fan's Last Request," "Turnpike Tom," "Talk Backwards," and "Vegematic," among many others, was once a safety patrol captain who proudly enforced the rules.

My cultural diet was thin. As a family, we did not go to operas, ballets, or classical music concerts. In fact, I knew virtually nothing of these highbrow tastes, except when Richard would take me and a few other friends to the Chicago Symphony for one of their children's programs. My mother would make sure I was properly scrubbed, dressed in a shirt and tie, and wore polished shoes. It was a magical time for me. I would look over the lush, gilded concert hall and be transported into a world of luxury and unattainable opulence. I didn't so much aspire to be able to afford such frills as I was satisfied that, for one short moment, I knew how the rich lived.

Opera may not have been our world, but my mother exposed me to music that had a great lifelong impact on me. She loved Broadway musicals. I think she liked to imagine herself in a starring role, standing in the floodlights and bowing to never-ending applause. Her one indulgence was to get us tickets to the hit musicals and then buy the soundtracks afterwards. I was not a mere spectator. I was Harold Hill, dancing and singing in River City. I memorized all the lines. I had a whole town enthralled and eating out of the palm of my hand. I had absolutely no musical or dancing talent. I would go so far as to say I had anti-talent. That did not stop me from singing at the top of my lungs in the house, sometimes to get a rise out of my sister, but more often just for the pure joy of being on an imaginary stage.

Oklahoma and *Seven Brides for Seven Brothers* brought me into worlds of color and heart-thumping music and dance. Then there was *How the West Was Won*. As a fourteen year old, I wanted to know more about what they were doing when the woman followed the man into the cave to see the "varmint" and exited with her clothes askew. I saw the play

Yankee Doodle Dandy, and, when it became a movie, I would it watch again and again every July 4th, marveling at James Cagney playing George M. Cohan. The optimistic, proud patriotism of George M. Cohan was infectious, and I stirred to his musical love affair with the country that welcomed him and millions of other immigrants, including my family. I knew I could never be the brash, extroverted, supremely-confident George M. Cohan, who could tap dance anyone else off the stage, but I could be patriotic soul mates with him. I could not get enough of these musicals, and I would replay their dreams again and again.

Best of all was *My Fair Lady*. For me, Henry Higgins wasn't just a confirmed old bachelor and likely to remain so, or an unrepentant misogynist. He was a man of contradictions. He was erudite yet ignorant of what mattered most, comfortable in his own skin yet uncomfortable in the presence of a woman, unfeeling yet sensitive, quirky yet traditional. In the end, he knew what he wanted, and he got it. I would walk around the house singing "I'm just an ordinary man," while knowing that Henry Higgins (and by extension, in my imagination, I) was anything but that. Yes, the lyrics reverberate in my head whenever I long for a moment of repose:

> " *I'm an ordinary man,*
> *who desires nothing more than just an ordinary chance*
> *to live exactly as he likes, and do precisely what he wants.*
> *An average man am I, of no eccentric whim,*
> *who likes to live his life free of strife,*
> *doing whatever he thinks is best for him.*
> *Just an ordinary man ..."*

I was envious of Henry Higgins. What I coveted most was his library – double-storied, wood-paneled, over spilling with books and endowed with inviting, strategically placed reading chairs and couches. Every proper Victorian English gentleman had his library. It was his inner sanctum, a shrine far removed from the babble of the day. Only those invited, and there were few indeed, could enter the oasis. Those walking by ought to tiptoe and wear slippers so as not to make unnecessary noise. It was the place where a gentleman could be at home with himself and fear no intrusion. As Henry Higgins continued with his exalted, distorted view of himself:

> "I'm a quiet living man,
> who prefers to spend the evening in the silence of his room,
> who likes an atmosphere as restful
> as an undiscovered tomb.
> A pensive man am I, of philosophic joys,
> who likes to meditate, contemplate,
> free from humanity's mad inhuman noise.
> Just a quiet living man."

When I later learned that meditative, personal libraries were of this world and not merely an invention of Hollywood, and when I read of Oscar Wilde's sacred library at his house at 34 Tite Street, Chelsea, London, the word "covet" failed to convey my longing for such a refuge. For Oscar Wilde, it was his Holy of Holies, a sacred space. To compare the Victorian library to today's "man cave," as some do, is to confuse a Rembrandt with the graffiti art of David Choe. As Thomas Wright described in *Built of Books*, it was "here a man sat alone, mediating on his life, chronicling his thoughts in the diary or the letters he penned there …"; it was "a symbol of his personal history as its contents bore witness to the various stages of his life and literary career." Equivalent of a man's cave? Nonsense. And, for me, it all started with Henry Higgins. Oh, how I would dream of my Higgins library.

I was a voracious reader, but my tastes as a young boy were decidedly narrow. I loved the Tom Swift series, which took me on outer space adventures. But it was in the fictional city of Bayport where I spent many afternoons and evenings. I was obsessed with the Hardy boys and devoured every single one of the original fifty-nine books in the series. I followed Frank and Joe Hardy and their friends Chet and Biff on each adventure, and I could not be pulled away from an engrossing episode, leading to the occasional yelling from my mother to come to the kitchen table for dinner. My vocabulary increased with each reading as I added "chum," skullduggery," "roadster," "swell," "by jingo," "culvert," "bedeviled," "taunts and jeers," and "trousers" to my pre-adolescence world. I learned about exploring caves, changing tires in driving rains, creeping around rugged coastlines, donning disguises and the sheer thrill of catching the culprit. The Hardy boys and their father, Fenton, were my world in print.

It was not all musicals and movies and books. My friends and I grew up on a steady diet of guns, soldiers, and Western TV shows. We would gather around a large console television in our rarely used living room to watch gunslingers save the world in black and white. My heroes were broadcast to me each week. I rarely missed an episode. They were uniformly tough, fearless loners, chivalrous protectors of the weak, and they were constantly victimized, but they were never victims, quiet but never silent in the face of villainy. I marveled at the strength and determination of Matt Dillon, played by James Arness in *Gunsmoke* (1955–1975). I saw myself mounting my steed to go wherever I was needed to wrong an injustice just like Paladin in *Have Gun Will Travel* (1957–1963). Lucas McCain (played by Chuck Connors) in *The Rifleman* (1958–1963) was so adept at using his rifle that I thought it was a third arm. *The Life and Legend of Wyatt Earp* (1955–1961), *The Cisco Kid* (1950–1956), *Davy Crockett* (1954–1955) and *The Lone Ranger* (1949–1957) all repeated the same themes and portrayed strong, resolute determined heroes. There were no ambiguities in mission or rightness: bad guys were dead or gone and good guys got back on their horses to do it all over again. From the ages of eight to twelve, these Westerns were as much a part of my education as school and family life.

There were two other shows, starring boys my age, which gave me my Walter Mitty moments. *Fury* (1955–1960) was the story of a horse and the boy who loved him. I would go on weekly adventures with Joey and Fury at the Broken Wheel Ranch. For thirty minutes, I would be Joey, and Fury would be my horse. For that half-hour, we were inseparable, and Fury was my protector. Then, there was *Spin and Marty* (1955–1957), a show about a know-nothing city boy, Spin, and a cowboy in the making, Marty, at the Triple R Ranch. Spin was sent to the ranch to toughen up and learn about life. At first, Spin and Marty were antagonists befitting the worst of enemies, but competition turned to cooperation and then into a deep friendship. As they rode horses, fixed fences, roped cattle, and met one challenge after another, they grew up, morphing from Tybalt and Mercutio to Porthos and Athos. And I was there every step of the way, imagining that I too were on the ranch, overcoming every obstacle and gaining the respect of those around me.

Alongside the strong heroes and resolute values of honesty, determination, resiliency and self-sacrifice for the protection of the vulnerable, the episodes showcased their horses, their essential, loyal, non-verbal partners in fulfilling their missions. To this day, I like to quip that, for a show or movie to be good, truly good, there must be a horse. "Where's the horse?" I like to say. People hear me, but they do not understand what I really mean.

I thought about westerns all the time, and loved to reenact them. Toy guns were the perfect birthday present for me. I would walk around with an air rifle, shooting at imaginary enemies. It was my cap guns (and I had many of them) that provided the most disruption in our apartment. They came with a paper roll that had a series of nubs, which, when aligned with the hammer of the gun, let off a loud pop, a whiff of smoke and a sulfurous odor. I delighted in sneaking up on people, mainly my sister, and firing, sending off a loud crackling sound and a whiff of burning paper. She would jump, I would delight, and she would scream for parental protection.

My toy soldiers and cowboys, Indians and horses preoccupied me for hours. My dad would bring home large bags of plastic toy soldiers of WWII vintage. I had every kind imaginable, from infantry to sharp shooters, flame throwers, hand-grenade launchers, radio operators, bazooka specialists, and assault troops from privates to generals. Along with these figures, I had the associated paraphernalia. I had it all. They numbered in the hundreds, and filled four large bags. When I add in the plastic cowboys and Indians and their horses, I had a child's award-worthy treasure trove. I would set them up all over the house, on tables, chairs, window sills, radiators, and TV sets, positioning them with precision. For hours, I would plan and then execute precise military maneuvers, complete with sound effects and dying men, falling all over the floors. Peter the Great may have used his vast collection of expensive lead soldiers to plan his expansion of Russia, but I had far braver soldiers and far better equipment for my imaginary theatres of combat. I would have challenged his grand army with my ragtag soldiers, cowboys, and Indians any day.

It was a short distance from my fantastical war games to the real world of school. Spanning the block between me and the school was a large playground that became my and my friends' after-school destination of choice, where parents knew they could always find us. That gravel park, with baseball diamonds and net-less basketball hoops, took up the southeast corner of the intersection nearest my apartment house. On the northeast corner was a large, yellowish brown apartment complex, and the northwest corner had two single-family homes, which sat incongruously among the apartments. In the ten years I lived in Albany Park, I never learned who lived there. Those who lived in single-family homes were in a parallel universe from mine. But it was the large, dark-brown apartment structure on the southwest corner that drew our curiosity and had an air of foreboding. It was the local home for unwed teenaged mothers to be. When we walked past it, we fell quiet. We knew not to talk about it, and, when we did, we whispered. We rarely saw anyone going in or out. When we did get to glimpse one of the girls, she would hold her head down and scamper into their building, trying her best not to be noticed. It was our neighborhood secret – but not our only one.

The other was at the end of our street, Harding Avenue, dead-ended about four apartment buildings along from ours. The barrier was only a chain-link fence, but it could have been the Great Wall of China as far as we were concerned. We did not have to be told. We knew never to even think of scaling the fence to go inside. When we looked through the chain links, we could see a beautiful vast open green space, dotted with trees and, in the distance, brick buildings. It was a tuberculous sanitarium, but, to a child, it aroused the same fear as a leper colony. So, on the one block between the home for the unwed pregnant teens and the foreboding sanatorium, I lived an ordinary childhood, surrounded by ordinary people making an ordinary living, and living an ordinary life. How extraordinary it all was.

Chapter 5

THE ANT FARM

While I didn't know the term at the time, I flirted with the idea of becoming an entomologist when I was in elementary school. I experimented with any bug I could find. When I was in the fourth grade, our teacher, Mrs. Wender, brought an ant farm into class, and my interest in insects took on a new focus. The farm was a box measuring about 18" x 12", 2" wide with clear plastic on each side so we could watch the ants at work. It was filled with a granular sand and about forty ants. I was fascinated by their work ethic and their cooperation in carving intricate paths through the sand in their plastic home. Each day I would come to class early so I could watch the ants at work. They never seemed to tire or rest, and they kept building more and more pathways with a purpose that escaped me. I never tired of watching them and wanting to know more. I had a Eureka moment: I would forgo being a shortstop for the Chicago White Socks to become a myrmecologist.

As the two-week Christmas break approached, Mrs. Wender asked if anyone would take the ant farm home, care for the ants and bring it back when the vacation was over. I immediately raised my hand. I walked the two blocks home carrying my valuable cargo. I held it steady, not wanting to upset the delicate tunnels the ants had cut into the sand. I walked up the three flights of steps ever so carefully and breathed a sigh of relief when I entered the apartment having got them safely home. I spent the next few days watching the ants. But they kept doing the same thing over and over again, and I was losing interest. I had never heard of Euripides, but my eight-year-old brain had somehow learned to "question everything," and I thought it was time for an experiment. What if I gave the ant farm a few vigorous shakes and destroyed all the tunnels? How long would it take the ants to reconstruct them? Would they build the same design? Would the tunnels be built to be stronger? Would all the ants join in the effort to rebuild or would some decide it was time for a holiday? These were the questions that pulsed through the mind of this would-be probing scientist. So, I took the ant farm and shook it. Again. And again. I must have shaken it five or six times. Vigorously. When I stopped, I had succeeded. All the pathways had collapsed. They were gone. There was no evidence they ever existed. I felt good. My experiment was on its way. But then I looked more closely. Where were the ants? I expected to see ants in every corner of the ant farm, some on top of the sand, some at each layer, digging their way out. But they were gone. I looked more closely, and could see dozens of ant bodies compressed by the sand gravel. The ants were not moving. They were dead. They were all dead. I shook the ant farm once again, hoping to wake up the ants. Maybe I could shift some of the sand and free the ants, bringing them back to life. Everything I tried failed to revive any of the ants. What was I going to do? There were ten more days left of the vacation, and they felt like the worst days of my life. I had killed all the ants. What was I going to tell Mrs. Wender? What would my classmates think? I was dreading returning to school. Then, one day before the end of vacation, I came up with a plan. I knew what

I would say. It would be fascinating. It would stimulate a whole discussion in class about the nature of ants. We would all learn a new truth.

The next day, I carried the lifeless farm to school. I was the last student to enter the classroom. I walked up to Mrs. Wender, who was sitting at her desk, and, looking down to avoid meeting her eyes, I said, "Here is the ant farm. The strangest thing happened. The ants were working away as they usually did. I fed them. Gave them water. All of a sudden, they started fighting. I saw them in all the tunnels. They killed each other. Look, there are no ants anymore." Mrs. Wender took the ant farm, examined it closely and confirmed there were no ants left alive. She did not embarrass me by explaining to the class that ants from the same colony do not kill each other. She did not ask what happened to the tunnels. She did not ask why there were NO ants left, no victors left alive. She did not mention that it looked like the ants had been crushed to death. She did not ask why traces of sand could be seen at the top of the farm. She simply said to the class that it was very odd, and it had never happened before. But she assured us that she would order more ants, add them to the ant farm, and, in no time, we would have tunnels again. I sighed with relief. I had escaped detection. Or had I? I went home after school, feeling dejected. I should have been elated; after all, my story about the ant fight had been believed, and I had escaped the consequences of my own stupidity. But I did not feel good at all. I knew I was responsible for the death of the ants when it was my job to make sure they were safe. More importantly, I felt ashamed for lying to Mrs. Wender. The next morning, I was the first one to get to class. Mrs. Wender was sitting at her desk. I went up to her. I hung my head, looked at the floor once again, and confessed. "The ants did not get into a war and kill one another. I shook the ant farm because I wanted to destroy the tunnels and see if the ants would rebuild them. The ants all died because I shook it so hard." She looked at me and said she knew. I was dumfounded. She said that the ants would not kill each other, and, even if they did, the tunnels would still be there and some ants would still be alive. But she was very glad that I had told her the truth. More important than keeping the ants safe, which I did not do, was owning up to what I had done, which, finally, I did. I was embarrassed, deeply embarrassed, no doubt about it, but I was spared living with myself as a liar and deceiver. And, when the new ants arrived, Mrs. Wender entrusted them to my care, giving me a chance to redeem myself. I fed them, gave them water, and occasionally slipped in a small twig or piece of lettuce. I would not let anyone harm the ants, and I hovered over them whenever a classmate got too close. I was given a second chance to look after them, and this time I knew what that meant.

I was not through with my youthful misadventures with bugs. The death of the ants gave me an idea. What if I could bring flies back to life? Summers in Chicago were brutally hot and humid. And they were full of flying bugs, most of them pests. Yes, there were the lightning bugs, those soft-bodied beetles that flew slowly in the air, giving off blinking flashes of light during the twilight hour. Their bioluminescence operated as a mating call, which attracted females, often waiting on the ground for the luminous call to mate. But they also attracted curious kids like me. They were easy to catch and would perch on my fingers. I would lift my hand and give them a gentle push back into the sky so I could see them light up once again. It was the mosquito and the fly that ruined the nights. All I could do about the mosquitos was slap my skin and kill them if I felt their bite quickly enough.

But the house flies, oh, the flies. They would get into our apartment and buzz around as if they owned the place. I would follow them with a fly-swatter, missing more often than I successfully swatted them. House flies live for only twenty to twenty-five days. Toward the end of their life cycle, they lose their energy, flying slowly and compromising their ability to launch quickly to escape the attack of a killer kid. Their slow end-of-life take-off gave me an idea that never even occurred to Charles Darwin. I decided to play God by freezing the flies and then bringing them back to life. I would capture and put a few flies in a cylindrical plastic tube intended for storing coins. I would then put the tube in the freezer for a couple of hours. While they were being frozen, I prepared the rest of my cryonics experiment by opening the steam valve on one of the cast-iron radiators, causing the corrugated metal to become very hot (and making an already uncomfortably hot room unbearable). I took the tube from the freezer and rested it against the hot metal radiator fins. I waited and observed, looking at my watch so I could record how long it took for the flies to come back to life. But they never did. Once frozen, forever dead. I tried other methods. If the flies were in the freezer for only fifteen minutes – and not hours – they looked dead when I took them out, and they revived when I put them on the radiator to thaw out. I varied the experiment by adding more flies to the tube, altering the time in the freezer, putting the tube in boiling water, letting the frozen tube simply sit on the counter, shaking the tube, adding food to the tube, and so on and so on. Although some hardy flies could withstand a few minutes in the freezer, for the most part I had come to the conclusion that once dead, always dead. My interest in entomology died along with the frozen flies that failed to cooperate with my grand plan for their resurrection.

Chapter 6

THE CAR

On Harding Avenue, one of the most extraordinary events was the arrival of a new car. I don't mean a brand new car, which seldom happened, but a new, used car. Word would quickly spread about the arrival of a new four-wheeled machine, and neighbors would vie for the right to be one of the first to inspect it. The men wanted to know the size of the engine, the mileage, the power components, the number of seats and, most importantly, the price. The answers to these queries helped determine the pecking order on the block.

My earliest memories are of my dad driving a black Ford that literally had a hole in the floor on the passenger side. We would have fun looking down and seeing the asphalt below. But things were about to change. One day in 1959, we were driving by a used car lot, and my mother shouted out, "Lou, stop the car." She had spied a salmon-colored 1957 Plymouth Belvedere, a four-door hardtop with rear wings that were guaranteed to lift the car off the ground. In about an hour, the transaction was done. The black Ford was gone, and we proudly drove our "new" car to Harding Avenue. My father loved driving that car, and showing it off. He loved the push buttons that changed the gears from drive to reverse. For the first year of ownership, he would walk down three flights of stairs at least once a day to look at the car parked on the street, just to make sure it was still there. I was only eleven, but I had big dreams. I wanted to drive. I would have to wait.

Five years later, in late 1963, a major event in our life was to happen. The Belvedere was still a good looking and well performing car. But our economic fortunes got a modest boost. My father still worked as a milkman, but my mother, ever sharp, attractive and yearning to do something outside the house and add to our income, got a job. She started in a clerical position at the Bankers Life and Casualty Company, then owned by John D. MacArthur, whose foundation now bestows the prized "genius" awards. By her own determination and hard work, by the time she moved from Chicago to Los Angeles in 1969, she was the highest ranking female at the company, but unable to break the glass ceiling for women, as officer positions were reserved for men. She wrote their "computer" handbook at a time when computers meant punch cards. She was proud of this achievement, and we were proud of her. The job at Bankers gave her an important identity outside the house, and it validated her inherent intelligence, business savvy and ability not only to work well with people but to lead a large team of other women. And she brought in an extra income that allowed for a few additional treats, like a visit to Hackney's for the best hamburger a teenager could imagine. But the extra I remember most was the brand new 1964 Chevy Impala.

We all can point to some material possession with pride. It is more than an object. It is a symbol. Perhaps of success, of aesthetics, of achieving a certain station in life. Perhaps it is a reward for a life of hard work. For my father, the 1964 Chevy Impala was all these things. When he parked it on Harding Avenue for the first time in late 1963, nearby apartments emptied. People came to see, to admire, to envy. And to sit. They asked to sit behind the wheel, to sit in the back, to open the hood. To inhale the new car smell. And my father was proud. It was silver blue, with blue cloth interior, a four-door hardtop, white-walled tires. Air conditioning, no. Too much money. But it did have power steering and power brakes. For my dad, nothing could be better. His dream came true. "Only in the America [back then the United States and America were synonymous] could a milkman buy a brand new car," he would repeat again and again.

Dad's dream faded shortly after I turned sixteen on January 26, 1964. I already had my learner's permit, and my father was a good instructor. He was so good that I was ready for my driver's test soon after my birthday, and I passed. He reluctantly let me drive the car around the narrow streets of our quiet neighborhood without him. I was not allowed to have any friends in the car, but that was OK. I just needed to drive it and be seen. Spring came. Chicago could be the most beautiful place on earth in the spring. Green, vibrant, cool, light breezes off the lake, and girls. Girls without coats. Girls with legs showing. Girls with exposed arms. Girls with long hair. Girls, girls, girls. I *was* sixteen after all. "Dad, can I take the car for a ride?" He answered, "Where do you want to go?" "Nowhere really (my usual response), just a drive around the block." He said, "Be back soon."

I raced down the three flights of stairs, turned on the engine, and maneuvered out of the tight parking space. And I drove around the streets. Harding south to Argyle, left to Hamlin, right to Ainslie, left on Lawndale, going back north. Windows open. All four of them. Soft breeze. Sun coming in. Perfect. I was driving back to Argyle, and about to make a left for quick trip back home, when perfect became sublime. I saw a girl walking on the north side of Argyle, long hair, spring to her step. She must be beautiful, but I could not see her face. I turned left onto Argyle, with my eyes focused on the only thing that mattered:

getting a look at the girl. The car veered to the left, and, to straighten it out, I turned to the right. But my sixteen-year old eyes stayed fixed on the girl, and I forgot to stop turning to the right. Before I knew it, I had plowed into a parked car. The right front of my dad's Chevy crumbled. Glass everywhere, grill pushed in, bumper jammed. It was a mess. The police came, I put a note on the other car with all the relevant information, and I was given a ticket.

My car was still drivable, and I drove the few blocks to our street. I lacked the courage to park the car outside our apartment – I needed more time before I told my dad. So I made a right turn onto Harding, a quick left into an alley, and parked at the car wash on Pulaski Road that was right behind our building. I sat in the car for what seemed an eternity before walking home. I still do not know what words I used to tell him that I had been in an accident, but his face turned red, and he asked if anyone was hurt. "No," I said. "Where is the car?" I was able to get out the words, "At the car wash." We went down the three flights of stairs and, for the first time, I wished it were twenty floors and not three. I needed more time before he saw what I had done. We walked on back to the car. He saw his pristine joy crushed in the front. He did not yell. He did not scream. He just cried. It was the first time I saw a grown man cry. And it was my father. He stood there and cried. And then I cried. And I cried and I cried. And then he hugged me, and said, "It is only metal. It can be fixed. No one got hurt, so it is OK." I cried some more.

Chapter 7

VENTURING OUT

In retrospect, elementary school was rather uneventful, as it should be. There were no great traumas or challenges. I was an ordinary kid, getting above average, but, for a largely Jewish school, expected grades. By the fifth grade, after I had completely adjusted to my new school, I developed a strong crush on Paula Albelda. She was petite, with light-brown hair, and as cute as can be imagined. Even her braces aroused desire. My eyes followed her everywhere, but I never let her know how I felt – heaven forbid. From the seventh grade, Volta sponsored dances at the Eugene Park Recreation Center. These were very tame socials, heavily laden with chaperones and characterized more by boys' immature antics (daring, pushing, wrestling, throwing cups of juice) than by dancing. But I somehow got up the courage to ask Paula to dance with me, and my skin still feels the rush when, as Fred Astaire would sing, we danced "cheek to cheek." Yes, I was in heaven. There were a few parties where we played "seven minutes in heaven," which really meant I would go into a closet with Paula, and we would wait out the seven minutes with awkward giggling and whispering, exiting the closet with embarrassed smirks. Paula remained my hidden and unrequited love for the remainder of my time at Volta. She was probably unaware of my crush, which, while that was my aim back then, was disappointing. Even worse than an unrequited love is an unknown one.

My traumas were outside of school. Like the time my mother relented and agreed to send me to Boy Scout camp at the Indiana Dunes. My mother never understood the attraction of camping, sleeping outdoors and contending with the elements, and she very effectively communicated that to me. But my friends were going, and I whined sufficiently to get her OK. It was spring, but when we got to the camp site, it could have been winter. Blistering cold, sharp winds, and piercing sand flying everywhere. Dinner was actually a treat – hot dogs and baked beans – but there was nowhere comfortable to eat it. I was miserable. The first night, I shivered in my sleeping bag unable to fall asleep, and the sun came up fast and far too soon. The scoutmaster told us to get dressed and start making breakfast, which was easier said than done. I picked up a carton of milk, and it was frozen solid. The eggs were frozen. The water was frozen. And I was frozen. I somehow made it through the weekend and got home, with a running nose, a hot forehead, flushed cheeks and 102-degree fever.

My mother decided my scouting days were at an end, but not before she called for our doctor, Dr. Izbicki. He came on Monday, and I remember looking out my parents' bedroom window as he parked his shiny black Cadillac in front of our house. I could not believe it. A Cadillac on Harding Avenue. It was worth being sick just to see the car. Dr. Izbicki got out of his car, shoulders slumped, carrying his ubiquitous black bag and walked upstairs. My mother let him in. His first words were, "Shirl, make me something to eat." He was about fifty, mustached and looking weary. My mother went to make him a sandwich while he came into the bedroom to examine me. He took my temperature and gave me a shot. Of what, I have no idea. "Doctor," I said, "you are so lucky to have a Cadillac." He looked at me with bloodshot eyes and said in a voice without flavor, "You think so? I have a boy like you, but I hardly have time to see him." I felt deflated. What I had intended as a compliment bounced back as sorrow. Perhaps that is why growing up I never seriously considered medicine for a career. He left the room, went to the kitchen to eat his sandwich, and, as he left the house, I heard him say, "Shirl, no more boy scout camping." That suited my mother just fine, and so it was. I too was relieved.

But getting sick at an inopportune moment deserved a repeat performance. First, though, I had to get through the seventh grade at Volta. My teacher was Mrs. Marble, aged about sixty (or so it seemed to my twelve-year-old eyes), just shy of rotund, with minute red blood vessels meandering across her pink cheeks and wispy white hair curled in the front and on the sides. What I most remember is a bump on her head. It was large. Like half of an egg, with the narrow part pointed up. I never knew what it was, and no one ever asked her. We never talked about it among ourselves. She was kind and dedicated as a teacher. She was also my first mentor, the first teacher who expressed a belief in me and made me feel that I had something special to offer.

When several of my friends were promoted to skip a grade, Mrs. Marble made sure that I did too. Sure, I would miss being in her class for another semester, but the push forward more than compensated. When I entered eighth grade, the class was told about a city-wide competition sponsored by Independence Hall Savings & Loan Association. It was an essay contest. We had to write an essay on the subject, "What my country means to me." The prize? An all-expense paid trip to Philadelphia and Washington D.C. to see the historical sites of the U.S. I had never entered, let alone won, a competition before, and I had no interest in spending time on this extracurricular project, when I could be playing basketball or football. Although no longer my teacher, Mrs.

Marble saw me in the hallway and asked me if I was writing an essay. I knew she had singled me out as her star pupil, and I did not have the heart to say, "No." So, I said, "I think so." She said I must, and I did.

To my amazement, I won with the best essay from Volta Elementary, and during spring break in 1961, along with about thirty other students, each of whom had won from their respective public or Catholic school, I was set to go on the trip. I was ecstatic. I had never been to Philadelphia or D.C., and had never been on a school trip with peers my own age. But I was also nervous. I did not mix easily; I had friends, but they were from the neighborhood, and they were of long standing. I was shy and not good with strangers. And my group was not just strangers. They were other thirteen year olds, and they came from schools with names like St. Mary of the Angels School, Sacred Heart Schools of Chicago, and St. Benedict Preparatory School. What was I doing? What was I thinking? Still, we bought clothes, a suitcase, stationery, snacks (in case they did not feed us enough). We were to leave on a Sunday for two weeks steeped in U.S. history. That Friday, I came down with a fever and Dr. Izbicki was back at our apartment. "Shirl, he's going nowhere. Keep him home, give him aspirin and soup, and call me in a few days." Several days later, thirty thirteen year olds were having a grand time at Independence Hall in Philadelphia, and my mother was able to tell Dr. Izbicki that this thirteen year old was feeling a lot better in Chicago. Was it separation anxiety, as my mother claimed, or just a coincidence? I don't know, but the Savings & Loan Association let me go the next year – 1962 – with that year's winners.

The trip was an immersion into United States colonial and Civil War history. It provided me with the intellectual and historical anchors of my patriotism, a bookend to the emotional moorings I earlier embraced from *Yankee Doodle Dandy*. Intellectually, I came away with a fourteen year old's' understanding of the Enlightenment, which formed the building blocks of the government and civil society our founders were striving to achieve. I was most affected by their firm belief in the power of human reason to build a better society based on freedom and liberty, and their insistence that people, not government, were endowed with natural rights. The role of government was to protect those rights, not to provide them. If government did not trample on the individual rights of man, and if people used their reason to solve common problems, society would inevitably improve. I was emotionally overwhelmed by Independence Hall, where the Declaration of Independence was debated and then signed on August 2, 1776 (the Declaration was adopted by the Second Continental Congress on July 4, 1776). A tour guide rose and went to the front of the Assembly Room, and in a booming voice he read the first few paragraphs of the Declaration of Independence to a silent, enthralled group of teenagers. When he solemnly intoned that "We hold these truths to be self-evident, that all men are created equal, that they are endowed by their Creator with certain unalienable Rights, that among these are Life, Liberty and the pursuit of Happiness," I was hooked. There was no music playing when he uttered these stirring words, but I was moved. It was my baptism into political philosophy. When United Airlines returned this kid from Albany Park to Chicago, I was on a collision course with my socialist, utopian grandfather. But that is another memory.

Not all our doctors were like Dr. Izbicki. There was our dentist Dr. Ira Feinberg. His office was spotless, and he wore a very official looking white medical smock. He was serious and looked like he knew what he was doing. Dr. Feinberg was a most unusual dentist. He did not like needles as he thought they hurt his patients and he did not like hurting his patients. When it came time to filling a cavity, he did not use Novocain: he just drilled. My feet would stretch out in pain, and I would repeatedly gag. It was torture. But, because he did not want to hurt his patients, Dr. Feinberg would keep the drilling to a minimum. Just a light touch. This meant that he often did not drill deeply enough or remove all the decayed material. As a result, his filings frequently became loose, leading to more visits. It was not only his aversion to drilling that was a problem. There was also the stock market. We all knew he invested heavily in the stock market. We knew because he would talk about it all the time. We came to learn that when the market was down, Dr. Fienberg was in a foul mood. Better stay away from his office on those days. And we did. We never hesitated to cancel appointments at the last minute after checking on the latest market results.

I thought I had adopted a keen strategy for avoiding Dr. Feinberg. One morning before school, I heard my parents talking about an appointment with Dr. Feinberg later that afternoon. Several hours before the anointed time, I went into the living room, laid down in front of the television, put my head on my outstretched right arm, and pretended to be asleep. I was confident that, if my parents saw I was sound asleep, they would never wake me just to go see Dr. Feinberg. I was getting uncomfortable in my adopted position, and my right arm was starting to tingle. I was fearful of moving as I did not want them to think I was awake. I made fine adjustments, but did not stir. Eventually, my mom and dad left the house for Dr. Feinberg, leaving me alone. It had worked. They had left me to sleep. I was ecstatic, confident that I had devised a winning strategy for avoiding the drill. They came home about 5:00 pm and told me they had made an appointment for my annual checkup with Dr. Feinberg in a month's time. It turned out that I wasn't even on the schedule for that afternoon, and I had wasted several hours laying on the floor for nothing.

Eighth grade was, well, just eighth grade. My memory is cloudy, but for some unfathomable reason I was elected class president and gave a forgettable speech to an auditorium full of proud parents, relieved teachers and restless siblings. I did not know it at the time, but it would be many years before I achieved a distinction as elevated as class president of the June 1961 Volta Elementary School graduating class.

I don't want to give the impression that my adolescence followed in the steps of the Sharks and the Jets, but I was no male Pollyanna either. Sure, I was not above pilfering plastic streamers for my bike handles and then paying for it with a thumping heartbeat as I raced home and recurring anxiety as I thought of the moment. Or slipping out of a diner without paying. Or taking two comic books but paying for only one. A group of us once ventured into Eugene Field at night on our bikes. Just being in the park in the dark was an unsettling experience. We took stones and threw them at the glass-encased lamps resting on high metal poles. We would see the glass shatter and then hear a loud hiss as something escaped from the broken cover. We quickly biked to the next lamppost and repeated the vandalism several more times. We did not get caught, but I never did it again. I imagined the sense of shame I would feel if my parents ever found out, and I had no desire to live on that edge.

During my teens, Chicago had a 10:00 pm curfew for people under sixteen. One night I went out with my friend Tony and, by the time we headed for home, it was past the curfew. We jumped on a bus, got off on the corner of Foster and Pulaski around 11:30 pm and started to walk the mile or so back to our apartments. We had not moved more than a few steps when a police car turned the corner and slowed down right beside us. Two cops got out and asked for our IDs, but we had none. "How old are you?" We answered, "Fifteen." They arrested us, and we were pushed into their squad car and taken to the station. Once there, they called our parents. We were never booked or fingerprinted, and no mugshots were taken. We didn't even have to sign anything. We got off with a stern warning and a promise to lock us up if we were ever caught again violating curfew. It was a prophylactic detention, designed to scare us into becoming good teenage citizens. It worked.

My mom came to get me as my father was fast asleep and had to get up in a few hours for work. She arrived at the same time as Tony's father.

He was angry. His face was twisted in fury, and he shouted at Tony as his face turned purple. He grabbed Tony by the arm and yanked him down the steps to his car. I knew Tony was going to get a real beating that night. I don't think it was because he had done anything intrinsically wrong by staying out late, but because the whole incident had inconvenienced his father. His anger at Tony was because the call from the police had interrupted whatever he was doing in his basement and he had to leave to get his son. The next day, Tony denied that he got a beating, but I didn't believe him.

I was scolded by my mom on the way home, as she told me how lucky I was to have escaped the evening without anything on my record. She was concerned about my future and impressed upon me that, being on the wrong side of the law, for whatever reason, could only limit my horizons. I got the point. By the time we were home, we were laughing about the whole incident, and we broke into hysterics as she said she would now have to introduce me to her friends as "my son, the ex-con."

Yes, there were still times when I broke curfew, but I was constantly in fear that a cop would see me walking and arrest me. Rather than walk on the sidewalk, I would bend over so that my back was parallel to the ground, lurk in the shadows and stealthily walk along the sidewalk side of parked cars. While I was less conspicuous to cars driving by, anyone who happened to see me would have been *certain* I was up to no good, possibly even trying to steal a car. The last block home would always be a sprint, and I did not let up until I was safely inside the door to the hallway of my building. I wanted to make sure I stayed an "ex."

Chapter 8

NOT STRICTLY BY THE BOOK

Most of my teenage sex education was caught piecemeal from my friends. I recall boys at school passing around a tiny photo of what they claimed were a woman's "private parts," as we called it. We were in the grip of group delirium as we pushed and shoved one another to get a closer look at the forbidden photo. I could not tell what it was. It looked like some unidentifiable part of the anatomy of a monkey. So much for the long-awaited photographic revelation. The anatomy of a woman remained a mystery to me.

There was one exception to learning about sex from my friends. No, I did not discuss sex or my rush into puberty with my parents. That would have been much too embarrassing for me and uncomfortable for my father. In fact, I have no memory of my father ever telling an off-color joke or making a casual immodest remark about women. So far as I could tell, there was not a salacious bone in his body. He would no more talk with me about sex than about women's shoes. Neither was within his consciousness. My mother? She was much less inhibited and would have welcomed the opportunity to probe and intrude, but the *last* thing I wanted to do was have a discussion about sex with my mother. That was just never going to happen. Period.

One day, I was going through my mom's dresser drawer, just snooping. "There must be something interesting in there," I thought. Under her clothes, I found it: pay dirt. It was small, only about 4" x 6 ½". Published in 1958, it was a paperback book with the intriguing title, *What to Tell Your Children About Sex?* This promised to be serious stuff. But what was it doing there? No one had told me anything.

For a young adolescent, this discovery was as exciting as an archeologist finding the lost Ark of the Covenant containing the tablets of the Ten Commandments. Just as the Ark mysteriously disappeared when the Babylonians destroyed the First Temple in Jerusalem, I feared that, if I did not take immediate action, the book too might vanish. So I snatched it and hid it without saying a word to anyone. When no one was around, I would secretly read passages.

The book was largely organized around chronological stages of development, from youngsters to pre-adolescents to teenagers, and posed questions that kids would likely ask their parents, along with answers. There were also illustrations. This promised to be a gold mine.

I immediately immersed myself in the answers to a few pressing issues. Is masturbation dangerous? I was relieved to read that it would not lead to injuries and was not a sign of severe mental illness. That was good. But I read further, and it warned that *excessive* masturbation may be a sign of inner disturbance that required professional intervention. I started to worry. I had no idea what "professional" intervention meant. The only professionals I knew were medical doctors, and I could not imagine explaining to my mother that I needed to talk with Dr. Izbicki. But more importantly, what was *"excessive"* masturbation? Was it determined by an allotted number each day or was there a maximum number per week or year or in a lifetime? Did each occasion use up the permissible times, over which any additional masturbation would be *excessive*, in the same way that there is an average number of heartbeats before the heart muscle expires? The book did not answer these logical follow-up questions, and I was not going to ask my parents. I read still further that, if masturbation were limiting one's outside activities or if he (this section only spoke of boys) seemed listless or depressed, he needed to get help. That did not sound like me so I thought I passed the test. Maybe I shouldn't have been so eager to read the book after all; it only seemed to cause me to worry.

Other parts of the book were equally unhelpful. I learned that wet dreams should be explained to the son by his father when they take a walk together, but, since I seldom took a walk with my father and wet dreams would never have been on the tip of his tongue if we did, I never received the personal explanation. There were short discussions of "sexual disturbances," such as sterility, impotence, and frigidity; and "problems," such as homosexuality (which the authors assured us could be cured), prostitution (which we were told was no preparation for marriage), and "venereal disease" (which made sex seem but a prelude to antibiotic "wonder drugs"); but these were so far from my experience as to be background noise to my real interest. What was sex all about?

I got very excited when I saw a chapter entitled, "Facts of Life Illustrated." Now I would actually be able to see female body parts in detail. An earlier chapter had told me that women had breasts because they made milk for babies. But I knew there was much more to them than that. I was acutely interested in breasts, but I had no interest in babies. All women had breasts, whether or not they had babies. Besides, they looked good (at least from the outside), and men paid a lot of attention to them. None of that had anything to do with milk or babies. Now I was going to be able to see for myself what all the fuss was about. But the book's illustrations looked more like the schematics of electrical circuitry than anything useful to satisfy my adolescent curiosities. The drawings of the female body with her internal sexual organs resembled the outlines of the skeletal head of a steer with curved horns on either side; I now know that the curves were fallopian tubes, but back then they were cattle horns to me. The "illustrated facts of life" gave me less insight into the mysteries of sex than the life lessons given by Lucy to Charlie Brown in the comic strip *Peanuts*.

I had to return the book before it was discovered missing. I put it right back where I found it. Then, a couple of weeks later, I grabbed it back. There must be something really useful (a euphemism for titillating) in there. Then I found it. In a chapter entitled "Looking Ahead To Marriage," which I had passed over the first time as being unlikely to contain anything interesting, there was a section called "What happens in sexual intercourse?" In two and a half pages, despite somewhat clinical language, the authors gave a detailed, step-by-step description of the process – emotional and physical – ending with the assurance that, when it is all over, the body is satisfied and there is an "after-glow of contentment and relaxation." This was what I was looking for. I dog-eared the precious pages and returned the book to the dresser drawer. I would retrieve it whenever I needed to be aroused by readily available entertainment.

Neither my mother nor I ever mentioned the book, and she never tried to initiate a discussion about sex. The book was my secret treasure trove. I cannot help but wonder whether she put the book in her drawer in the hope that I would find it. If she were looking for signs that I had, the dog-eared pages would have given me away.

My teenage sex education continued one night at Deborah Boys Club, on West Ainslie at the corner of Kimball Avenue. It was our community center, with a huge gymnasium, wood shop, arts and crafts, locker rooms, kitchen, and after school programs. The club hosted sports and dances. When I first got there, they served 1600 kids each year. Many of us formed what was called Social Action Clubs. I joined one of the SAC's with my friends from Volta, and we wore specially-designed black jackets with red stitching and letters on the back spelling out Centurions, the name of our SAC. They were specially made by Ned Singer's Sports, which seemed to have a monopoly on jackets for the SAC's. We used the club mainly for playing sports, like basketball, in competitions with other clubs. It was good, clean fun, until the night of the sleepover. I was twelve or thirteen, prior to entering high school, when our team decided to have a sleepover in the gym. We brought our sleeping bags, plenty of snacks, and ordered in hot dogs and hamburgers. That night we played basketball for hours, munched on potato chips, fries, popcorn, and other equally unhealthy snacks, and downed gallons of Coca-Cola, orange drink, and Kool-Aid.

Finally, around midnight, at the end of the umpteenth basketball game, the chaperon entered the gym and ordered us to turn out the lights and get into our sleeping bags. We groused but complied. Twenty boys in their early adolescence, high on hours of vigorous sports and junk food, were not going to bed quietly. It started with guys from all over the gym yelling out inane comments, asking dumb questions, and bravely shouting the isolated swear word. One guy would scream something crude to another or holler out to the room itself, just to make sure he was heard. Someone would respond with an even more obnoxious retort, followed by laughter and the throwing of wet paper towels and cups. Then someone said, "I'm jerking off and you guys don't even know how to do it." The response was predictable. "You dumb shit, you don't know the different between your thing and a broom handle." "Yah, your mouth and your A-hole are the same thing." And it went downhill from there.

Then there was a voice that set off the ultimate challenge. "Hey, I can shoot my wad a lot further than yours." In the pitch darkness, I did not know who said it, but I had a good guess. It had to be Tony. "You don't have a wad," came the response from the corner. (While I thought I knew what a wad was, I wasn't sure I had one, and I surely wasn't going to say that.) Lots more laughter, although I doubted it was all genuine rather than defensive. Other responses came pouring in, each trying to outdo the other. A sibilant echo added, "Your wad smells like a stinkin' snake," even though it made no sense. "Mine went clear over to the wall." "Yeah, but mine hit the window." Then came the Superman boast. "I just hit the ceiling." The room exploded with cackles from every corner. Superman continued, "And it's right over your head and about to drop." Hee haws. Hysteria. "Gross. Everyone, cover your heads." There was pandemonium. The lights went on, boys leaped out of their sleeping bags and started running around the room, looking at the twenty-four-foot ceiling, thinking they would find the telltale sign. It took thirty minutes for everyone to calm down and get back into their sacks. I did not join in either the attempted one-upmanship of insults or the competition for who could be the most vulgar, but I did pretend to laugh. Yes, I was uncomfortable with the impious banter and had neither the desire nor the personality to out-gross the others, but the last thing I wanted was for my friends to see me as a wimp and exclude me from our newly-formed band of brothers. What occurred that night was a typical, all-male adolescent bonding experience for "we few, we happy few." For us, those who were not there that night must "hold their manhoods cheap." That evening was our Feast of Crispian.

Chapter 9

THE CATCH

Professional sports lore is filled with stories of feats that not only elevate their actors to super hero status, but embody supreme confidence, reflecting the glow of an "I can do attitude." There was Babe Ruth, coming to bat for the New York Yankees against the Chicago Cubs in Game 3 of the World Series in 1932. In the fifth inning, with the game tied 4-4, Ruth came to the plate. The pitcher, Charlie Root, threw a strike. The fans shouted insults at Ruth and mocked him as he positioned himself at home base, ready for the next pitch. He then pointed toward center field. Strike two. He again pointed toward center field. This time, Root threw a curve ball, and Ruth hit it more than 440 feet into center for a home run, right where his finger promised it would go.

Then there was Willie Mays, playing center field for the New York Giants in the first game of the 1954 World Series. In the top of the eighth inning, with the score tied 2-2, Vic Wertz of the Cleveland Indians came to the plate. The Indians had runners on first and second base. Wertz belted the ball deep into center field. Mays, with his back toward the diamond, ran at full speed toward the warning track and caught the ball on-the-run with an over-the-shoulder catch, turned around in one fluid movement and threw the ball toward the infield, preventing any runner from scoring. It is often called one of the greatest plays ever.

My favorite was Johnny Unitas, who played quarterback for the Baltimore Colts from 1956 to 1973 and is credited with leading his team to a NFL Championship in 1958, with a stunning drive in the final two minutes of regular time left in the game. It is now referred to as "the greatest game ever played" by sports writers. But my most enduring memory of Unitas is not the 1958 game, but a long pass that he threw at the end of another game. Right after the ball left his hand, but before it was caught by the wide receiver, Unitas turned his back and walked away, toward exiting the field. He was later questioned about why he did not wait to see if the receiver caught the pass. He responded something like "It was my job to throw the ball, which I did. It was his job to catch it, which he did." Unitas once said, "There's a big difference between confidence and conceit. To me, conceit is bragging about yourself. Being confident means you believe you can get the job done, but you know you can't get your job done unless you also have the confidence that the other guys are going to get their jobs done too." I marveled at his self-confidence. Where did it come from?

And then there was Cary Lerman. I was around twelve years old, and we often played football. No, not football with uniforms, padding, helmets, mouth guards, cleats, shin guards, and hard tackles. Size, weight, muscle, and hard-headedness did not matter. We played touch football, where speed, agility, and the ability to catch a football and then run as fast as you can by striving to achieve take off velocity. I vividly remember a day we went to River Park, just off Foster Avenue between N. Albany Ave and N. Francisco Ave. It was a beautiful, thirty-acre park, where we played in the Mighty Mites baseball league (our equivalent to the Little Leagues). It could be reached with a long bike ride, but we preferred being driven by our parents. But they were not keen on driving us around, especially when others parks were nearby. As a result, going to River Park was a rare treat.

One Sunday, a bunch of us got together and somehow got to River Park to play touch football. It was just an informal, pick-up game, without uniforms, coaches, umpires, or watching fans, and no official score keeper, hardly a blip on the radar screen of a young person's life. I was a fast runner and played receiver. Our team huddled. I was to run as fast as I could, and the quarterback would throw me the ball. That was the play. Simple. I lined up, the center snapped the ball to the quarterback, and I took off like the fate of the world would be decided on my speed. I zigged and zagged to evade the defender, and then ran straight down field. I looked up and, out of the corner of my eye, I could see the football soaring high above my head. I picked up my pace, and, without ever looking back or turning my head from side to side, I caught the ball over my shoulder in a dead run toward the opponent's goal line. I ran into the end zone and scored a touchdown. Yes, everyone on my team cheered and marveled at my once-in-a-lifetime catch. But the play didn't matter in life's balance sheet. The game didn't matter. No one was really keeping score. The day is remembered by no one except me.

But what a memory it is. When I caught the ball, I was overwhelmed by a feeling of exhilaration. For that moment, that one brief shining moment, I could do anything. I was Babe Ruth, Willie Mays, and Johnny Unitas rolled into one. I have often called upon that remembrance to shore up my resolve when my confidence was lagging. Each time I replayed that catch, the same emotion would swell up within me. I would feel the confidence to move forward, knowing I was capable of more than my echoing doubts. From that one otherwise forgettable moment, utterly insignificant to everyone else that day but alive in my memory, I found a life-changing truth. Remember your finest moment, and then do it again.

Chapter 10

USE YOUR SECHEL

In a metaphysical sense, my mother's family was split. There was the Chicago Rottstin contingent on my mother's maternal side. And there were the Shapiros, on her paternal side. In Chicago, my great-aunts Lil and Ann, from the Rottstin side, also lived in Albany Park. They lived together and loved each other fiercely. They fought and argued and yelled with as much vigor as the love they shared. We would often go to their apartment for family get-togethers and dinners. After the dinners, my father would go to play pinnacle and poker. The cigarette smoke was heavy and lingered above the dining room table. Their brother, Uncle Phil, was a wonderful, warm man, who would shower us all with gifts from the hosiery and underclothing store where he worked. On birthdays, he would surprise us with the biggest, best toys, reminding me today of Uncle Herr Drosselmeyer in the opening scene of *The Nutcracker* ballet. He once gave me the basic American Flyer electric train set, which I enlarged over the years. It was 3/16" scale and perfect in every way. Then, in mid-life he got married. His wife, Rose, was also warm and fitted right into the family, but she put a stop to the OMG gifts – except for my cousin, Raymond. Lil, Ann and Phil had had another sibling, Nathan, who had died young, leaving a widow and two children, one of whom was Raymond. Uncle Phil was particularly protective of Raymond, and he continued to shower his nephew with over-the-top gifts. I was envious, but I understood. Family takes care of family, and Raymond's needs were greater than mine. Instead of spectacular toys, each birthday I received underwear, undershirts and socks from Uncle Phil. My mom was thrilled, and I wore the best underclothes of any boy in Albany Park.

Raymond was several years older than me, broad-shouldered and strong, and, although we did not see each other often, I have two unsettling memories of him. When I was around eight years old, the extended family went to a family camp in Wisconsin where we swam in a cold lake, swatted mosquitos, and ate bologna sandwiches. Raymond was there, and I looked up to him. One day, we all went to the camp store that stocked all manner of sundries and odd items. My eyes fixated on a sword in a jewel-encrusted case. I wanted it so badly that my excitement was evident. I held it in my hand as if it were a precious, fragile artifact, examining it from every angle and speaking in high-pitched, rapid tones of its singular beauty, as if it had been just taken from the tomb of Tutankhamun. But I had no money and my mom was not about to buy it for me. I pleaded with her but she would not budge. An aunt was there, and she was equally unwilling to treat me. Raymond then offered to pay for it, but I said no. For some reason I cannot explain, I was uncomfortable with having him pay for the sword. He wanted to do something nice for me, yes? It was a wonderful gesture, no? Was it just stubbornness on my part or was there a legitimate reason for my uneasiness about the whole matter? A couple of nights later, I wetted my bed, a very rare occurrence. Somehow, Raymond learned of it, although I tried to hide it as best I could. I begged him not to tell anyone. He said

"I won't tell if you let me buy you the sword." I was thunderstruck, as I immediately felt something untoward going on. I felt uncomfortable, sensing his use of an emotional lever. I was caught between the proverbial Scylla and Charybdis. I would be humiliated if it were known that I had wetted my bed, but I knew I would feel humiliated if I acquiesced and let Raymond buy me that sword. Which humiliation would I choose? I saw no way out. I opted for the emotional blackmail. He bought me the sword. It immediately lost its magic by virtue of the tarnished transaction, and I felt cheapened in the process. I felt more soiled than the sheets on the camp bed. I had managed to achieve the worst of both worlds. I had both wetted my bed and succumbed to a threat, a form of extortion. I vowed never to allow myself to be put in that position again.

When we were teenagers, Raymond and I would have another misadventure that left me feeling adrift. It reverberates inside my brain whenever I know I am contemplating not playing in the middle of the field but instead skirting the outer boundaries of what is proper. My mom needed to move a mattress from our Albany Park apartment to my Aunt Lil's, only a few blocks away. Then we were to take a different mattress from Aunt Lil's to a new apartment for my grandmother, who was moving out of our place. Our job? Simple. We were to haul the mattress down three flights of stairs, meet my father, who was waiting outside, and help get the mattress on the top of the car. We carried the mattress down half the first flight, and were preparing to make a sharp right-hand turn and continue down the stairs. But straight ahead of us was a large rectangular light-well above an air shaft that went all the way down to the first floor. So we could continue to struggle with a very heavy, cumbersome mattress down all the stairs – or do it the easy way. God gave us brains to make a choice, and the choice was easy. We threw it over the bannister into the air shaft. The sound of the mattress hitting the bottom was deafening, reverberating upwards toward the light-well. My mother came running out. "What's the matter? What happened?" She saw the two of us starring down the air shaft, and joined us looking down. "You didn't, did you? You couldn't have." We all ran down the stairs to inspect the mattress. It was obvious upon first sight: it was ruined. The mattress was folded onto itself. The spring coils were bent and deformed. My mom starting screaming at us like we were imbeciles, which we were. "What is wrong with you? You have no *sechel* [Yiddish word for brains or common sense]," she screeched. In our home, there was no insult greater than telling someone they had no "*sechel*." It stung, going straight to the emotional solar plexus. We were ashamed. We were silent. Anything I said would only make matters worse, as there was no rationale that could possibly excuse our decision. We were lazy, we tried a dumb shortcut, and it cost my parents money they could not afford. I later learned that Warren Buffett would famously tell his managers to conduct their behavior as if an aggressive reporter for the *New York Times* would find out about it and publish an account for the world to see. I had learned at the age of thirteen my mother's analogue of this principle. It was simple and boiled down to three words: "Use your *sechel*."

We did successfully move the second mattress to my grandmother's new apartment without mishap. My grandmother, Sylvia, my mother's mother, had earlier moved to Los Angeles with my grandfather in an attempt to save their failing marriage. They had little in common with one another and came to loathe each other. They were very considerate, though, about their divorce. They waited, cursing and hating each other, until all the children were married. After they divorced, my grandfather met and then married "that other woman," as my grandmother would curse. Her name was Charlotte, but we were not allowed to say her name in my grandmother's presence, and heaven forbid that we should ever invite her to a family event.

Chapter 10: Use Your Sechel

Grandma would alternate between living in Chicago and Los Angeles. Before she got her own place in Chicago, she lived with us and contributed mightily to the clouds of cigarette smoke in our apartment. She often cleaned out the men at the family poker games. Her voice made the walls vibrate. But to me, her grandson, she could not have been warmer or more loving. She exuded love and acceptance and would wrap me in arms that felt like eight tentacles swaddling me in protection. She had few material possessions, and yet she would literally give anyone in her family the last shirt on her back. Her love poured out, consistently and inexhaustibly, like Niagara Falls. When it came to cooking, she had a specialty, and everyone knew it. No one even tried to compete with it. It was her strudel. Not a German apple strudel. It was an Eastern European red raspberry strudel, surrounded by a dough so thin that when it flaked, it became almost transparent. She would bring it to our apartment in a shoebox, with wax paper separating row on top of row of this delicacy that put Burny Bros. Bakery to shame. When I opened the box and smelled the freshly baked strudel, I knew it was just for me. It had to be. Who else could it be for? Of course, my sister did not agree. After the family ate about half the box over the course of a week or two, I would hide the remaining strudel in the pantry, pretending it was all gone. I would strategically eat a piece and hide the crumbs. But I also would take out a piece and eat it in front of my sister, to taunt her as only a younger brother could do. "Where did you get that," she shouted, "I want some." I just smiled, making her yell some more. Oh, how I miss that strudel.

My love for my grandmother's strudel was matched by an equal and more powerful opposite reaction to cheese, a lifelong anomaly for a person who sees himself as a student of reason, a devotee of the Enlightenment. It is more than an anomaly. It is a phobia, which the textbooks call turophobia, the fear of cheese. I cannot pinpoint when it started. There was a time when I loved grilled cheese sandwiches; I recall devouring my mother's grilled cheese sandwiches when I came home from school for lunch. I had no problem. And then, as Joseph Heller would say, "something happened." I was no older than ten when cheese became my lifelong *bête noir*. It would be wrong to say I disliked it – I loathed it. I could not tolerate the aroma, the touch or even the look of cheese. When my parents brought pizza into the house, I had to run out of the room. At times, the smell would trigger dry heaves. The phobia grew to the extent that I would not eat anything that had touched cheese or had even been on the same plate with it. And this meant all cheeses. Every kind. No exceptions. The phobia eventually extended to white milk, cottage cheese, cream cheese, sour cream, yogurt, cream in its liquid form and butter in its solid form, and to any flavor of cheese cake. But ice cream was not just permissible: I loved it. I would drink chocolate milk, and we always kept a large supply of Bosco chocolate syrup on hand. I would eat whipped cream but not cream poured into another drink. I would *never* eat butter on bread, but I had no trouble putting melted butter on popcorn. But when it came to cheese itself, there was no room for any margin of error. It was all verboten.

What was the cause of this affliction? I have no idea. The experts tell us that phobias are displaced anxiety, often induced by a traumatic childhood incident. Did I once eat rancid cheese? Was my phobia somehow related to my father being a milkman? Was it an outgrowth of seeing my father's animated revulsion to my mother serving us beef Stroganoff? Had I somehow – unintentionally and unknowingly – transformed the Jewish prohibition on eating meat and milk products together into one that forbade eating cheese and related milk products altogether? I will never know and have never tried to find out. I subscribe to the Irish proverb "better the devil you know than the devil you don't know," but I also think it is better that some things remain hidden.

Chapter 11

NOT MY FAVORITE BEACH

Countless scientific studies have confirmed that an adolescent's brain is not fully formed. The frontal lobe, which is responsible for decision-making, rational thinking, and impulse control, is still evolving; it continues to mature until about the age of twenty-five. This is the part of the brain that assesses risks and decides on risk avoidance behavior. It is well known that teenagers perceive short-term rewards more favorably than do adults. It is said that the teenage brain is wired for impulsivity. It could be dangerous for the inhabitant of such an underdeveloped brain to make choices for himself.

In the summer of 1963, I learned this lesson first-hand without having to conduct any scientific experiment. It was all about skin. The Shapiro side of our family has bronze-toned skin, and my grandfather, mother, and Aunt Myrna had an olive hue to their skin that bronzed beautifully in the sun. They also had semi-Asiatic eyes, particularity as they aged. We often speculated that there had to be Asian ancestors somewhere in the family tree. My mother loved the sun, and, on vacations, she would sit brazenly in the open to maximize her access to the rays. She would bake to her heart's content without any evident effect. My father, like all the Lermans, had skin so fair that it burned at the mere thought of the sun. He avoided the sun whenever he could, and wore a hat when he was outdoors. He did not tan. He got red and redder and then he would burn. When my parents would go to Florida on vacation, I would chuckle at photographs showing my mother lounging with others at the pool, soaking up piña coladas and ultraviolet rays with equal intensity, while my father drank hard whiskey at a canopied bar by himself, in the safe protection of the shade. My skin was closer to my father's, though not quite as susceptible to the sun.

Summertime in Chicago. Hot, humid, humid and hot. Miserably hot. No wonder my father loved the song by the Kirby Stone Four called "In the Good Old Summertime/Take the Lady," with the lyrics "Take the lady to a place that's shady and you gotta have a wonderful time; whenever the summer heat is hot, you just gotta find a spot …" He played the song over and over again, so much so that I can still sing the lyrics after more than fifty years. So, during the tropical Chicago summers, my friends and I would jump on a CTA bus and go to Foster Beach. Yes, there were real beaches in Chicago with wide areas of sand stretching along the edge of Lake Michigan, the fifth largest freshwater lake in the world. During the summer, the water could warm up to eighty degrees, more than pleasant for swimming. We would jump into the water from a pier, oblivious of whatever man-made dangers lurked below the surface, including concrete buoys and protruding rebars. Mostly, we just sat on blankets, listened to music on the transistor radio, drank pop, and hit each other in the arm, looked around for pretty girls who we saw only as mirages. Did we have a beach umbrella? Of course not. Did I wear a shirt to cover my skin? "What ya tike me for, a fool?" as

Eliza Doolittle would say. Did I put on sun screen? Why would I want to be a greasy spoon? Did I do anything at all to protect my skin? Not me.

Three days later my shoulders hurt and, as the day wore on, they turned a deep red and hurt more and more. Eventually, my skin began to peel all across my back shoulder from right to left. I decided to help the peeling along and, by the next weekend, I made sure that the epidermis layer of my skin across my shoulders was gone. Did I tell anyone about my condition? No. Did I rest, protect the damaged skin, add moisturizer, use an anti-inflammatory cream, make a cool compress, take a cool bath, stay hydrated, stay home, wait for the skin to heal? Not me. I did nothing to help heal my skin. I didn't need to. I was fine. I knew better. Nothing was going to happen to me.

That next weekend we went to the beach again. And I exposed my damaged shoulders to the same strong ultraviolet rays that I had the weekend before, without making the slightest effort to mitigate any further damage. It felt fine. No problem for this teenager.

This time it did not take three days. The very next morning, I was in agony and could hardly move. My shoulders were on fire. Every time I moved, I felt like my skin was tightening up, about to crack. Taking off my tee shirt to survey what was going on was an effort. Each movement sharpened the pain. I finally removed the shirt, and, craning my neck ever so slightly, I saw a series of inter-connected blisters, some pin sized but others several inches wide, across my shoulders. Some were white but others were discolored, a sickening shade of yellow. I now had second-degree burns, which damaged the dermis layer of my skin. The burns were not only extremely painful, but they could have caused permanent damage to my tissue and increased the chances of skin cancer.

At least this time, I made two smart moves. I showed my skin to my parents, who were shocked. My mother screamed, "What is that?" and pointed to my shoulders. She yelled at me for my stupidity so loudly and for so long that is was hard for me to get out the story. When she calmed down, she called the doctor. The second wise decision was that, this time, I did not try to help Mother Nature along by bursting the blisters. The doctor prescribed a regimen of careful rinses with cool water and an antibiotic cream. I spent three days at home trying not to move, fearful that I could pop a blister and bring on an infection. The burn eventually healed, but not my memory of the experience. I had a new-found respect for the power of the sun and for my ability to be, well, just plain dumb at times. My adolescent brain realized that I was neither invincible nor savvy. And I knew I needed to spend more time with my father under an umbrella.

Chapter 12

CALIFORNIA DREAMIN'

Many of my mother's relatives on the Shapiro side had made the migration to Los Angeles. By 1960, the LA contingent consisted of my grandfather and grandmother; my mother's brother, Marty; his wife, Phyllis; their two sons, Chuck and Rick; my mother's sister, Myrna, and her husband and kids; my grandfather's brother, Leo; and others. These were the ones who got away, and who, in our imagination, were living the life.

My grandfather was one of the most unusual men I have known. And he was the happiest, at least after he divorced my grandma and married Charlotte. He would reminisce about his idyllic life as a child in Pavoloch, a shtetl about 60 miles southwest of Kiev. That life was not so ideal as to prevent him from emigrating to the United States around 1905.

I still picture him sitting in an easy chair being yelled at by one of the many women (my Mom, Aunt Myrna, Charlotte, friends from his dance group) who thought it their mission or duty to do so. He would sit still, with an enigmatic smile on his face, hands in lap, twiddle his thumbs, and pretend that he was listening to Mozart rather than female anger. It worked. He could not and would not be perturbed. Stress was the second ugliest word he ever heard. (The ugliest was capitalist, but more about that later.) I learned a key survival skill from him. To this day, I have the ability to let wayward remarks, feigned challenges, and collateral sleights roll off my back, touching but not penetrating me. I choose not to let them infect my psyche, to weigh me down or to define who I am. I treat them like rainwater on my skin, momentarily uncomfortable but ultimately harmless. And I owe this adaptation for emotional survival to my grandfather.

Grandpa lived a healthy lifestyle. Yogurt or cottage cheese with fresh fruit every morning, followed by twenty minutes of standing on his head. He exercised his core and would dare us to punch him in the stomach. Recalling what happened to Houdini, I never took him up on it.

He had too many vital things to do than be bothered with earning a living. The real world of work bored him and demanded too much of his limited time. He loved to paint, and he would paint on any surface: burlap, wood, steel, and plastic. Some of his oeuvre consisted of Chagall-like figures leading a heavenly life in rural regions of Ukraine. He generously bestowed his masterpieces on family members, who would quickly try to pawn them off on someone else. He fashioned himself as a poet worthy of England's poet laureate. Every birthday, anniversary, or celebration of any kind, he would insist on reading his latest poem in which every other line was sure to rhyme. He learned the piano by ear and played and sang at family gatherings, even when no one was listening. He did not care; he was enjoying himself.

His greatest artistic love was dance. He and Charlotte didn't dance so much as perform with dramatic effect. Charlotte, a seamstress by trade, made all their costumes, using bright colors and bold patterns, borrowing heavily from the folk costumes of Ukraine and Eastern Poland. Grandpa loved these outfits. The more outrageous the better for him. No amount of frills was too much to show off. And they did not just dance for themselves. They traveled to community centers, nursing homes, and senior citizens' complexes to perform, and, frankly, to show off to his age peers how spry they were. Charlotte was reserved, revealing a faint shadow of blush and offering a shy mischievous smile when she would say in her Yiddish-accented English, "He is so sexy." I knew what she meant, and it made me blush too. Unlike Charlotte, Grandpa was a born exhibitionist: he preened his way onto the dance floor and needed to be pried away. He thrived on attention. I recall one home movie when he suddenly jumped up from a lounge chair, stripped off his clothes, and proudly displayed his birthday suit. He wanted everyone to admire and adore him. He was vain and tried to cover his balding head by letting the hair on one side of his head grow long so he could comb it over the top. When that no longer worked well, he wore a toupee that sat on his head like Moe's of the Three Stooges. The toupee had a will of its own and would move around his head at whim. This is the measure of the man who ultimately lured me to Los Angeles.

Our intellectual exchange started when I was in high school. Three national newsweeklies dominated the media – *Time, Newsweek*, and *U.S. News and World Report*. In the 1960s, the first two were either centrist or left-leaning in their politics. *U.S. News* was decidedly more conservative, leaning to the right. It was a more focused publication in that it emphasized serious national and international issues, like economics, education, politics, world affairs, and health, and all but ignored the more popular news like sports, Hollywood, and what was then called "women's issues," such as art, home furnishings, cooking, and child rearing. I gravitated to *U.S. News*, and, for a while, it became my bible. Any article printed on its pages had to be true.

It was before the days of computers and when long-distance telephone calls were for emergencies only. Grandpa and I wrote to each other, pontificating on politics. He was a committed socialist and believed firmly that there was no worse sin than capitalism, which exploited the worker. The fact that his only son was a very successful and prosperous capitalist who succeeded in his own business caused him existential pain. My grandfather was not an intellectual. He never graduated high school. His understanding of the realities of life in the Soviet Union and the economics of communism was equivalent to a fifth grader's comprehension of the theory of relativity. But that did not stop him from telling anyone within earshot that the Soviet Union was the greatest country in the world, with free health care for all, guaranteed jobs, resort spas that charged a nominal fee, and no religious discrimination. He would never acknowledge that the free health care ranked among the lowest in the world in terms of facilities, training, medicines, mortality rates, and life expectancy. As for the guaranteed jobs, he had obviously never heard the Russian joke: "They pretend to pay us, and we pretend to work." Yes, there was no religious discrimination (unless you were Jewish and wanted to openly practice your religion or go to Israel), but there was no religion allowed at all. The health spas? He may have had something there. He and Charlotte would vacation at a resort on the Black Sea every three or four years. He paid very little for it and loved the resort and the food. While the accommodations would not qualify for the Pocono Mountains, they were luxurious for him. The power of his convictions came from his feelings and the belief that a utopia was not only possible but real. And the only thing standing in the way of spreading that utopia was the capitalists' greed.

I would get his letters extolling the virtues of this imaginary, peace-loving country, and I felt it my moral duty to set him straight, often with direct quotes from *U.S. News & World Report*. I would regale him with the American dream, the rags-to-riches stories, where any person who got an education and worked hard could prosper. He responded with Montgomery Alabama, George Wallace, and tenement slums. He would never hesitate to show utter disdain for our system when he uttered his third ugliest word: "Rockefeller." If Hitler is the embodiment of evil to me, to him, Rockefeller was synonymous with "bastard capitalist." I insisted he pay homage to the First Amendment with its guarantees of free speech and free press. He pointed to the Soviet Constitution, which enumerated even more rights than the U.S. Constitution. When I said that the Soviet's rights were on paper and not put into practice, unlike in the U.S., he said "what about Joe McCarthy, loyalty oaths, blacklists of Hollywood writers, the House Un-American Activities Committee, and political witch hunts against Communists?"

I thought I had him when I mentioned the threat to world peace by the Soviets when they brought nuclear missiles into Cuba. But he asked who had first invented and used the nuclear bomb and placed nuclear missiles in Turkey adjacent to the Soviet border? I responded that the Soviets could at least show gratitude to the U.S. for saving them from Hitler, and he replied that the Nazis were thrown back by the Russians at Stalingrad, and the Russians were the first to reach Berlin. Well, I reminded him, there would have never been a World War II if Stalin hadn't entered into the Non-Aggression Pact with Hitler in August 1939. And he said that the U.S., France and England threw Stalin into Hitler's arms by being aloof and unserious when it came to making a treaty with the Soviet Union. I boasted that the United States spills the blood of its youth so that other people can be free. He countered that the Soviet Union lost 27,000,000 people in World War II and that 16,000,000 of them were civilians. And on it went.

I kept up this correspondence for three years of high school. I eagerly awaited his letters so I could throw back the next verbal punch. For a man who never went to college, he held his own in this exchange. He never changed my views, and I never made a dent in his, but I learned an important life lesson from debating him. I learned to understand the other side's arguments by viewing the issue from their perspective. I was able to see the issue as he saw it. Years later, as a young lawyer, I would hear Charlie Munger, Vice-Chairman of Berkshire Hathaway, tell us that we had to learn to understand an opposing argument fully, by looking into the other end of a telescope and viewing it from your opponent's perspective. This advice was not new to me. I had first learned it from my grandpa.

For many years, we would make trips to Los Angeles to visit Grandpa and the rest of the family, sometimes during the summer and often during the Christmas break from school. We would ride on the El Capitan, part of the Atchison, Topeka and Santa Fe Railroad. There was no sleeping car for the Lerman family. We sat in the coach seats that leaned back about thirty degrees for the forty-hour trip. But I didn't mind. I loved it. I would jump out of my seat for the freedom to walk from car to car, always landing in the Big Dome Lounge car, where I gawked at the impossibly mammoth open spaces and dreamed of something other than Albany Park. But it was the dining car, with its smooth white table cloths stretched so taut that there were no wrinkles and real cloth napkins, a luxury beyond my imagination, which made me feel like royalty. The waiters were dressed in white – white pants, white jackets and shirts and black bowties – and they were my visual transition from Chicago to Los Angeles, from the old world to the new.

The new world became a magical reality in 1960 when my grandfather took me to UCLA. I was in my early teens. It was December, but the weather was glorious. Warm, in the seventies, blue sky, no breeze. All around me was green: trees luscious with green leaves, green lawns stretching beyond the horizon. And set against the green were reddish-brown brick buildings that stood stately and imposing. All I could do was think about why anyone would stay in Chicago, where it was so bitter cold my tears would turn into strips of ice and where the winds were so fierce I could hardly turn my body. Even the Aleuts would not put up with it. And then my grandfather tapped me on the shoulder. "Do you see that couple there, under the tree?" I nodded my head yes. "Do you see him kissing her?" My nod picked up momentum. "Do you see him touching her breast?" At this point, my head was moving up and down like a bobblehead statue. It was moving so fast that everything became a blur. "You will do that someday." I was lightheaded. My fate was sealed. I knew my future. I was moving to Los Angeles the first chance I had.

Chapter 13

BAR MITZVAH

1961 was the year John F. Kennedy was inaugurated, the United States sent its first astronaut successfully into space, and I had my bar mitzvah. We finally joined a synagogue and my parents found the most reformed one they could. It was called Temple Beth Israel, located at the corner of Bernard and Ainsley in Albany Park. The clergy was headed by the esteemed Rabbi Ernst Lorge, who had escaped from Nazi Germany in 1936, became a U.S. Army chaplain during World War II with the 69th Infantry Division, served in England, France, Germany, and Belgium, witnessed the liberation of Buchenwald, and was the first Jewish chaplain to aid the survivors at Auschwitz. He was a champion of the civil rights movement in Chicago and a towering public figure. But all of that was lost on me as I approached my thirteenth birthday with trepidation.

   I was not looking forward to my bar mitzvah. But my family certainly was. It was time to get me a suit for the party to come. We went to a glitzy men's clothing store in West Rogers Park, the "better" neighborhood that was a few miles to the north and east of Albany Park. I can still recall the suave salesman with a small slick moustache who knew just what I should wear. Not some ordinary suit, no. He pulled out a burgundy silk sports jacket, paired with black slacks, a white shirt, and a flat black tie in the shape of an X. He even added a white pocket square. My mother couldn't stop with the superlatives. She loved it. The salesman beamed. And I sulked. I wanted something that would make me blend into whatever space I was in, yet the two of them had settled on something I might wear if I got my handprints fixed in cement on the avenue of the stars in Hollywood. The more they pushed, the more I pulled away. The more my mother said, "You look so handsome," the more I wanted to find a hole for refuge. The more the salesman said, "This sports coat is you," the more I doubted who I was. My sulking gave way to stubbornness and then to sheer determination. I was not going to wear that outfit. Period. We left the store without buying anything, and I was miserable. I had disappointed my mother, and I could not forget the frown on the salesman's face when we left. I spent the next few days rethinking what had happened. The more I thought of the salesman, the more I remembered how his face had turned from disappointment to devastation. "Could I have caused such hurt simply because I was so stubborn?" I thought. "He and my mom only wanted me to look good. What is wrong with that? It is only a suit of clothes." We returned later that week and bought the whole shebang. It made all three of us feel better.

I was diligent in mastering my Torah parasha. It was not the whole parasha. This was an über-Reform congregation after all. I had it nailed. Every line was memorized. No problem there. I wrote my speech and wove it around the election of President Kennedy. Even my father had a part. He was to read a paragraph from the prayer book. He practiced and practiced. But there was one word he stumbled over. Again and again. The word was "consecration." He kept saying "consegregation." My mom, sister and I would roll in laughter each time he mispronounced the word. But he was determined. He was not going to make that mistake in the Temple on my bar mitzvah day. That was the only time that counted.

It was the January 28, 1961, the Saturday morning of my bar mitzvah. Performance time. I aced my Torah reading and speech. I was still sitting on the bimah, facing the congregation. Up came my dad, looking handsome in his new suit, and confident in his stride. He marched up to the bimah and gave me a wink. He was ready. He was going to nail it. And when he came to the word, out came "consegregation." I looked over at my mother and sister. Barb began to snicker, my mother tried to stifle a laugh but failed to hold it in, and it became infectious. I started to laugh and then I laughed some more and couldn't stop. Barb and my mom couldn't stop. Our private joke had morphed into a public spectacle. The great Rabbi Ernst Lorge gave me a look, first of surprise and then of dignified disapproval, but I couldn't stop laughing. Nevertheless, I did get my bar mitzvah certificate, showing the benefit of joining a very liberal, reformed Temple. But I think it was signed by the assistant rabbi.

The worst part of the bar mitzvah for me had to do with my pairing. There were two bar mitzvahs that morning, and the other boy was David Kornbluth. I was average Jewish height for a boy of twelve, which meant that I had barely reached the shoulder of my 5'2" mother. I was anxious about that. Why wasn't I growing more? One of my favorite pastimes was to mark my height on an interior doorpost in my house with a pencil. I must have done it three times a week. I would even stretch sometimes so that the horizontal lead mark would be a tab higher than before. I still remember meeting David six months before our bar mitzvahs. He was huge. Not just big for a Jewish bar mitzvah boy, but big by any standard. He was as tall as the Rabbi. And, by the time six months had passed, and I stood next to him on the bimah, he had grown even taller while I still waited for my growth spurt. (I am still waiting.) I was told that I would become a man on my bar mitzvah, but I felt like a child next to David. I still think about how that felt, and I wonder if he ever gave it a moment's notice. I doubt it.

My parents hosted a beautiful bar mitzvah luncheon party at the Ridgeview Hotel in Evanston. The party included my family from Chicago and Los Angeles, my parents' friends, and my friends from Volta, complete with a band, a large cake that I dutifully served to my mother, and the indispensable Horah danced to the tune of Hava Nagila. The highlight of the party was the candle lighting service, the ersatz Jewish ritual of honoring the special people in one's life by asking them to light a candle. One candle was reserved for my all friends, who were represented by one boy and one girl. Who was the girl? Of course, it was Paula Albelda, and she gave me a kiss on the check that amused my father and thrilled me. The kiss still delightfully tingles on my cheek.

But what I remember most was the gift that came all the way from Los Angeles, brought by my very successful Uncle Marty and Aunt Phyllis. It was a self-winding Bulova watch with a pearl face and brown metal band. It was not only my first watch, but the finest piece of anything I had ever been given. It was a priceless gift from a promised land and spoke to me not only of my uncle and aunt's generosity, but of the riches to be had 2000 miles away in the Golden State.

Chapter 14

ROLE MODELS

After my bar mitzvah, I made a decision that, to this day, as Winston Churchill once said, "is a riddle, wrapped in a mystery, inside an enigma." I was popular, sports minded, reasonably well adjusted, and had many friends. Graduating eighth grade meant going to high school. We lived within the district for Roosevelt High School, which was where my sister went. Virtually all my friends were going there. I took the path less traveled, and it made all the difference, and not necessarily for the better. I decided to apply to Lane Tech High School, located on Western and Addison, several bus rides away. Why I did that, I do not know, but I have a couple of guesses; that is all they are, guesses.

At the time, Lane Tech was one of the premier public high schools in Chicago. It was all boys (girls were not admitted until 1972) at a huge campus with a building large enough to accommodate all 5000 students in grades 9-12. It would be an exaggeration, but not by much, to say that its football team was a feeder for the National Football League. It prided itself as the best college preparatory school in the city for those wanting to become an engineer. It had advanced math and science classes and a two-year mandatory tech requirement. Back then, tech did not mean computers, as we didn't know what those were yet, it meant: woodworking, electric, auto, aviation, foundry, or machine shop. But did I yearn to be an engineer? My mother wanted me to be a lawyer and never hesitated to drop hints, but she was not opposed to engineering.

Role models are critical. Unlike mentors, who have a personal, one-on-one, relationship with and influence on a person, a role model does not need to be immediate. He or she only needs to be a person who is elevated as a figure to be emulated. My mother's paternal family, the Shapiros, had several potential role models for me. For a first generation family from Russia, they were remarkably well educated and successful. My paternal great grandfather on my mother's side was Pincus, who came to the U.S. in 1905. He changed his last name from the Russian-sounding Sopofsky or Sapinsky to Shapiro, a more American sounding name, or so he thought. He was a garment presser and attributed his self-sufficiency to the fact that he owned his own very heavy iron. My only recollection of him is that he would walk with his hands behind his back and hum. Always humming. It was not a musical hum but more like a monotonous low vibration. I have been told that I am somewhat tone deaf and cannot carry a tune. I think I inherited my musical abilities from my Zede Pincus. Pincus came directly to Chicago with his wife, Ruchel, with his three children – Louis, Betty and Maurice. Once in the U.S., Pincus and Ruchel had two more sons – Leo and Henry.

My grandfather, Louis, came with his parents to escape having to serve in the Czar's army. My grandfather was drafted into the U.S. cavalry for World War I but never served abroad. He fell off his horse during training and received a small disability pension for the rest of his life. As the eldest brother, my grandfather did not have the luxury of a higher education; rather he was expected to work so his brothers could be educated. He became a bookkeeper and fulfilled his role as big brother. His brother, Maurice Shapiro, became a Certified Public Accountant and learned how to invest in the stock market. He became wealthy from his stock investments, or at least rich by our standards, and he bought an apartment on the Gold Coast of Chicago, on Lakeshore Drive. He freely offered his financial advice and charmed us with a warm twinkle in his eye. He was a possible role mode. My grandfather's brother, Henry, became a lawyer, but he tragically died young from a kidney disease. Brother Leo also became a lawyer, moved to Los Angeles before World War II, played the piano for silent films to make extra money and changed his name from Shapiro to Shephard. By the time I was born, Leo was out of sight and out of mind and not a ready candidate for the honorable position of family role model.

Then there was my mother's brother, Morris Shapiro, who became an engineer after graduating from the Illinois Institute of Technology. Soon after my birth, he borrowed money from my mom and dad, bought a car and headed west to Los Angeles with his bride, Phyllis. Uncle Marty was tall and handsome, with dark wavy hair, and exuded an in-born confidence. My Aunt Phyllis was also tall, blonde, and very attractive, with a cool demeanor. Leaving their West Side Chicago roots behind, they carried themselves as if they had been raised in a country club. Morris too changed his name when reaching the Golden State, from Morris to Martin and Shapiro to Shephard to avoid anti-Semitism. He started his own business as a manufacturer's representative for the semi-conductor industry and his success outstripped that of anyone in our family. He and Aunt Phyllis bought a house in Culver City. I recall visiting it at a young age and seeing something I did not realize private citizens could own: a real backyard. To me, it seemed a grand expanse of green. It required a lawn mower, which meant a luxury. No, I do not mean that the lawn mower was a luxury. Having a lawn that *required* a lawn mower was the luxury.

By 1961, when I was considering Lane Tech, my uncle did something that was unheard of in our family. He and Aunt Phyllis built their own home in Encino, California, a sprawling ranch style house complete with a swimming pool and a view of rolling hills and unbounded greenery. It did not get better than that. They were the epitome of a rich, glamorous couple and proof positive of the reality of the American dream. To a young adolescent who lived in a two-bedroom apartment in Albany Park, their home seemed both unattainable and aspirational at the same time. Marty Shephard clearly occupied the exalted position of role model for our family, and, I now realize, for me.

I visited my Uncle Marty many times in my teens, and my stays in Encino helped seal my own version of "California dreamin'." John Wooden, the Wizard of Westwood, once said everything we know, we learned from others. And that an "other" could be someone at a distance. I learned a lot from Uncle Marty. I recall one evening when we sat down to watch home movies in his home. He took out a movie reel, guided the film through the spools on the projector and pressed the power switch. The tape moved forward except there was no picture. The bulb was blown. I went with Uncle Marty in his Cadillac to a drug store to get a new bulb. At the store, he bought not one but two bulbs. "Why did you buy two when all you need is one," I asked. I could not fathom spending more money than you needed to at the time. He answered, "if one bulb blows out, I have a spare in the house. I don't need to run out to the store as we are doing now and leave everyone waiting for our return." A light bulb went on in my head. In a flash, I learned several important lessons. One was to anticipate something going wrong because, if it can, it eventually will. But the insight went further than that. I needed always to have a backup plan. I had to make sure I had a spare. Equally important was realizing that I needed to have the resources for the spare. Just like Uncle Marty, I needed to make sure I had enough money in my pocket to buy that extra light bulb, even if I were not going to need it right away

Whether Marty, the family engineer, was the deciding factor in my decision to go to Lane Tech is part of the puzzle, but he was undoubtedly an influence. The other was the boy who lived on the first floor of my apartment building, Michael Waitsman. He was in the same class as me at Volta, but he was a person apart. He was different, odd even. He had no friends, except for me and a fellow student at Volta named Alan Losoff, who excelled at math and science and also decided to go to Lane Tech. Sports were as alien to Michael as snow cones from Mercury. But he was smart, really smart, indeed brilliant. And he had interests, far from the contours of the crowd. He loved board games, inventions, and oddities. We designed school science projects together, testing theories of electricity. We had our own phone system, a cord dangling from my third-floor bedroom to his first-floor bedroom and two connected headsets powered by batteries. There were sufficient vibrations that allowed us to talk every day. We were close, but not closer than I was to several other friends who were more in the mainstream of school life. His mother, Bernice, was very smart, astute, hard-working, and a flurry of activity. She was an elementary school teacher, but only because it was 1961 and not 1991. Otherwise, she would have been a business executive. She and my mother were best of friends. Our families were close. So, when he said he was going to apply to attend Lane Tech, the idea started to germinate.

Chapter 15

NOT IN KANSAS ANYMORE

Lane Tech was a mistake. A big mistake. And I knew it from the beginning, but I stuck it out. Picture an entering freshman class of 1250 boys, most of whom were not only not Jewish but had never met a Jew and were not terribly fond of all the Jews they never met. It seemed as if most of my classmates were Polish, and they made no effort to hide their disdain for Jews. "Hey sheeny, what you doing?" "Sheeny?" What is a 'sheeny?'" I asked myself. I had never heard the word before. But their tone and mocking gestures could not be clearer. It was an insult on steroids. "Hey, you wearing a beanie?" they would shout, even though I clearly had nothing on my head. I was never threatened physically, but I internalized the feeling that I did not belong. And then there was the absence of girls. Sure, I knew when I applied that it was an all-boys school, but to be in a building with 5000 testosterone-pumping boys without any girls in sight was, to put it mildly, depressing.

I quickly learned that I was not in Kansas anymore. It was the first day of my first class at Lane Tech: mechanical drawing. It was 8:15 am. I was nervous. We were all nervous. The teacher was Mr. Richard Olson, about thirty, lean and muscular, blond and sporting a crew cut. He wore a white shirt and non-descript tie. He welcomed us to our new school. His speech was clipped, precise and concise. There was no effort at warmth or concern for our first-day anxieties of what was to come. After Mr. Olson greeted us with "Welcome to Lane Tech. Do your best," we heard the national anthem played over the PA system in our room. Several of the boys were restless, standing awkwardly, shuffling back and forth on their feet. Several were whispering to one another. There were a few snickers in the room. All typical boys' stuff. When the anthem was over, most of the boys quickly sat down, but Mr. Olson remained standing. He looked at us with anger in his eyes. "Get up. All of you. Stand straight." We complied. And then he bellowed, "I fought in Korea for this country. I saw my buddies die in rice paddies and on mountain tops. They died for you. So you could stand in this free country and honor our national anthem with your hands over your hearts. You have disgraced them with your disrespectful behavior when the anthem was played. I never, never want to see that happen again." And it never did.

I was required to take two years of mechanical drawing, which included one semester of architectural draftsmanship. The mechanical drawing classes required me to draft schematics of tools, equipment, bridges, and similar industrial objects. The architectural drawing class was exactly as it sounds. I drew floor plans, building façades, details of bookcases and furniture. My essential tools were a large, solid wooden drafting board, high-quality paper, thin tracing paper, a T-square, triangles, protractors, compass set, lead pointers and, of course, a really fine eraser. While this equipment was available in the classroom, I had a lot of homework, which required a duplicate set of tools at home. Not only were the lines to be precise, but I had to print labels with clarity and aesthetic appeal. I used to work at home from our dining room table, maneuvering the T-square up and down the board, positioning the triangles to get the perfect corners and lines. I struggled. Graphic art did not come easy to me. But I was able to turn to my father for help. He had a natural talent for drawing and could do the pristine lettering required. He would spend hours with me, demonstrating just how to letter the labels, draw a precise semi-circle with the compass, and get the right perspective. Hauling milk crates was his work, but working with me on the technical drafting was his delight. I got high grades in these classes, and his help was the reason why. As I sat next to him and marveled not only at his ability but his joy in drafting, I could not help but wonder how different his life would have been if he had been able to pursue a different vocation. Yes, life did not deal a fair hand to everyone, which was his misfortune, but I also knew that my parents were doing their utmost to provide me with the opportunities they never had, which was my good fortune.

At the end of my first year, I had to select a foreign language. The choices were Latin, German, Russian, Spanish, and Polish. I could understand offering Latin, as that unlocked the mysteries to many classics and the romance languages derived from Latin. Spanish was practical and useful not only in parts of the U.S., but in all of Central and South America and in Spain. It was also closely related to Portuguese and Italian. Russian made sense as we were in the midst of a cold war and needed to understand our adversary. German? Well, Berlin was ground zero in the cold-war battle with Russia, and besides scientific and technical sources were still written in German, and it was a first language to almost 100 million people. But Polish? Why Polish? Its popularity at Lane Tech could be found in the numbers. As I mentioned, Lane Tech's largest ethnic group was Polish. The demand for the language was there, but I do not think anyone who was not Polish took the class.

I selected German. My teacher was Mr. George Meierdierks. He was tall, very tall, about 6'5," with an enormous head, a long face, and hands the size of a Ferris-wheel car. His voice was deep and gravely. He resembled Fred Gwynne's Herman Munster character in the sitcom *The Munsters*, except that Mr. Meierdierks had a kind smile, and he was a gentle man. And he gave me all A's. Those grades still baffle me since I completed two years of German without knowing how to speak a word of the language. We drilled every day to learn how to use the German definite articles *der, das, die, dem, den*, etc. He taught us a nifty ditty that we used to figure out when to use which article, and it went something like this, sung to a forgettable tune: der, das, die, die, dem, das, die, die – and on and on. At a moment's notice, I was able to stand in class and recite the ditty without error, which is probably why I got A's. It was certainly not because of any ability to read, write or speak German. To this day, I can still sing much of the ditty.

I had no friends at the school. Even Michael Waitsman moved away to the suburbs after the first year, leaving me alone. But I had an idea. While I was still not tall (probably 5'4" when I entered Lane Tech), I was fast and athletic. Or so I thought. It was time to try out for the football team. Yes, the other kids would be bigger, but I was faster. Lane Tech has its own stadium, and tryouts were after school. I showed up. The other guys looked like they were already in the NFL. Several weighed over 200 pounds and were over six feet and growing. But I was fast. All the coach wanted was to time us running 100 yards. I was ready for that. Ready, set, go. I raced, faster than I ever ran before. I could feel the wind hitting my hair and my feet picking up the pace as the yards went by. I could hear the coach click the stopwatch as I passed by. I ran a bit further to cool down and proudly walked back, waiting to hear that I was on the team. All I heard was, "Thanks, kid, for trying out." That was it. It was over. They didn't even offer me the position of water boy. I hadn't even qualified for the bench. In retrospect, the rejection probably saved my life. I returned to school the next morning and signed up for the slide-rule club.

Lane Tech had a massive cafeteria, as would be expected for a school of 5000 boys. There was not a lot being served that I would eat. Each Friday, in keeping with Catholic tradition, fish was served. I was not a big fan of fish back then, even though the pools of oil in which it was served was not a deterrent for me. Each day offered a special, but it was often ham or pork chops or some other meat I avoided. Daily staples included pizza, macaroni and cheese, pasta with parmesan, and other cheese-laden fare, so I avoided them. Hot dogs might be an option, but they were made of pork, so I demurred. The best-selling item on the menu was, no surprise, hamburgers. While I had no problem at the time with eating non-Kosher meat (but never ham or pork chops), these hamburgers were out of bounds. They were served in buns dripping with butter. They needed to keep the cafeteria line moving fast, and they succeeded by not taking any special orders. I could not get a hamburger that was not already ensconced in a butter-soaked bun. My father's angry words came to mind when he learned that beef Stroganoff was made with sour cream. My stomach curdled at the thought of eating the hamburger. I opted for sandwiches from home: peanut butter and jelly, bologna, and salami. At Lane Tech, even lunch time was a disappointment.

The school may have set back my social life by years, but I did learn a few things. I learned what privilege was about or, more frankly, what not having privilege meant. At the end of each school year, an enormous spreadsheet was plastered on the wall outside the administrative offices. It listed each student in each grade level, ranked by their grade point average. At the end of the first year, I looked at the sheets containing the names of 1250 boys to find mine. I started at the top. I knew I was not number one. I did reasonably well, but I certainly did not get all A's. I went down and down and down and there, around #120, was my name. Respectable, but, as Groucho Marx would say, "No cigar." The problem was that there were two freshman classes of thirty kids each who were in an honors track. They took all their classes together and floated through the school in their own bubble. They rarely mixed with us ordinaries. They got the better teachers and the better schedules. But here was the kicker: if an A were worth four points, their A was five points. Their B was four points instead of three. And so on. They started the class ranking race twenty yards in front of everyone else. And, because they were in the honors track, teachers tended to give them the benefit of the doubt – an A or B but never a C. This extra point applied to all the substantive classes, like English, math, and science, but not to P.E. or the practical trade classes like woodworking or electric shop. So, the top sixty or so places were taken up by these guys who got extra points just for being in a separate track. Yes, Woody Allen was right. All they had to do was show up to get that extra point advantage. That grade preference was bad enough, but they walked around with a superior attitude, looking down at the rest of us from their privileged perch.

Is success really the sweetest revenge? Could be. My English teacher in the eleventh grade petitioned to have me join the twelfth grade honors English class. It was very rare for one to cross over the divide, but I somehow qualified. I remember walking into the class, feeling like an imposter. I was nervous. How could I possibly compete with these academic superstars? Who was I kidding? They all knew I did not belong in the honors track. I knew it too. They kept their distance from me, maybe because they were concerned that my "ordinariness" would rub off on them. Or perhaps they thought that they could not possibly learn anything from me. We were given our first assignment, to write an essay. I wrote on the *Prince and the Pauper* by Mark Twain. I started the paper with quotes by Napoleon, Alfieri, and Marcus Aurelius. I then had the temerity (or was it gumption?) to include my own quote, citing my own name. Several days later, we were sitting in our seats as the teacher handed back the essays, redlined and graded. As she was walking around the room giving out the graded essays, she said, "The student with the highest grade is Cary Lerman." Silence. No one was more shocked than me. I looked around the room at faces that were aghast. How could this have happened? they thought. Who was this guy? That is all it took to be accepted by them as a member of their rarified club. It was the twelfth grade, high school was almost over, and it was just one honors class. But it felt so good to see all those emperors with no clothes. When the school year was over, I was #102 out of almost 952 graduates. Not terribly distinguished, but not bad for someone in the second tier.

Chapter 16

THE ALCHEMIST

By the time of my second year at Lane Tech, I was not burning to be an engineer, but I was not sure what I wanted to do either. After a semester of wood shop and another semester of electric shop, I signed up for a semester of foundry. I had never worked with molten metal before, and, what the heck, I thought, my parents could always use anther ashtray. Between them, they smoked three packs a day. I was not great with my hands and never showed any aptitude for shop work, but I thought I would give it a try. The teacher was Fred Dix, tall, angular, and with a voice that boomed throughout the room. And it was a large room. It had to accommodate fifteen work stations for the students, two large casting furnaces for melting metal, and storage rooms for the supplies and the finished projects. Even when the casting furnaces were fired up to full blast to melt the metal, sending pulsating noise to every corner of the room, Mr. Dix's voice dominated the room. He was no nonsense. No horseplay in his shop. It was dangerous work. Aluminum, which was one of the metals we commonly used, melted at 1190 degrees. We also worked with copper, which melted at 1084 degrees. Mr. Dix instilled seriousness and purpose in us. He took fifteen jocular, silly boys and, by the end of the semester, taught each of us to understand danger, calculate risk, respect fire and molten metal, and produce something we could be proud of. He loved to take a shovel and, when no one was paying attention, bang it against metal, causing an ear-piercing clank to reverberate around the room. He delighted when we jumped in surprise or fright at the unexpected noise.

I loved foundry. Every part of it. I had never experienced anything like it. There was the smell of the fire and the molten metal. The glow of the liquid metal was other worldly to me. It was magical. We made molds using sand and had to be sure it was not too fine or too coarse, not too loose or packed too tight, not too dry or too wet. We had to slowly build up the sand around the mold and carefully, oh so carefully, remove the mold without compromising the sides of the impression left in the sand or leaving any grains of sand, no matter how fine, inside the impression. We would then carefully prepare a funnel in the sand to receive the molten metal. Some may have found it tedious work, but every step in the process fascinated me. It taught me to pay attention to detail and that an investment in the prefatory work would pay enormous dividends in the finished product. The end was determined by the beginning: an important lesson that has carried me through life. There were no shortcuts.

Mr. Dix was in charge of firing up the furnace and pouring the metal. We would help carry the cauldron of liquid metal to the molds, but the job of pouring, well, that was his. After the metal had cooled, we carefully removed the top layer of sand, lifted the new metallic object and inspected it for imperfections. Many a time, the ashtray or house number or bookend was imperfect, and it went back into the furnace. But if it looked OK, we filed off the rough edges and polished it until it shone. I made all sorts of trinkets, but I was most proud of a pair of bronze bookends in the shape of an Indian chief with a full headdress. After all, our school was called the Lane Tech Indians.

When the semester was over, Mr. Dix did the unimaginable. At least, unimaginable to me. He asked me to stay on for another semester as shop foreman. I didn't have to think twice. I grabbed at the chance. The next semester, fifteen new boys came in, clowning around and being frivolous around the hot metals. I got to see Mr. Dix, like a drill sergeant, turn them from childish putty into firm young men, just as he was able to transform the liquid metal into the perfect solid shape he desired. I grew stronger that semester. I learned how to teach by doing, how to gain respect by example, and how to work harder than I ever had. And it was all because Mr. Dix saw something in me that Mrs. Marble also saw. Through their eyes, I began to see myself differently.

At the end of the semester, when my stewardship as shop foreman was coming to a close, I excitedly told my mother I needed to talk with her. She was the architect of our lives, the one who directed me, was ambitious for me, and pushed me forward. She was the decision maker in our family. Her word was law. When I told her in an excited tone that I knew what I wanted to be, she asked, "What?" "I want to be a foundry man," I said with pride and conviction. She looked me straight in the eye and did not miss a beat. "After you go to law school, you can become a foundry man." I knew she had outsmarted me. She did not say "no," which would have caused reflexive teenage outrage, but she knew how to deflect and deter. I knew in my heart that my foundry career would go no further than Lane Tech.

Chapter 17

A LAWYER'S OFFICE

I was pushed further down the road to becoming a lawyer in the summer of 1964. One of the stores on my father's milk run was Sears, Roebuck & Co. He got me a summer job in their administrative offices. Each morning, I put on a white short-sleeve shirt, tie, and nice pants, and took two buses and the El train to downtown Chicago. For a sixteen year old, this was real freedom. My job was in the mail room. The head of the mailroom was an Italian named Bill. He was around forty, had a respectable paunch, and lived with his mother. It was clear that the mail room was the zenith of his ambition. He was warm, funny, and welcoming. Then there was Tommy, a Cuban, who flitted around at a frenetic pace, pretending, preening, and scheming to be the assistant head of the mail room. There was another full-time employee and two other summer workers, both high school students like me. One of the other students, Sandy, was Polish and went to a Catholic school. She was very pretty and had a cool reserve that alternated between alluring and off-putting. The other student was Paul, also from a Catholic school, who was likeable but forgettable.

I really enjoyed the work. I became a master of the copying machine, learning how to repair it after paper became stuck. I became expert at removing and polishing the mirror-surfaced drum that determined the quality of the prints. I would deliver mail to the offices on my floor twice a day and got to know the clerical and white-collar workers. And then there were the corner offices, housing the executives and the in-house lawyers. I would deliver packages of legal correspondence and court documents to them, and I wondered what was in them. The lawyers, and they were all men, were in suits and constantly rushing around as if they were doing something important. They had their own offices, their doors were made of wood (and were usually closed, which only heightened the importance and mystery of what was behind those doors), the floors were carpeted, not only in their offices, but in the entry to their offices. There was an air of "this is the place to be." As a sixteen year old whose mother told him first go to law school, my proximity to lawyers kept me on that path.

Occasionally, and only very occasionally, I got a plum assignment. I had to leave the offices to deliver a package several blocks away to the outside lawyers for Sears. This was truly heady work. I would clutch the parcel as if it were my life jacket to make sure I didn't drop or lose it. I recall so vividly going into an impressive building and then up the elevator to the lobby of a law firm. I stepped out. It could have been out of a movie. The reception room was dimly lit, giving the space a somber and serious ambiance as if only weighty matters crossed the threshold from the elevator, and throughout were burgundy leather couches and chairs, dark wood paneling, low tables with magazines and newspapers. The receptionists, and there were two of them, were young, pretty, and professional. They spoke in soft voices and carried themselves as if they too were privileged to be privy to important people and their work. Once, they asked me to stay, as there was a package I had to take back to Sears. As I sat and waited in one of the chairs, I imagined myself opening the door to the interior offices and looking out into the reception area to welcome a client or guest. I knew on a gut level that there was a schism between my world and that of the lawyers who walked at a fast clip in and out of the elevator. I was just another young kid in high school delivering packages. But that was the outer me. Inside, I was the kid who knew he wanted to be a lawyer and to get to LA as soon as possible.

My movement toward the bar picked up speed that summer when I read two books. One was John Henry Falk's *Fear on Trial*, about the blacklisting of writers and actors by McCarthy in the 1950s and the author's legal battle to rescue his name. The other was *My Life In Court* by Louis Nizer, who regaled me with his courtroom battles, making himself and the legal profession appear to be a twentieth-century amalgam of Robin Hood and King Arthur's Knights of the Round Table. Both books showcased the power of lawyers to achieve remarkable results for clients in a public arena on important issues. I was getting hooked. And then there was the television series *The Defenders*, about two lawyers, a father and son, teaming up to tackle important public cases and winning. Yes, the lawyers' offices were fast becoming more appealing than the foundry.

That summer was not all work. Not at all. It was the summer when I closed and opened a door on sex. I was sixteen and had the Chevy to drive, if I could find a compelling reason for my dad to give me the keys. He had more or less forgiven me for the crash, and I had become a better driver. At least I had learned to keep my eyes on the road (an important lesson for a driver). Still, I did not have a girlfriend and had never had a real date. Spending five days a week with Sandy at work was about as close to going out as I got. In my own timid way, I tried to coax some interest from Sandy, but that fell flat. She showed more enthusiasm for Paul, whom I saw as unexceptional in every way, than for me. She would joke with him and, when it came time to punch out at the end of the day, would walk with him. When it came to me, however, she declined a suggestion to go to lunch together, avoided me during our breaks, and answered my questions monosyllabically. I took the hint, but could never figure out why Paul was allowed to be a part of her orbit.

Then Tommy, the "assistant" head of the mail room, invited me and Paul to his apartment to watch some porno movies. I was hesitant as Tommy made no secret of his orientation: he was gay. Paul thought it would be fun and, after I confirmed with Tommy that the movies would be of men and women and not of men and men, I agreed to go. One weeknight, Paul and I went to Tommy's apartment. It was a decent enough neighborhood, and his apartment was small and neat. He had set up snacks, opened some beers (which I declined) and put on the movies. They were shown in an eight mm reel, and, sure enough, they were of heterosexual couples in various positions. The quality was really bad, there was no sound and the whole thing was, well, creepy. But I pretended it was great. We left around 9:00 pm, and I drove home. No damage done.

The next week at work, Tommy kept bringing up movie night and wanted to know how I liked it. "It was OK," I said. "Let's do it again. I can get even better movies next time," Tommy responded. "That's OK, but not necessary," I said, hoping he would take it as a firm no. I still had not learned how to explicitly say no. Tommy was not to be deterred by such a tepid response. All week he kept bringing up the promise of encore night, and I kept deflecting it in a most incompetent way. Then, one afternoon, I was standing and sorting the mail. There were more than 100 mails slots, and I was focused on getting the mail in the right slot. Tommy was to my right, and he too was sorting the mail into the slots. All of a sudden, without word or warning, Tommy took his right hand, reached across and put it on my crotch. Without thinking about my next move, I acted instinctively. I slugged him hard in his left arm. It was not a knockdown, as I was not that strong, but it took him by surprise and pushed him far away from me. Not a word was spoken. I did not look at him. I pretended nothing had happened. So did he. He never bothered me again.

Chapter 18

THERE'S SOMETHING ABOUT MARY

Whether it was in response to Tommy or just my raging adolescent hormones, I went to see Mary that summer. I had not lost complete touch with my Volta friends, even though they went to Roosevelt High School, and I didn't see them on an everyday basis at school. During breaks, we still got together. In that memorable summer of 1964, I was surprised when one of my friends, Tony, told several of us about a prostitute he had been to see. I had never spoken with my friends about a prostitute; I had never seen one, and I had no idea where to find one. Tony said that he went to the West Side, in a Black area, with some other guys, and they had Mary. Talk led to jokes and jokes led to boasting and boasting led to dares and dares led to action. Mary cost $10 a person so money was not an issue. The four of us were all going to go together, but there was a problem. We didn't have a car. Or did we? They said my dad's Chevy would be perfect. "No way," I said. "He wouldn't let me take the car out at night and drive to a place like that!" They would not give up, and said "Oh, he will never know. We will be back by 9:00 pm. Don't tell him. No harm, no foul." I gave in, and Tony, Carl, Marvin, and I made plans.

I remember taking a shower that night and waiting for Tony, Carl, and Marvin to arrive at my apartment. It was still light outside when we left, after giving my mom and dad some vague excuse about where we were going. Tony directed me from the front seat. We headed south and to the east (even though we were going to the "west" side) and the neighborhoods began to look ever more sketchy. I was getting nervous. Tony became unsure of where we were going, and kept telling me to make right turns, then left, then right again, left, left, and I thought we were going in circles. The area was filled with red-bricked apartment buildings that seamlessly adjoined other apartment buildings, and they all looked the same. Each one had a stoop and each stoop was crowded with people, all of them Black, sitting outside to escape the summer heat and humidity. I said "This is enough. You don't know where you are going. I'm going home." Just then, Tony recognized something, perhaps a local store or a billboard, but whatever it was he now knew where to direct me. Within a couple of minutes, I was parked about 100 feet from Mary's apartment. The atmosphere in the car had changed during the ride. It started out with four excited boys, laughing and teasing one another, each of us putting on a veneer of bravado. Then, as we got lost, it became tense and the only talk was about what we should do. Once parked, the car became silent. I was scared. My heart was racing, I felt slightly light headed and my knees seemed disconnected from the rest of my body. "Why am I doing this," I thought? But there was no turning back now. We all got out, I locked the doors to the car. It was starting to get dark. We were four white sixteen year olds who, in this neighborhood, were as out of place as a Roll's Royce in Albany Park, and we passed scores of Black teenagers and parents looking at us intently. They knew where we were going. There was no other possible reason for us to be on that street. Tony found the building, and we went in.

We walked up at least three flight of stairs in a dark hallway and knocked on the door. A big guy answered. He looked at us as if we had come to rob the place. "You 'all here for Mary?" "Yes," one of us answered. "I's her brother. Get in." We shuffled in and sat on a couch. The room was dark, smelled of dust and had a feeling of mold. We each gave him $10, and he disappeared. He returned and said "Who first?" Tony jumped up, and said he would be. I didn't know if that was because he had been there before, knew the drill and couldn't wait for the repeat performance. Or, was he showing off? Both? Anyway, he was gone for about five minutes and returned with a Cheshire cat grin. Marvin went next, and he too was gone for only three minutes. I did not want to be last, so I got up. The "brother" told me to wait a few minutes, and he then took me through a door where there was a bathroom straight ahead and a bedroom to the right. He closed the door and left.

I could see that there was a girl in a bathtub. I looked into the bathroom and a young girl, probably no older than I was, sat in a tub of water with a blue cast to it. I had no idea what made the water blue, and I did not ask. "What you lookin' at? Get outta here and go to the bedroom." I did as I was told. I sat on the bed, and Mary walked in wrapped in a white towel. She was dark, very dark, with dark eyes surrounded by stark, scleral white. Her hair was matted and plastered close to her head. She dropped the towel. She was not tall, maybe 5' 3" and she was about ten pounds away from being plump. She was not a Rubenesque figure, but she was not Twiggy either. "What you sittin' there fo'? Get them pants off. I ain't got all night." I took off my pants, underpants, and socks but kept on my shirt. I was so hard that it ached. Before I knew what was happening, she put a condom on me, laid on her back, and told me to get on top of her. She didn't tell me or show me what to do. She grabbed a hold, guided me, and, before I knew what was happening, I was done. She was taking off the condom and wiping me off with a hand towel while I was still processing what had just happened. That was it. I was no longer a virgin, but I knew nothing about making love either. I dressed and went back to the living room.

Then it was Carl's turn. He went in and five minutes passed, then seven, then eight. We all heard Mary's loud voice shouting, "Hurry up already. What taking so long. Get it already." But Carl did not come out. We waited. The "brother" got up and went into the bedroom to see what was going on, and he returned. All he said was "Damn fool can't get it done." Finally, Carl came out, looking embarrassed and said he couldn't come. Poor Carl, and he didn't get his money back, not that he would have asked for it.

Years later, whenever I heard the Jacques Brel song "Next" from the production *Jacques Brel Is Alive And Well And Living In Paris*, I would be brought right back to Mary's living room with these lyrics:

> *I was still just a kid*
> *When my innocence was lost*
> *In a mobile army whorehouse*
> *Gift of the army, free of cost*
> *Next, next*

We were all done with Mary, or more accurately, she was done with us, and that should have been the climax of the evening. I wish it had been, as what happened next took five years off my life and cured me from any more adventures like that. We literally ran down the stairs to the street. It seemed there were twice as many people on the street than when went in. We ran to the car, and I can still feel the stares of people boring holes in my back. When we got to the car, I made no effort to check to see if it had been damaged. I just wanted to jump in and drive off. And what difference would it have made? If I had seen a dent or scratch, would I have tried to find out who did it? Not on my life. I stood by the driver's side and fumbled trying to find the keys. I always put them in my left-front pocket but they weren't there. Did I leave them at Mary's? The mere thought of that possibility made my stomach regurgitate sour acid. They were not in my right-hand pocket either. The situation was turning from humorous to serious to desperate. "I can't find the keys, I shouted." They looked at me with hopeless resignation. Then I remembered. When we first arrived at Mary's and her "brother" asked for the money, Carl couldn't find his wallet. He left it in the car. I threw him my keys, and he jolted down the stairs to get his $10, while Tony went in to be the first with Mary. Carl never gave me the keys back. "Carl, you have the keys," I shouted, "give them to me." Carl was startled, had a Eureka moment, and found them in his pants' pocket. He threw them to me, and we were in.

I was shaking so hard I had trouble getting the key into the ignition switch. Finally, when I turned the key, the engine would not turn over. There was this awful muffled grinding sound. I tried again. Same. Damn it. What is wrong? This is a new car. I smelled gasoline. Then I knew. With my overloaded anxiety, I had flooded the engine. I pressed down on the accelerator too long before turning on the engine, and I had allowed too much fuel to go into the combustion chamber of the car. All we could do was wait. Each minute seemed like an eternity. Ten minutes went by, and I was afraid to try to start the car. If I hadn't waited long enough, I could make the situation worse by stepping on the accelerator again and adding more gasoline into the carburetor. I had a panic attack at the thought of having to call my dad. Call him? How could I call him? What would I tell him? And there were no phones around. Fifteen minutes. I could see people on the stoops starting to point at us in animated gestures. Laughing. Twenty minutes. Tony, Carl, and Marvin yelled at me to do something. "Start the car already. Let's get out of here." I waited some more. Twenty-five minutes. Some of the folks were leaving the stoop and coming over to the car. Carl was stamping his feet, "go, go," he pleaded. I thought he was going to cry. I felt I had no choice. My heart was outside my body, with each beat pressing heavily against my chest. Was I the only one who could hear my chest pounding? I was sweating, breathing heavily, and hoping the thump of my heart would stay inside my chest. I turned the ignition, and the engine turned over. At that moment, I knew there was a God. Luckily, there was sufficient space between the front of my car and the car ahead of me to get into the road with no effort. We were moving. I never wanted to see Mary again.

The ride home was a mixture of animated vocal jockeying as we retold what had just happened and absolute silence, as we each withdrew to our internal world to reflect on the momentous events that had just occurred. I drove to Albany Park without incident and dropped the three friends off at their places. I drove to Harding and found a parking spot. It was around 10:00 pm. Any high from the adrenaline rush of the evening was long gone. Instead, I felt exhaustion and relief. I had dodged a bullet. I would never forget Mary and the 1964 Chevy. They would forever be woven together in one memory of fantasy and folly.

Chapter 19

FIXING IT?

I didn't think my parents had the perfect marriage. I had no concept of what that might be. But I thought they had a good marriage. It seemed to be working. Oh, they would fight now and then. I can still hear my mother's voice, loud and angry, over something or other. She usually started the fight and my father would start to yell back, but he mostly just wanted to retreat to a safe, neutral corner. When they fought, it was often about money. The lack of it. I knew my mother wanted to buy a townhouse in the suburbs like some of her friends or to go on nicer vacations, but that never concerned me. I was quite content living in the apartment in Albany Park. I never felt deprived. I had what I needed, and everyone around me was just about the same; even at school, no one was rich, or so it seemed. We were, I thought, a content family.

But one evening, when I went to bed in the room I shared with my sister, I could hear my mom and Barb talking in the dining room. The bedroom opened onto the dining room, and, even with the door closed,

I could easily hear them. The two of them had a close relationship, and they were often huddled together to talk about the great social issues in my sister's life. (Later in life, they talked so often that I thought they should get a dedicated telephone line.) This time, however, the hushed conversation was not about Barbara. I could tell my mother was distressed. She was unhappy, very unhappy. And the unhappiness was because of my father. This is how she put it or, I should say, how this teenager heard it. "He doesn't excite me. He doesn't challenge me. I want a husband who, when he walks into a room, lights it up. Who mingles, who talks to everyone. Who people want to talk to and be with. Someone with electricity. Lou is just *there*." I was shocked to hear these words. I don't know if I were more troubled by what I was hearing about my father or about how my mother saw my father. I feared for their relationship. I needed a plan. I had to do something.

There are times at night, often when we lie still in bed, when we are our most creative or, we think, we are the most brilliant. I find that my mind races. I give speeches that would make the Gettysburg Address simply a footnote in William Safire's book *"Lend Me Your Ears."* I conjure strategies that would win a presidential election. I see clearly solutions to the most intractable problems. I make an argument so persuasive that Leopold and Loeb would not just have been spared the death penalty, as Clarence Darrow did, but they would have been pictured on a Wheaties box. Of course, when the fog of night is over, and I awake in the morning, all is gone. Reality gives way to the faintest memory of last night's rather ordinary free association. So it was that night. I knew the way out of the problem. I had an irenic solution. I would talk with my father the next day. I would help him at this critical hour. I would tell him everything my mom had said, and urge him to be a charismatic, charming extrovert who could and would dominate a room. He just needed to be Cary Grant. Simple. I fell asleep, confident in my ability to give him the key to solve the problem. When I awoke, it was not so easy. How could I have that kind of talk with my dad? I would be too embarrassed. I would hurt his feelings. But, more importantly, I did not have a solution. I would be asking him to be someone he was not. He could not change in that way. What if he did not want to change, even if he could? I decided to do nothing. There are times when doing nothing is less harmful than doing something badly. And it is a lot easier. I let it go, but I never forgot it either. What kind of person was I, and what kind of man would I be? Would I be someone who was forgettable in the larger, social world or would I be the light that my mom wanted my father to be? It took me a long time to realize that this was not the right question. The question that mattered was whether I would be the best version of myself that I could be. Hopefully, that would include being a slight ray of light and hope for my family, my friends and my community.

Chapter 20

THE LUCKIEST KID IN THE WORLD

The troubling eavesdropping of the conversation between my mother and sister faded, my parents' marriage seemed to fall into a comfortable rhythm, and I achieved a sixteen year old's dream. And it was all because Barbara was getting married to Neal Schiff. She was twenty years old and more than ready to leave the house and become a wife. Neal was not her first suitor but he was her first successful one. Besides being to Barbara's liking, a potential husband had to pass two difficult hurdles. The first was me. I was true to form as the obnoxious young brother. I would use a self-made slingshot to shoot little wads of paper at her boyfriends' derrieres. I was able to hide behind my bedroom door and, with great proficiency, shoot the tightly balled-up paper through the space between the door and the door frame. I got to be quite good at it. How these guys reacted was definitely revealing of their character, although I am not sure which reaction was better. There was Shane who, upon being hit, turned around with an angry, gnarled face and a few expletive gems. Barbara would curse at me too, along with the traditional refrain of "Ma, make him stop," her all-weather response to my antics. Shane had to go. Then there was another Neil, spelled differently, and my mom and dad thought he was the one because his father owned a wrought iron factory. When my slingshot proved true to a bullseye, he sloughed it off as if it didn't happen. I shot again, another success, but he could not be fazed. He was dismissed as too phlegmatic. In other words, Barb found him boring. But if Shane was too reactive and Neil too passive, Neal Schiff was just right. I liked him right away.

It was the second hurdle that really counted. He had to get the approval of my mom. She was a tough jury and judge. But as soon as Neal walked into our apartment for that first date, we knew he was the one who would get the maternal nod. He had white shoes, white pants, a nice dress shirt and tie, and a blue sports coat. His hair was light brown, combed perfectly, and his smile bounced us off the walls. He was charming, gracious, and engaging. He was warm, caring, and genuine. He was also from Albany Park, but from the other side of Lawrence Avenue, which made him a bit exotic. He had graduated college and was working for a pharmaceutical company, which meant he had a steady job and potential. We didn't know exactly what he did, but we knew he had a good job.

If the way to a man's heart is through his stomach, the way to Barbara's heart was through our mom. When he would come over, he would say hello to me, my dad, and Barb, and then go into the living room to talk for hours with my mom. It was rare for our living room to be used, but Neal was gladly given this honor by my mother. They really hit it off. Barb would cool her heels, waiting for Neal to finish talking with my mom, and occasionally interrupt with, "Neal, we have to go." Oh, he was also a good dancer, at least I was told so. He had it all, and, on August 1, 1964, they got married, and I, at only sixteen, was best man.

Neal was an only child, and picking me to be his best man was a sign of both his acceptance of me as a brother and my new station in life – the only kid left in the household.

But the best part, for me, was that Neal drove a 1963 Chevy Impala convertible. In Chicago, a convertible? They were rare, and, if you had one, what were you doing in Chicago? You should be driving it on Sunset Boulevard. Neal's car was beautiful, and, while made in a factory in Detroit, it seemed like a marvel of nature to me. Burgundy with black leather interior. Black power top. Power steering, power brakes and power windows. 305 V8 engine. That meant a lot of power. And bucket seats. A stereo radio with speakers in the back. It was a fact of life that Neal was cool. But he was beyond cool. Just as he was about to go off on his honeymoon to Florida with Barb, he gave me a honeymoon too. He handed me the keys, and said "Drive us to the airport and, after that, while we are in Florida, take good care of it until we get back." He knew about my crash in my father's Chevy, but showed his confidence in me by entrusting to me his four-wheel prized possession.

And did I drive it, for ten glorious days. I was working in downtown Chicago that summer, and could not wait to come home and drive the convertible. It stayed light until after 8:30 pm so I had time to enjoy it. I would pick up a few friends, and, with the top open and my left arm resting on the top of the door with the window down, I felt like the luckiest kid in the world. I didn't go anywhere special, but there was no need to. Driving the car was special enough. I just wanted to be in the car, smell and feel the leather, and drive it around. The most remarkable transformation occurred when I was driving that car. I no longer felt I was in Chicago. I was in Los Angeles. I was dreaming about year-long warm weather and greenery everywhere. But, most of all, I was dreaming of that girl under the tree who was just waiting for me to come and kiss her.

Chapter 21

LEAVING LANE TECH

To my amazement, I was invited by Gloria Gurtz, a girl I had known from Volta but with whom I had had no contact for three years, to take her to the senior prom for Roosevelt High School. Gloria had always been one of the "nice" girls at Volta, and I was excited to get the invitation. It was my first (and only) prom. I put on a suit and tie and, with friends, we rented a car to pick up our dates. All I recall of her is seeing hair under her arm pits and wondering why it was there. It should have dawned on me that she had decided not to shave, but simple explanations went over my head. I had not yet learned about Occam's razor. My only distinct memory of the evening itself was going to a restaurant afterwards with Gloria and others. My head was pounding. I seldom got headaches, but, by the time we reached the restaurant, mine had overtaken me. I sat at the table and, when the waitress came to take our orders, I said, over the din in the space, that I wanted a "Bayer." She said I was too young for a "beer." (I was seventeen and looked fifteen.) Everyone laughed. "No, I don't want a beer. I want a Bayer." "A beer?" she shouted over the noise. "No, just some aspirin." I finally got my aspirin, returned Gloria home after our chaste evening, and my only high school date was over. I was ready for college.

There was never a question about college. I was going to college, and my mother had already decided I was going to law school. I knew where I wanted to go: UCLA. I was ready for Los Angeles. I applied there and also to the University of Illinois in Champaign-Urbana. My parents offered me an option. If I went to the University of Illinois campus then being opened in Chicago, they would get me my own car, and I would live at home. I didn't even bite at that. I wanted to be on a college campus (the only one I had seen had been UCLA), and the thought of staying at home in Chicago never entered my thoughts. I was accepted by both UCLA and University of Illinois in Champaign-Urbana, and I made my pitch (or I should really say plea) to go to Los Angeles. My mother did what she was so good at, which was saying no by not saying no. She said they could not afford to send me to UCLA and that the University of Illinois, which charged a modest tuition for in-state residents, was where I would go. But, she added, if, after one year at the University of Illinois, I still wanted to go to UCLA, they would find a way to make it work. There it was. Not a flat no, just a deferral. Her words mollified me, as I could dream of UCLA after just one year in Champaign-Urbana. But she knew me better than I knew myself. She knew that, once ensconced at the University of Illinois, I would stay to the end. I had not learned that about myself, yet.

I finished my senior high school year without any major incidents. I rounded out my extracurricular activities with the coin and stamp club, which, along with the slide-rule club, was probably a refuge from my first year's football tryout trauma. When I look at my year book, filled with photos and names I cannot recall, one stands out. There is a note to me written by someone lost in the haze of memory. He wrote "Best of luck in law school." While I had a growing interest in the law, he knew my future better than I did.

I have no memory of the graduation ceremony at Lane Tech. According to the program, it occurred on June 23, 1965, and I was on the Honor Society and the Honor Roll, whatever that meant. But I was glad to be leaving. At the beginning of my last year, during a physical education class, one of the assistant football coaches, Michael Pacucko, decided we were old enough for an important life lesson. He was lean, muscular, and had a rough voice. His head was thin and his ears protruded under a crew cut. He wore a white tee shirt with the sleeves rolled up à la James Dean, with a whistle around his neck. His eyes were small, and they darted around. He looked over the thirty seniors sitting in front of him and started to talk to us as if we were in the locker room during half time, and he was going to give us the secret sauce that would win the game. His words are etched in my mind. "Boys, you are going to graduate soon. And I know a lot of you are looking forward to that day. I know, there is the great temptation to get out there and make the big bucks right away. I know many of you can't wait to drive that semi across country, to be on the open road, just you and the trailer, and to be feeling the dollars in your pocket. I know all about it. But don't do it. Stay in school and go to college." I looked around the room. "Semi?" Big bucks"? "Just me and the trailer?" What is he talking about? Who is he talking to? I had no more intention of graduating and driving a semi rig than I had of becoming a ditch digger. Yes, I had flirted with the idea of foundry work, but my mother put a quick end to that. I looked around the room. I saw faces starring at the coach in great seriousness and nodding their heads up and down. He got to them, and he understood them. They knew exactly what the coach was telling them. They took note. They got the advice. They wanted the advice. They needed the advice. "Who are these people I have been going to school with for four years?" I asked myself. I didn't really know them. My classmates were strangers. And that is how I left Lane Tech – with the realization that I had spent four years of high school with strangers.

I worked another summer in the mail room at Sears Roebuck after graduation. Sandy ignored me once again. That was disappointing. Tommy was still there too, and he left me alone. That was encouraging. I got the occasional assignment to go to the plush corporate law offices. That was exhilarating. The rest of that summer was spent worrying about college, where I would live and what my major would be. That was exhausting.

Chapter 22

SNYDER SANCTUM

It was September 1965 and time to take me to Champaign-Urbana. On the Saturday before the start of classes, my dad, mom, Barb, Neal, and I squeezed into Dad's Chevy and drove the three-and-a-half hours to Champaign. It was only 138 miles, but it took what seemed forever to get there. In 1965, there were no interstate highways to take us directly to Champaign. I was puzzled by all of the cornfields we passed. Miles and miles of cornfields. We used to eat corn on the cob, especially in the summer and fall, and always if we went to a barbeque. But I had no idea that people ate that much corn. I later learned, to my embarrassment, from one of the rural boys who would become a friend in my dormitory, that the corn was not for human consumption. It was for livestock. I had never before thought about what cows ate; I knew only what people ate or, because of phobias, would not eat. The fact that great industries were devoted to agriculture shook me out of my metropolitan bubble and gave me an insight into the wider world.

We drove past the cornfields and into Gibson City, one of the soybean capitals of the country. I was overwhelmed by the smell that came from the processing plant, and the proud banner on one of the mammoth storage tanks that said "Gibson City – Soybeans." My first reaction was to question why anyone would want to proclaim that they were all about soybeans. But I then remembered back to Mr. Dix, who was proud of his foundry, and to my father, who took pride in his milk route, and to my experience in the honors English class, when I was proud to get an A+ on my first essay. I realized that it was the pride of having accomplished something, and not necessarily what was accomplished, that mattered. Gibson was as proud of its role in producing the finest soybeans as Hemingway was of writing a great story. And they were letting the world know it. That was as it should be. I was a long way from Chicago and just beginning to take notice of a different world, one far from the Windy City and so unlike Los Angeles.

We arrived in Champaign in early afternoon and my dad drove around the campus. This was the first time I had been on any college campus since that exhilarating day at UCLA. I was going to a college that I had never even visited. My first impression was of just how huge it was. There was a beautiful quad just south of the student union. Liberal arts buildings framed the perimeter of the quad. Red brick and stately. As an undergraduate, I was required to live in the dormitory for the first year, and my dorm was Snyder Hall, located among a group of identically looking dorms toward the south side of the campus. All the dorms were single sex and there were rules absolutely forbidding the opposite sex from visiting our rooms. We parked the car and went up to my room on the second floor. We walked in and found my roommate, Robert C. Dillier, Jr. – but we just called him Bob. He was the first person I knew who was a Jr. I learned that sons were named after their fathers, which was usually prohibited in Judaism, as one could not be named after a living person. Bob came from Effingham, a small town in south central Illinois with a population around 12,000. Bob was short, a bit of a dough boy, and unsure of himself. He had no idea what he wanted to do in college, and I got the impression that he did not really want to be there. Getting to know Bob and others in the dorm was my first experience with people from small-town America. They had a sense of identity that I lacked. They were not just from a place, as I was a person born and raised in Chicago, but they *were* the place in which they were raised. It was deeply embedded within them. Yes, I was from Chicago, but I could leave Chicago physically and emotionally. They were forever tied to their towns and had no desire to escape that identity.

My mother got to work lining with paper the small dresser for my clothes, and helped me set up my desk. Then we went out and took a tour of the futuristic looking basketball stadium called "the Assembly Hall," which looked like a UFO that had just landed in a corn field. I still recall a photo we took, with all of us standing in front of the stadium. I had a lonely feeling, but I hid it. After dinner, they left to go back to Chicago, and I went up to my room. I was 5'7", weighed 120 pounds, and felt like I had been abandoned. But that feeling did not last long.

Back at the dorm, I met several of my other neighbors. Across the hall was Fred Harms, who was a freshman on a football scholarship. He wasn't as big as most of the players, but at about 5'10" he was built like a truck, with legs the size of a sequoia tree. He spent most of his time working out. He was the one person I knew during my freshman year who had a girlfriend. She was gorgeous. Fred's roommate, Al Cicmanec, was from a small suburb of Chicago. He was gangly and quiet. He wanted to be a mathematician, which gave him an aura of awe in my eyes. Also on my dorm floor and living next door to me for part of the year, was Ted Neumann, who would become a lifelong friend. He was from Paris, Tennessee, and was the first person I met from the South. We hung out in the dorm, eating most of our dinners together. I consumed calories and Ted inhaled nicotine.

One of the biggest influences on me would be Danny Gibb, a junior and dorm master of our second floor, which was called Snyder Sanctum (East). His job was to make sure the floor ran smoothly, and, to do that, he had to know everyone. And he did. Danny was the first truly WASP person I ever got to know. (Or at least I thought he was a WASP. Decades later I learned that Danny and his family were Mormons.) He was also the first Republican I ever met. In fact, he was an officer in the University of Illinois chapter of the College Republicans. He was from Biggsville, Henderson County, Illinois, population 363. He had sandy brown hair and a crewcut. His clothes were always impeccably clean, neat, carefully pressed, and he usually wore a button-down shirt. One would never find Danny in blue jeans, work shirt, or flip flops. His shoes had a military, spit-polished shine. Always. He was outgoing and loved simply talking to people. Danny was as far removed from my world in Chicago as a crater on the moon.

Danny tried to entice me to join the College Republicans, but I would no more join them than become a Catholic. I was from a proud, loyal Democratic family, in which it was forbidden to say a nice word about a Republican. I was indoctrinated to believe that they were all rich, elitist anti-Semites. I also had an aversion to joining groups and committees. I could be characterized as a committed social isolationist. I had many friends and really enjoyed getting together with them, but they were individuals I picked out for their unique merit and not because they belonged to a larger group that I wanted to join. But Danny did make me more aware of politics, which formed a part of his core identity. We would argue about economic and foreign policies for hours. He suggested books that would widen my awareness of policy and its implications. Danny talked about going in into politics, musing about becoming a Congressman. I had no intention of going down that road.

I thought back to politics in Chicago, which was a family affair. The Chicago political family included everyone. If you snubbed the family, the city owed you nothing. Chicago was ruled by Mayor Richard J. Daily for over twenty years (1955–1976), and I never knew another mayor for the city. Chicago was a Democratic city run with a steel hand. Albany Park was no exception. The city was divided into wards, with each ward having an alderman, and each ward divided into precincts. The precincts were basically local neighborhoods units and everyone living within the same precinct voted at the same polling station. Each precinct had a precinct captain, whose job was to get out the vote. This local, grassroots organization gave the Democratic machine a tremendous advantage, ensuring that votes would get cast and residents would vote the right way. I recall the precinct captain knocking on our door on election days. "Shirley and Lou, you haven't voted today yet." My mom and dad would dutifully go to the polling station and pull the lever, visible to all as the privacy curtain was always gathered to the side, to vote for the full slate of Democratic candidates. Voting regularly and Democratic was not necessarily a political act, though it was. My parents could never fathom voting Republican. Being a Democrat was more religion than political affiliation. It was also a self-interested act. Want your son to get a summer job with the city? Want that parking ticket taken care of? Need to get a permit approved? Having trouble passing your driver's test? Having a problem with a school administrator? If you didn't vote and pull that full slate lever marked "Democrat," so all could see, you were on your own. And you did not want to be on your own in Chicago. Chicago was a *quid pro quo* town. If I had thought deeply about it, I might not have liked the one-dimensional political ethos that defined our city, but it was my town, and rejecting it would feel disloyal. Danny had no chance of turning me into a Republican. Besides, I intuited back then that politics was the art of making hypocrisy look like principle, which life experience has confirmed. I would talk and argue about politics, yes, but I had no interest in organized political life, regardless of the party.

The start of classes was still a few days away, and I joined my new friends and others to go drinking on a Saturday night at the most famous watering hole on campus, Kams. Some called it "the home of the drinking Illini." I had never been a drinker. I don't think I had had a single drink during high school. We made the twenty minute walk to Kams, talking cheerfully, comparing class schedules and trying to learn from one another whatever survival information we needed. The drinking age in Illinois then was twenty-one, but that did not get in the way of Kams serving prodigious quantities of beer to undergraduates. The place was buzzing with students. The noise made it hard for me to think. I smelled putrid beer everywhere. Smoke intruded into every corner of the large space, students stood shoulder to shoulder at the bar, and the weathered wooden tables were covered in pools of beer. We found a table, and the beer kept coming in what seemed ever larger pilsner glasses. I had never drank beer before. It was bitter and unpleasant. But, heck, I was not there because I was thirsty. I was there for part ritual, part bonding and part learning how to be a college student. After two or three mugs of beer, the bitterness disappeared, and all I could taste was liquid. Each table had a large bowl of peanuts, and they helped a lot. I alternated a gulp of beer with a handful of peanuts. All night long. We left around 11:00 pm, but the crowd at Kams had not thinned out at all.

I was drunk. I had never been drunk before. My head was spinning, and all I wanted to do was lay down. Somehow I got back to my dorm and threw myself on the bed, curled up in a ball, and quickly fell asleep, clothes and all. I woke up around 2:00 am, sick to my stomach. And then it happened. I vomited up gallons of beer and buckets of peanuts. It covered my blanket from top to bottom. My roommate, who was also drunk, didn't stir. I had to do something. I couldn't just sleep in all that muck and, anyway, I didn't want anyone to know that my maiden voyage to Kams had ended in such an ignominious way. I fell out of bed and balled up the blanket, trapping the gunk inside. Fortunately, my mom had made sure to show me where the washing machines were, although I had no idea I would need them this soon. I went to the basement where the washing machine room was, and no one else was there. I was lucky. Of course, who would be there at 2:00 am? I put the blanket in the machine, added quarters, and, not having any soap, I turned the machine on and waited. Forty minutes later, the wash and spin cycles were over. I took the blanket out, and, to my horror, peanuts lined the washer. I tried to take some of them out, but just couldn't manage it. I put the blanket in a dryer, added money, pushed the on switch, and waited about an hour until it was done. The blanket looked reasonably well laundered, and I could not make out much of a foul smell, though, in my still drunken state, I was not exactly in a position to give it an accurate smell test. I got to my room, threw the blanket on top of the sheets, and passed out. I woke up the next morning before my roommate did, straightened out the blanket, threw my clothes in the hamper, and went down to the cafeteria for breakfast. When I got back to the room, Bob was just getting up and had no idea of my ordeal. And I did not tell him. It was my secret.

The Kams experience put two roads in front of me. One led to learning how to tolerate and then love beer, to become a good old boy and make drinking part of an occasional bacchanal, as so many did. The other road was to put beer on the no-go shelf. The experience of coughing up so much beer and peanuts caused me to smell the rancid stew whenever I recalled the Kams' outing. Reliving that night was just too vivid and dispiriting. If the smell of a madeleine was enough to trigger sharp and unforgettable memories for Marcel Proust, the smell of beer would forever do the same for me. Kams was not going to be on my list of hangouts, and beer would forever be something I would drink rarely. Peanuts, however, would become a staple. I have no doubt that favoring legumes over hops was the better life choice.

Chapter 23

LIFE CLASSES

Monday, the first day of class, came too quickly. I still hadn't recovered psychologically from the Kams debacle. After breakfast, I loaded my book bag, which was basically a blue canvas sack tied tightly by drawstrings, swung it over my shoulder and set out. The first campus fixture that captured my attention was girls. This was a novel and welcome sight for me. After four years in a girl-free zone, I was in danger of getting whiplash from the distractions all around me. Never mind that in 1965 the boys outnumbered the girls by a large margin. Never mind that I was too shy to approach a girl. Or that I had no idea how to talk with one. I loved the new, co-ed environment.

My classes that semester were not memorable, except for one: a mandatory class called rhetoric. I had no idea what a rhetoric class was or would be. I soon learned that it was a class in effective writing, accompanied by essays on the subject or essays that were exemplars of effective and influential writing. Two aspects of that class had a lifetime impact on me. First, there was Devillo Begando. She was tall, about

5'7," blonde and stately. And beautiful. No, she was stunning. She artfully walked with a sweater draped over her shoulders and held her head high as if waiting for the photographer from Vogue to show. It was as if she were on display, and she knew it. She sat in the front of the class in the right-hand corner. I sat toward the back, and was able to keep my eye on her. I fell in love with this goddess without ever speaking to her. Words were not needed. I would get to class early just to wait for her to enter. After class, I would sometimes follow her, at a distance to avoid detection. She would often walk to another classroom or to her all-female dorm. In class, I tried to make eye contact with her, but that didn't work. I was invisible to her. I did not have the courage to approach her in class. The thought of making contact outside of class terrified me. I defaulted to the neutral position – do nothing. The year ended with my second unrequited love disappearing from my life without so much as a word. First it was Paula and now Devillo. I was pathetic. Devillo walked out of my life before she even walked into it. Was Sir James M. Barrie, the creator of Peter Pan, right when he said, "Let no one who loves be unhappy, even love unreturned has its rainbow?" Yes, in a narrow sense, as the feeling or giving of love may be its own reward. But it is only a pale rainbow.

The second and most memorable part of the class was the teacher and the material he assigned. He was a graduate student teaching instructor named Mr. Spencer Cosmos. He was about twenty-seven, with short-cropped, dark hair, wiry, intense eyes, and he was very animated. He quickly showed that he cared about his students, learning our names, asking about our interests, probing our reasoning, and giving us detailed feedback on all our assignments. For the first time, I was introduced to complex intellectual ideas. I was challenged first to understand them, then to analyze them, and finally to critique them. And all this had to be done in clear and persuasive writing.

This class was my first introduction to well-reasoned, analytical essays on a variety of difficult topics. None were easy readings. I remember vividly the first essay. It was called "Highbrow, Lowbrow, Middlebrow," by Russell Lynes, and it had originally been published in *Harper's* Magazine in 1949. I did not know it at the time, but it was a classic. At first reading, and second as well, I had a lot of trouble understanding it. The language and concepts were foreign to me. I did not know how to approach it. I froze and went to the first class discussion of it baffled. I now know that it is a tongue in cheek exposition of different categories of people within our cultural milieu. It does not place people into silos based on wealth, education, ethnicity, or gender. It places them based on where they stand vis-à-vis our culture. Taste, rather than the ability to buy taste, was the determinant.

The Highbrows were the intellectual elites, often in universities, but they could also be found in museums, and some publishing houses, who liked to critique the culture around them rather than create it. Only they read certain authors or truly appreciated fine art. They were serious folks who abhorred the democratization of culture. They could take criticism, but only from other Highbrows. They saw their role as perpetuating traditional cultural ideas and values. Highbrows wanted to surround themselves with only the genuine article. They would rather do without than live with a facsimile. Their furniture, food, and wine all defined their exquisite tastes. If I were to nominate a signature type of Highbrow, it would be Oscar Wilde (although he both created and critiqued) and his intellectual progeny. Highbrows detested Middlebrows, whom they saw as pretentious and frivolous, using culture to satisfy their ambitions socially or economically. Middlebrows were blind to real art and beauty. The Highbrow felt no tension with the Lowbrow, who was not seeking to usurp the Highbrow's place in the cultural pyramid. The Lowbrow's art might be jazz, folk art, or movies, and he might even be oblivious to the existence of the Highbrow. The Highbrow was content to keep it that way. For the Highbrow, the Lowbrow was so off the cultural radar screen that he was not even sufficiently worthy to be considered a cultural philistine. They were not worth arguing with. It was the Middlebrow who drew the Highbrow's ire. They were the operators of the popular press, commercial galleries, purchasers of art to impress. They may believe they were promoting the arts, but, if so, it was at the expense of having to make a living doing so or obtaining the recognition of the Highbrow. Lynes divided them into Upper-Middlebrow and Lower-Middlebrow, and in witty dissections of their tastes, defined them in opposition to the Highbrow. They were the cultural philistines.

It was my first exposure to so-called Highbrow views of cultural distinctions and one's place in that order. It took me a lot of analysis, thought and class discussion before I really understood the currents of culture that existed in a universe outside of mine. I did not want to be a Lowbrow, ignorant of the greatest contributions of artists, musicians, writers, and philosophers, and seeking joy in pop culture. Nor was I seduced by the Highbrows, whom I saw as elitist snobs with a disdain for my own background. On the whole, they criticized but did not create. The Middlebrows were the economic engine for the purveying of culture, but I could not identify with them either. They prostrated themselves before the Highbrows, seeking their respect, but would never get it. I did not belong to any of Lynes' groups, and I had no aspiration to join any of them either. I would find my own path in seeking knowledge, appreciating the artistic bouquets around me, and drawing on the wisdom of others. But I first had to plunge headfirst into learning what was out there.

Spencer Cosmos' class exposed me for the first time to a rich brew of ideas and challenges that had been previously unknown to me, like the proverbial fish unaware of a world existing outside the water. I learned for the first time about the culturally-variegated possibilities all around me, and I wanted to experience them.

At the end of the year, Mr. Cosmos approached me for a private talk. He told me he really enjoyed reading my papers, and he wanted me to consider becoming an English major. At first, I thought he had confused me for someone else. I had thought I was invisible in the class. As we talked, and he mentioned a couple of essays I had written, I realized that he really meant me. I had written an essay on the book by Albert Camus called "The Stranger." My essay, entitled "Who is Guilty" argued that the protagonist, Monsieur Meursault, was ostensibly convicted of murder and sentenced to death for the shooting of an Arab, but his real crime was his flouting of society's conventions and his brazen disregard for basic norms. The essay raises difficult issues of guilt, what is it, how guilt is decided, and by whom. I see in the essay inchoate seeds of a legal mind at work, churning over issues of justice and questioning our use of euphemisms to make our actions more acceptable. Mr. Cosmos saw an English major. I never did change from my useless psychology major to English, but I should have. His confidence in my writing and encouragement of my intellectual curiosity served as a solid-fuel propulsion system, challenging me to strive for a higher orbit. And I did. Mr. Cosmos gave me two gifts. He introduced me to the world of ideas, and he gave me the confidence to dive into that world. When I got my grade, which was a B and not the A I expected, I knew I had a lifetime of work before me.

Chapter 24

THE OUTER CIRCLE

My social life the first year fell somewhere between a desert and an endless desert. Ted and I heard about a dance at a women's dorm, so we eagerly got dressed and quickly walked over, hopeful that the evening would end in success, however defined. We had no definition. We walked into the room, which was the dorm cafeteria sans tables and chairs. The place was crowded and popping. There was a band playing loud, pulsating music. I can still feel the bass to *Hang on Sloopy* bouncing off the walls. Songs like *Help Me Rhonda, (I Can't Get No) Satisfaction, Let's Hang On, Can't Help Myself, Let's Twist Again,* and *All I Really Want To Do* kept the mood fast paced and upbeat. I am convinced it was also the beginning of my hearing loss. There were three concentric circles. The innermost circle saw boys and girls dancing to the sounds. These guys were the Lucky Ones. They were the envy of the room. The next concentric circle was a ring of boys looking wistfully at the dancing boys and girls. They were in the on-deck circle and had a theoretical chance of getting a dance. They clung to hope over experience. They were the Potential Ones. The furthermost circle saw another ring of boys, but these poor souls could not even get a view of the dance floor and their sole purpose that night was to hold up the wall. These guys were "*Les Desesperes*," aka The Desperate Ones, the title of a Jacques Brel song. Ted and I leaned against the wall.

That first dance, and those that followed, made us believers in the scientific method – hypothesis, testing, and repeating results. The hypothesis was that because the University of Illinois, Champaign-Urbana, had such a lopsided ratio of boys to girls, due to its strong engineering program and the relative paucity of girls on campus, it would be hard to impossible for us to meet anyone at a dance. The test was going to the dances. The result proved our hypothesis. We never met any girls at the dances. In fact, we never even came close to meeting anyone at the dance. True to the scientific method, we had to repeat the experiment to see if we got the same results. We did, over and over again. Same results.

Most of my social life was spent at Snyder Sanctum, hanging out in one of the corner lounges on the second floor with other guys who had no social life. Danny would make us laugh with stories about the hidden secrets of Biggsville. Ted moaned about his dull life in Paris, Tennessee, while he chain smoked. My roommate, Bob, was constantly depressed about his fear of flunking out, which would not be a surprise since he never studied. Al, with an acne-scarred face, sat around listlessly and barely spoke, walking with his head down. His side of the dorm room was always in a predictably shambolic condition. He too did not seem to study much. Fred, the football player across the hall, was never around. He was out with Miss Beautiful and was "rushing" for one of the premier fraternities on campus. I drank sloe gin fizzes and Jim Beam whiskey, ate junk food, and fantasized about being in the innermost concentric circle.

If I didn't gain any experience in dating that first year, I certainly proved I could eat. I gained twenty-five pounds, largely because of the high-carb diet in the dormitory cafeteria. I had paid in advance for a three-meals-a-day plan for the entire year, and I never missed a meal. Even during the winter, when it was bitter cold with a twenty-mile-an-hour wind from the north, I would walk across the entire campus to return to my dorm for lunch. I was not going to spurn a paid-for meal by paying out of pocket for lunch at the Illini Union.

The University of Illinois was reported to have the largest number of fraternities and sororities of any college in the U.S. There were over fifty fraternities and thirty sororities. I never seriously considered "rushing" for one during my first year, but I had an awareness of their outsized presence on campus and perceived that they operated in a parallel universe to mine. They gave students the chance to move out of their dorms, and I knew that they offered a self-contained community and access to a rich social life. If I were going to join one, there was no doubt that it would be one of the many Jewish fraternities, which included ZBT, AEPi, Sigma Alpha Mu. The non-Jewish fraternities were totally foreign, or even hostile, territory for me. Jews just did not join the non-Jewish fraternities. Whether they were actually anti-Semitic, as rumored, was less important than their reputation. What's more, fraternities were more expensive than dorm rooms, and I was on a shoe-string budget. Also, I did not think of myself as a joiner, and did not aspire to be part of a larger social community with its rituals and mores

It was only in hindsight that I have been able to pinpoint the principal reason for shying away from a fraternity. I perceived, rightly or wrongly, the "frat" boys as coming from a higher socio-economic class than me. In my imagination, the fraternity houses were filled with boys from the wealthy suburbs of Chicago, whose fathers were doctors and lawyers, whose mothers stayed at home and occupied themselves with charity work, whose college preoccupation was a four-year social playground, and who thought of themselves as superior to the plebeians who were outside of the Greek system. In contrast, I was a working-class son of a milkman from a ho-hum part of Chicago, and I internalized an inferior view of myself compared to others whom I saw as wealthier and socially above me on some imaginary scale. I carried that self-image for a long time, and was not able to shed it until well after school. But when I finally did cast off the negative self-perception, I was surprised and overjoyed to find that what I had thought was a weakness was really my great strength. Apparent curses can often be blessings in disguise.

The fable of the blessing in disguise is told in many traditions. Like any tale of wisdom, it is not confined to any one ethnicity or community.

In the town of Kishinev, a Jewish peddler worked each day except on the Sabbath and relied on his aged horse to take him from village to village. The horse got lame and died. But the peddler's son came home one day with a strong, healthy new colt that he had found in the forest. The Jewish peddler asked his son how he had found the horse as he wanted to make sure it did not belong to anyone else. Satisfied that all was OK, the peddler took the colt, trained him and used him for his rounds.

His neighbors envied the peddler's and his son's good fortune. "You both were very lucky to find such a horse after your old one died!" the people said.

"Maybe," the peddler responded. "But what may seem to be a blessing, can also be a curse."

The man's neighbors dismissed the peddler. He was always saying that expression. What did it mean anyway?

The young horse grew and it needed more and more food. The peddler had to buy so much food for the horse that there was little left over for the peddler and his family, including the son. The neighbors said, "What a curse it is to have found that horse in the forest."

"Maybe," the peddler said. "But what may seem to be a curse can also be a blessing."

The colt grew into a strong stallion and the son started to race with the horse and make prize money. People also paid the peddler for the right to use the stallion for their mares. The stud fees made the peddler comfortable.

"You are so lucky," the neighbors said to the peddler. " You have a valuable horse."

"Maybe," the peddler said. "But what may seem to be a blessing, can also be a curse."

One day, the son was riding the horse when the horse tripped. He fell off the horse and the horse rolled onto him, breaking his leg. The doctor said it would take a long time to heal. During that time, the son could not help his father peddle his goods from village to village. And, the doctor said, the son would probably limp for the rest of his life.

"What a great misfortune," the town's folk told the peddler. "You never should have gotten that horse."

The peddler said, once again, "But what may seem to be a curse, can also be a blessing."

One year later, the Czar's soldiers came to Kishinev looking for soldiers for the Czar's army. All eligible men were drafted into the army for twenty years. Every physically capable young man from Kishinev was taken. But the peddler's son was rejected because he was lame. Every one of the young men drafted into the Czar's army died of either dysentery or battle wounds.

Sometimes, what seems to be a blessing can be a curse, and what seems to be a curse can be a blessing. Events and perceptions, whether ominous or promising, inevitably trigger a cascade of choices, decisions and consequences, which lead to more events and choices and so on.

With that, the Great Mandala continues. The stories of my life are an inseparable consequence of curses and blessings chasing each other as a dog circles in pursuit of its tail, and propelling me toward a new set of circumstances. I have come to appreciate that whether something is a curse or a blessing can only be judged with considerable hindsight, and then only after we have made a choice about how we are going to respond to an event.

I eventually came to see my humble background as a source of great strength and pride and not a disadvantage or weakness. I had learned the values of hard work, of resilience, of not taking anything for granted, of deferred gratification, of being grateful for the successes I had achieved, of recognizing and valuing the people in my life who helped me along the way, of appreciating the obstacles that were placed in front of others and how much perseverance it took to overcome those obstacles, of the critical importance of a stable, supportive and loving family, of the debt that I owed to so many and that needed to be repaid, and so much more. I was able to look back to my beginnings and to measure my self-worth, not by what I had been given or born into, but by what I had achieved and had given to others. When I came to realize that my working class background was a blessing and certainly not a curse, I was hit with a thunderbolt. My interior view was inverted. I chose to see myself differently.

Chicago, 1921, Louis Shapiro and Sylvia Rottstin at their wedding. To paraphrase Lao Tzu, "New beginnings often foreshadow painful endings."

Chicago, Shirley Shapiro, 1939, age 17.
Looks like a headshot for a Hollywood talent agency.

Chicago, 1942, my mom and dad soon before they got married.

Chicago, 1942, Louis Lerman and Shirley Shapiro

Chicago, November 5, 1942, Shirley Shapiro and Louis Lerman wedding photo

New Guinea, December 1944, my father while serving in the Army Air Corps accompanied by three indigenous men

Chicago, June 1950, Kiddyland, my father and me

Chicago, circa 1956, my father and me in our apartment in Albany Park

Los Angeles, circa 1956, Four Generations of Shapiro men. Back row: my uncle Marty Shephard, my grandfather Louis Shapiro; front row: my cousins Chuck Shephard and Rick Shephard, my great grandfather Pincus Shapiro, and me. Taken at the wedding of my mother's sister, Myrna, who was considered by her family a "late" bride at age 26.

Chicago, Illinois, circa 1955, Louis Shapiro, always the ebullient performer

Chicago, January 1961, me in my "stylish" bar mitzvah outfit.

Chicago 1959, Lake City Cleaners. I am the would-be baseball star in the bottom row, second from left

Chicago, 1961, Graduation from Volta Elementary School. From left: back row: me, Chuck Zis, unknown, Tony Mackin, Richard Eisenstadt; front row: unknown, Rodney Zolt

Evanston, Illinois, January 28, 1961, my bar mitzvah party at the Ridgeview Hotel. "The Kiss," under the amusing glaze of my father. From the left, my father, Paula Albelda, me and Michael Waitsman

Chicago, circa 1964, Neal Schiff and my sister, Barbara, around the time of their marriage.

Encino, California, September 1967. My father and me during an exploratory trip to Los Angeles, where he hoped to move with my mother after I graduated from the University of Illinois. He died six months later.

Chicago, circa 1970, Fred Dix, foundry teacher at Lane Tech High School

Champaign, Illinois, circa 1967, Jane Walsh, freshman at the University of Illinois.

Champaign, Illinois, circa 1966, Spencer Cosmos, teaching assistant of rhetoric, pictured in the middle wearing a black shirt.

Pittsfield, Massachusetts, Summer 1968 at Camp Winadu.
I am on the far left with seven, but not all, of my campers.

Champaign, Illinois, circa 1967, Ben Blakeman in a rare serious pose.

Israel, Kibbutz Malkia, Summer 1968, Hallie Tager posing as an IDF soldier in what could have been the IDF pin up poster of the year

Champaign, Illinois, May/June 1969, Hallie outside of the South First Street Apartments during my senior year

Champaign, Illinois, Spring 1969, me and Hallie outside of her parents' home. I have no idea who took the photograph, but it brings to mind Henry Miller's insight that "the one thing we can never get enough of is love."

Champaign, Illinois, April 1969, Hallie on the night she purportedly made me a delicious halibut dinner. Notice there is not a hair out of place.

Champaign, Illinois, Spring 1969, me and Hallie. The very short dress she is wearing made me forget about attending classes.

Northridge, California, July 1972, my sister, Barbara Schiff (nee Lerman), and Hallie

Encino, California, summer 1969, me and Hallie at my mother's apartment. My mother had no idea of the intrusion in store for her when she agreed to host Hallie and me in her one-bedroom apartment.

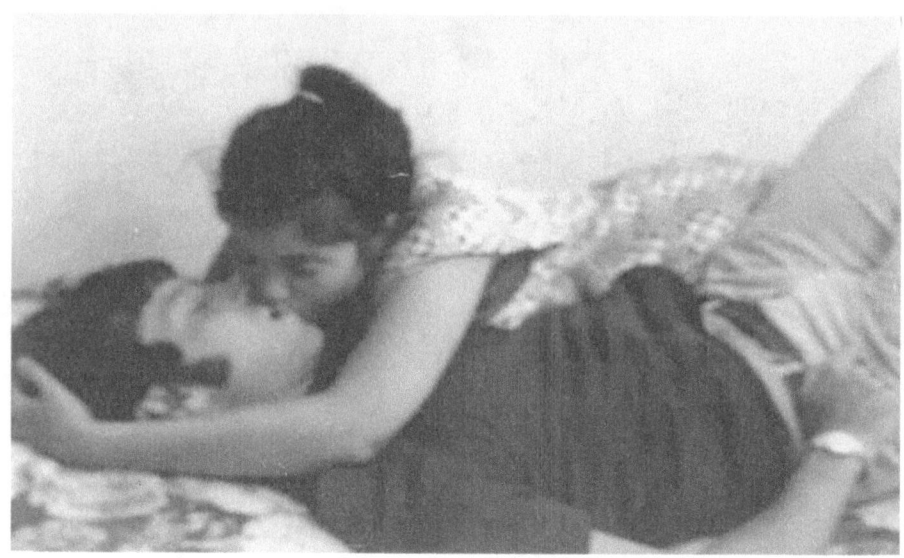

Encino, California, summer 1969, just another lazy afternoon at my mother's apartment

Northridge, California, August 1969, Barbara, Hallie and my mother.

Los Angeles, circa 1974, Forrest ("Woody") Mosten, who, even as a law student, was striving for greater and more affordable access to our system of justice.

Circa 1969, Professor Michael Tigar, UCLA School of Law

Los Angeles, Gary T. Schwartz, Professor of Law, UCLA School of Law

Los Angeles, summer 1970, celebrating at the wedding of Rick Romero and Claire Pike, from left, Steve McMurtry, Anita Ostroff, Bruce Dennison and Hallie Tager

Los Angeles, summer 1970, Claire Pike and Rick Romero at their wedding.

Los Angeles, circa 1970, me as the earnest law student

Champaign, Illinois, circa 1969, Hallie's mother, Ruth Tager, an engaging, energetic and charming force de la nature.

Champaign, Illinois circa August 1971, me and Hallie at our engagement party

Champaign, Illinois, August 4, 1972, Hallie's father, Dr. Stephen Tager, and my grandfather at our pre-wedding dinner on Friday night at a private home. My father-in-law, the high-brow, German-trained doctor, and my grandfather, the inexorable bohemian, really hit it off.

Champaign, Illinois, August 6, 1972, my grandfather, Louis Shapiro, performing at my wedding. He did not want to give up the dance floor.

Champaign Illinois, August 6, 1972; at our wedding in the best of "flower child" tradition.

Chapter 25

SECOND YEAR

In June, I packed up my dorm room and took the Illinois Central to Chicago, where my dad picked me up from the station. Instead of work, that summer I attended classes at Roosevelt University in downtown Chicago. I took a whole year's course in intermediate Spanish in eight weeks, wanting to complete the two-year language requirement as fast as I could. By this time, I knew that foreign languages were not my forte. I struggled, especially with the hearing and speaking parts. I was quite accomplished at opening the book and memorizing vocabulary, but I was unable to recognize the memorized words when I heard them. And the task of stringing words together to create an understandable spoken sentence was beyond me. I was looking forward to the next year of college without the pressure of a foreign language.

I returned for my second year at University of Illinois that Fall. I was beginning to learn another truth about myself. I was like a plant for, once I put down roots, it was hard to pull me up and away. Whether due to inertia or comfort, it took a lot for me to change my environment. Things had to be really bad for me to do it. And the U of I was not that bad. Yes, dating was more of a concept to me than a reality, but I had largely enjoyed my first year: I made friends, I successfully navigated the campus and I was content to return. The return was to Snyder Hall. The university required all its undergraduate students to sign up for the dorms, unless they joined a fraternity, were married or had a dietary requirement that the dorm cafeteria could not accommodate. I was single and would eat almost everything in sight, except for cheese and ham. Thus, I was back in the dorm.

My friend Ted was also back, and we got a corner room together with three beds. I don't remember who our third was. Danny was also back and was moving up in the hierarchy of the College Republicans, eventually becoming president. But Bob and Al did not return. I heard that they had flunked out. A new boy arrived. His name was Jack Benjamin Blakeman from Daytona Beach, Florida. He claimed his parents named him after Jack Benny, the comedian. I first saw him when I walked by his room, and he was sitting on the bottom bunk, playing the guitar. He had a large flop of reddish hair, a full mustache, wore glasses, and snorted when he laughed. In terms of personality, values and interests, we were far apart. But somewhere along the line, he became my best friend, my ersatz brother. If I carried within me a girlfriend deficit, his female longing shortfall was greater than the national debt. All he thought about were girls, and the more he thought about them, the further out of reach they were. He helped me and Ted hold up the wall.

Jack, who later became Benjamin at the suggestion of a girl he was dating (or wanted to date), was a contrarian extraordinaire. He made being difficult into an art form. His greatest pet peeve was when he had to agree with you; his greatest pleasure was disagreeing. He loved to argue, to quibble with everything. It was as if by expostulating he was affirming his existence. For Ben (which is how I now refer to him), nothing in the world was right. Everything was unfair. Everything was open to criticism, and he not only had a right, but a duty, to criticize, to complain, and to kvetch. Some singers have a very narrow vocal range, falling within an octave or two. Ben's personality octave went from cantankerous to curmudgeon. His ability to achieve this distinction prior to the age of twenty marked him not just as precocious but as a genius. Despite all this, we got along famously. I enjoyed arguing with him. I got his odd humor, which went below the radar of most people. He also got mine. Our humor was dry, drier than the Los Angeles River, and mixed with illusions to the absurd. Ben might say something outrageous, often just to gibe his audience. While they might look at him quizzically or even with disdain, I would grab his taunt and ratchet it up a notch by moving to the next orbit of inanity. Many people would not know if we were serious or not, but Ben and I knew instantly when one of us was disguising folly through humor. We were different in almost every way – values, politics, religiosity, life style – but we understood one another and were comfortable being ourselves in each other's company. We could be unforgivably nutty with one another.

Ben was smart, very smart, and, when it came to the hunt for girls, he had an indomitable will. He never gave up. His tenacity in the pursuit of the opposite sex, despite all failures, reminded me of the Oscar Wilde quote: "Marriage is the triumph of imagination over intelligence. Second marriage is the triumph of hope over experience." Ben never let experience temper his hope that the next "perfect woman" would still be "perfect" after two dates. Ben would begin a relationship with more hope than reason. A new girl would be "sweet," "perfect," "giving," and "one of the most remarkable people he ever met." Invariably, after no more than three dates, "sweet" would become "nasty," "perfect" would become "wretchedly flawed," and "generous" would become "self-centered and selfish." But these experiences never diminished his ardor for the ideal, flawless love that he had no doubt was destined to be his. He would have agreed with the unverified quote attributed variously to Winston Churchill or Abraham Lincoln that "success is going from failure to failure without losing enthusiasm." Based on this view, he was the most successful person I knew.

We developed a group of friends, a few guys and girls. One of them, Jane Epstein from New York, had a crush on Ben. She was smart, effervescent, and had a terrific sense of humor, and I encouraged him to take her out. They dated a few times, but Ben dropped her. "Why don't you go out with Jane, anymore?" I asked. Ben said, "I am not attracted to her, and, besides, she talks like Donald Duck." "What do mean she talks like Donald Duck?" I wanted to know. Ben said, "We can be having a pleasant talk, and, all of a sudden, she will say something in a voice that sounds like Donald Duck." I found that implausible and, even if true, it could be endearing, no? Several weeks later, we were in the cafeteria in the Illini Union, when Jane and several of her friends came by. They sat at our table. We were talking about nothing in particular. Jane was telling us something funny when her tone changed. Her voice sounded like she was letting out helium gas, and, before I knew it, she was talking in a squeaky, Donald Duck accent. She said something like "This is a fine kettle of fish." I looked at Ben and broke out in uncontrolled laughter. I could not stop laughing. Jane looked at me and said in Donald Duck lingo, "What's the big idea? I didn't think it was that funny." I never again suggested to Ben that he go out with Jane, even though the Donald Duck accent *was* that funny.

The second year of college had its bright spots and more than its share of disappointments inside the classroom, too. I took a full year's course on the history of England, with the first semester going from early origins to 1688 and the second semester from 1688 to the present. While the rhetoric class in my Freshman year fired up my interest in ideas, the history of England class began a lifetime love affair with learning about the past and the lessons that were right on the surface. I was enthralled with the stories, personalities, and the infinite "what if" scenarios. I concluded that the debate about what is more important in shaping history – the person or the times – was wasteful mental gymnastics. They both were primary. One influenced the other in ways that could not be separated. It was like the work in a foundry. One could look at the perfect heliarc weld and ask what was more important, the tungsten inert gas or the base metal. It would be a misguided question. Each was indispensable and each affected the other. The search for an indisputable cause of an historical event was also folly. It depended on the position of the observer or, in the case of history, the recorder. Causes were never simple. If there were a color to understanding history, it was grey. I was fascinated by these multifarious forces, and the way small changes resulted in consequential outcomes that rippled through centuries. Yes, I was absorbed by the "facts" of history, but it was the dynamic interplay of forces that gripped me. If it were a mistake not to become an English major, I compounded my error by not becoming a history major.

Instead, I stayed the course with a major in psychology. Introduction to Psychology and Introduction to Social Psychology set me off running down the paths of Freud, Watson, Pavlov, B. F. Skinner, Rogers, Maslow, Erikson, and Piaget, to name a few. I always knew I had no interest in becoming a psychologist, or exploring the deep recesses of the unconscious mind, or evaluating the personality ticks of the average person. Why was I a psych major and why did I stay with it until I graduated? Inertia, again. I cannot explain it beyond my inability to change course once I was on it. I view my undergraduate days as a missed opportunity. Instead of feasting on the bounty of English and history, I nibbled on a deficient diet of psychological theory. Mark Twain's quip comes to mind: "I was seldom able to see an opportunity until it had ceased to be one." It is only in retrospect that I see so clearly the opportunities I let pass.

Chapter 26

FAKIN' IT

In the Fall of 1966, I received an alarming call that would affect my entire life. My mother phoned to tell me that my dad was going in for surgery. He had been diagnosed with adenocarcinoma of the rectum. "How did this happen?" I asked apprehensively. "How serious is it?" She explained that he had bleeding hemorrhoids for some time but ignored them, self-diagnosing them as a recurrence of a wartime condition. Even as they got worse, he refused to go to the doctor. He did not want to take a day off work. His work ethic was not something he did; it was an inseparable part of his psyche. My sister finally insisted that he go to the doctor, and she drove him for an appointment, over his protest. The surgery was the next day, and I took the train up to Chicago. I went to the hospital and walked into his room prior to the surgery. By then, I had let my hair grow long, which was the prevailing style at the time. It signified nothing other than my fealty to my generation. But when I walked in and he saw me, he started to cry. He thought I had made a radical transformation, and he approved of it not one bit. I assured him that I just did not have the time for a haircut, and it meant nothing. I regret that one of the last images in his mind before being wheeled into the operating room was his son with long hair.

His reaction brought back an earlier memory, deeply buried. I was six or seven years old. Dad took me to a barber shop, and I got a crew cut. It was the first time I had ever had such a haircut. Afterwards, we stopped for cookies at the bakery next door. I was licking the cookies when we got home. My mother looked at me and said, "What a haircut. I can hardly recognize you," and she gave me a big hug and kiss. I only heard the literal. I started to cry. My mother did not know who I was. I was heaving and balling, unable to catch my breath. I finally calmed down, and she told me she was only kidding and kissed me again. But I never forgot it, and I would never get another crew cut after that. My father, too, succumbed to the emotional power of a haircut when I walked into his hospital room. Perhaps Fran Lebowitz was on to something when she said, "You're only as good as your last haircut."

After the surgery, Dr. Jerome Forman came to tell us the bad news. He had removed a large section of the rectum, which required a colectomy. He explained that he had to cut an opening in his abdomen wall, called a stoma, to collect fecal matter from the digestive tract. My dad would have an external bag that would collect the stool. That sounded horrible, especially for an active man who had a physically demanding job. But then came the devastating news. The surgery did not remove all the cancer. My dad had waited too long, and it had metastasized. There was no cure. He could not predict how long it would be, but we should think in terms of a year or two and not years. I was stunned. Only a few days earlier, my dad was a healthy, strong man. He and my mom had talked about moving to Los Angeles in the near future. That plan died in the operating room. My mom tried to get him admitted to the City of Hope Medical Center in Duarte, California for experimental treatment, but they refused, claiming he was beyond help. His future was shattered.

Neither Dr. Forman nor we told my dad the prognosis. He knew he had cancer and that his rectum was removed, but that was about all. The prevailing ethos at the time was not to tell a patient dire news. That could always wait. He was discharged from the hospital, and we all went about our lives as before. I returned to the U of I, my mother continued to work at Bankers Life, my sister went home to Neal, and my father went back to being a milkman, hauling heavy crates at 3:30 am as if nothing had happened.

I returned to school. I repressed my anxieties about my dad's condition, and went about my college life as if not much had changed. I came home for winter break. My dad had given up smoking cigarettes, but he now smoked cigars to hide the smell from his colostomy bag. All he accomplished was smelling up the house, but at least it gave him some comfort. We never talked about his condition. We all pretended that there was no elephant in the room.

Winters in Champaign-Urbana were brutal. It was not unusual for the temperature to be below zero accompanied by fierce uninvited winds. Unlike Chicago, where Lake Michigan served somewhat to mitigate the cold, the open country around Champaign-Urbana acted like a wind funnel to magnify the feel of the freezing weather. The walk from Snyder dorm to my classes could seem like a death march in the gulag. Only a couple of blocks from the dorm, and right on the way to my classes, was the Armory building shaped like a rectangle with a metal cylindrical roof. I would often walk through it on the way to class, giving me a respite from the cold. The floor of the Armory was a large indoor track, and students would exercise by running around it. Classrooms were on the outside of the track and in one corner was a full gymnasium, complete with all the workout equipment imaginable. It was also something of a secret. I rarely saw more than a couple of students in the gym. I started to work out with the weights, after finding a P.E. instructor to guide me and write up a program. I worked out three times a week and found that pushing the limits of my body gave me not only strength but energy. It took my mind off my dad's condition. It quickly became an integral part of my week, and I continued through graduation. I do not want to give the impression that I had become a jock or that I was trying to give Charles Atlas any competition. But I did develop muscle tone and was able to impress myself, though no one else, with my ability to lift free weights. I cannot help but wonder whether, by building up my body, I was trying to compensate in some meager way for the deteriorating condition of my father's body. I was required to take a second full year of P.E., which I satisfied with an American square-dancing class and a badminton class, not exactly the competition of choice for anyone aspiring to be jock of the year. Surprisingly, both square dancing and badminton caused me to work up a sweat, which gave me momentary insulation when I ventured out of the Armory into the bitter cold.

It was always a relief when Champaign emerged from the worst of the winter weather, but, even better, for spring break in 1967, Ben invited me and Ted Neumann to his home in Daytona Beach, Florida. We jumped at the chance. Ben's mother and father, Gladys and Charles, were delightful, warm, and welcoming people. I marveled that Ben grew up in a single-family home, which was a luxurious lifestyle so far as I was concerned. He took me to his father's army/navy store, which sold virtually any paraphernalia a college kid could want. Camouflage jackets, denim work shirts, blue jeans and bandanas were *de rigueur* at that time. Spring break in Daytona Beach had a reputation as a collegiate, party-going hades. Yes, the beaches were filled with scantily clad co-eds, obnoxious guys, and beer cans, but Ben, Ted and I never did find a party. Still, I enjoyed just going to the beach and appreciating the ambiance of a Floridian beach and ocean.

Ben was close to a family that had a daughter who was a junior in high school. Her name was Joy Trachtman. I was four years older than she was, and, at our ages, those four years were a large gulf. Yet I really liked her. She had a pretty cherub face, red cheeks, and gorgeous black hair. And, as Raymond Chandler said, "she gave me a smile I could feel in my hip." It was something I wanted to take away with me. Being in a party city without any party and being a sophomore in college without any girlfriend, I took an interest in Joy, and fantasized that I might have found a girlfriend. After returning to the University of Illinois. I corresponded with her several times, but the distance and the age gap doomed any real chance of building a relationship.

After spring break, I started to think about where I would live my junior year. I had had enough of university dorm life. The room was small, I had to share it with two other guys, sleeping only a few feet apart, and restrictions on visitation meant I could never bring a girl to my room. I did go out on a couple of dates, usually Jewish girls from Chicago whose dream was to have their future career as a teacher conveniently derailed by getting married. I don't think I dated any girl more than two times. But I was hopeful. I would be going into my junior year, and the law of averages meant that my social life had to improve.

I had also, finally, been induced to join a fraternity – or sort of a fraternity. It was called Praetorians. What distinguished it from a genuine fraternity (and the University of Illinois had the largest Greek system in the country at the time) were three factors: it did not have a fraternity house, it accepted virtually everyone who asked to join, and its members were people who abhorred true fraternities, with their secret codes, rituals, drinking, partying, hazing, and snobbish attitudes. Praetorians was perfect for me. I got my friends Ben and Ted to join too. Most of the guys in Praetorians were Jewish, but they gladly welcomed Ted. Mike Gruskin, from Chicago, also joined, and became a good friend. Mike had a unique combination of qualities. He had an ebullient personality, but also a serious, contemplative side to him. And he had a terrific sense of humor. He was an example of some people who are markedly improved by their other half. I do not recall if he was married at the time, but his girlfriend was Kathy, an adorable, fun-loving and level-headed person. She converted to Judaism for him.

My own observance of Jewish ritual was about to take a giant leap forward. I met two guys from Chicago who were members of Praetorians, Alan Weintraub and David Resnick. Alan was one year senior to me, and David was in the same year as I was. They asked me if I wanted to be their roommate the next year. They had an off-campus apartment in a building owned by the university. "How did you get out of the dorms?" I asked, as I thought that only married couples could get an apartment. "We keep kosher," said David, "If you have to keep kosher, you can get your own place because the cafeterias in the dorms do not have a kosher meal plan." "But I don't keep kosher," I answered. "No problem," Alan said, "become kosher." All I had to do was get a letter from a rabbi attesting that I needed my own apartment because I kept kosher, and I was free.

The problem was that I did not know of any rabbi, let alone one who would put their reputation on the line for me. After my bar mitzvah, we had dropped out of Temple Beth Israel and severed contact with any Jewish institution. I called my mom, told her what I wanted to do and what I needed. I got some pushback. "What do you want to keep kosher for?" she asked in a mocking tone. She had little respect for Jewish rituals and even less for the laws of Kashrut. She said she knew of one rabbi, and, after a lot of coaxing, agreed to call him. She contacted Rabbi Isaac HaLevi Small, head rabbi of a small, Orthodox shul called Poalei Tzedek, located a few miles from our home. She knew him because he had officiated at the funeral of my grandmother in March 1967. He signed a letter attesting to my desire to keep kosher without ever meeting or talking with me. I was ecstatic. I had my passport to residential freedom. I would not have lied if asked why I wanted the letter, but it was a relief that I didn't even have to look Rabbi Small in the eye and admit that I needed the letter, not because I wanted to be a kosher-observant Jew, but because I wanted more freedom. Keeping kosher would be a limitation on my freedom to eat whatever I wanted, but I was getting the letter so I would have greater, not less, freedom in my life style. I mistakenly thought that would be the last I would hear of Rabbi Small. I finished the second year more confident in my ability to navigate college life and looking forward to being a junior. I put my father's terminal illness out of my mind and thought about the future. It was looking up.

Chapter 27

LEAVING THE FOG BEHIND

I left college to go home for summer vacation in June 1967. My father, in his usual role as a dedicated job placement agency for me, once again got me a summer job. Despite his illness, he was still working, getting up at an hour when most Chicagoans were fast asleep. His work was a balm, affirming that he was not only a vital working man, but he was still the provider for his family and his cancer was not putting him at death's door. He would never allow his cancer to slow him down. He fought it by continuing as normal a life as possible. It gave him strength. And his strength gave me strength. Or, at the least, it let me live in denial about his condition.

The position he found for me was at a company called Screen Floc, which was housed in an enormous one-story brick building located in an industrial zone in Chicago. I took two buses to get there. It was summer in Chicago, so it was hot and humid. When I entered the building, I was immediately hit with a rush of hot air, so hot it felt like an oppressive blanket was securely wrapped around me. The company made posters and billboards using a silk-screening process. The dryers used to dry the paint were going full blast, full time. Large fans, which did little to cool the building, contributed a ferocious, ever-present racket. It was always there, but it became background noise after a while.

My job was to prepare the silk screens for stenciling. I would stretch the silk over an empty wooden frame until the mesh was completely taut and there were no wrinkles whatsoever. This sometimes required great strength, especially if the frame were large. Each layer of color in the design required a separate screen. For much of the summer, all I did was prepare the screens in this way, and I was judged by how many screens I made in an hour. Later in the summer, I was trusted with additional responsibilities. I was allowed to affix the stencil on the silk frame. I positioned the design on the tight silk and fixed it by removing a layer of the stencil, exposing a sticky surface. Then came the fun part. I added a layer of acetate around the stencil so that, once applied, the paint would bleed only through the porous spots of the stencil. I was never allowed to apply the paint itself.

The work was all manual labor and required no intellectual effort, but I came to enjoy it. This was a needed break from school. The best part of the day came once in the morning and once in the afternoon when we were given a fifteen-minute break. A food truck would miraculously appear outside the plant door just as we started our break, and I knew exactly what I wanted. The truck had honey-glazed donuts that were heated so that the sugar coating was soft and about to melt. The donut was warm and melted in my mouth. This was my steady diet, five days a week for eight weeks. It would be a long time before I had a more tasty breakfast.

I earned decent money and met many hard-working, hard-driving guys who were going nowhere. They viewed me as a curiosity, since college kids were rare at the plant. And the job taught me an important lesson. I came home each day with sore shoulders and a desire for one thing – sleep. I learned just how hard it was to earn a decent salary. And it made me appreciate why I was going to college.

I had a few dates that summer, but only one girl was memorable. I do not remember how I met her, but her name was Mary Pharr. She was my age, very pretty and had a Southern accent that was as out of place in Chicago as honey-baked ham at a Jewish wedding. One leg was a bit shorter than the other, and it was much thinner. She walked with a noticeable limp, but that somehow added to her attractiveness, or perhaps more to her uniqueness. We never talked about it. She lived at home with her mother, and I would drive my father's Chevy to her house, which was forty-five minutes away. We never did anything more special than go to a movie, and my primary focus was raw affection. I did not get much of it, or at least not as much as I wanted. After our dates, I would park the car in front of her apartment, we would kiss, and I would test how far she would let me go. It wasn't very far. But I persevered, as any adolescent boy in those days was expected to do, and gave her the chance to take the test several times. It became clear to me that, while she was the one taking the test, I was the one who was failing. After a few more dates, our relationship fizzled out.

In early September 1967, before the start of my third year, my mom, dad and I flew to Los Angeles to visit Barb and Neal, who had moved to Encino earlier that year. In many ways, it was an exploratory trip for all of us. My parents were committed to moving to LA once I graduated (assuming my dad's health held out), and I wanted yet another view of paradise. With the passing of her mother in March, there was little reason for my mom to stay in Chicago. My grandfather and his second wife were long settled in LA, my mother's brother and sister-in-law were thriving there, and, with my father ill, there was little chance that he would continue working at the dairy for much longer. In fact, they had talked about moving to LA, and my father starting over, perhaps as a clothing salesman. (I never thought he had the skills to sell and he was not even close to being a fashion maven, but what dreams aren't part delusion?) Barb and Neal moved into an apartment complex that was standard for the San Fernando Valley – rather new, with a common-area swimming pool, palm trees, on-site parking, abundant outdoor space, private patios – amenities that were unheard of in Chicago. And the rent was affordable. My mother and father liked what they saw, and talked more and more about the big move once I graduated. My mother knew Los Angeles was her future and, due to his illness, my father could only hope it would be so. I remained hooked on the California dream.

While we were out there that summer, I decided to look up a friend from my days in Albany Park, who had moved during high school with his family to Brentwood, a well-heeled area of Los Angeles, during high school. Rodney Zolt had been one of the popular kids at Volta Elementary, with plenty of guy friends and, as he put it at the time of graduation, a "harem" of girls. He was outgoing and very good looking. We were staying in the San Fernando Valley at the time. I wanted to drive there, but my dad insisted he would drive since I did not know where I was going. The fact that he did not know either didn't seem to matter. After dinner he borrowed Neal's car. He maneuvered onto the Ventura Freeway going east before turning onto the San Diego Freeway (also known as the 405) going south. We were chattering about nothing in particular, and everything was bright and clear when suddenly, like a wall, fog enveloped us. The fog surrounded the car, immersing us in pea soup. Dad stayed in the far right lane and drove slowly, up the steep part of the 405 going toward Mulholland Drive. Chicago did not have inclines that were 10 percent as steep as the one we were on. There was no more talking. Silence invaded the car as much as the fog. He leaned forward, as if he were trying to see further ahead, but it was no use. There was less than 10 feet of visibility. We kept going up and up and up, ever more slowly, moving further into a dense cloud. I heard the engine strain as the RPM's of the engine surged. We crested the top of the hill, just beyond Mulholland. Suddenly, there was nothing but clear sky in front of us. It was as if someone had removed a white sheet that had been covering our eyes. The road was open, stars were above, mountains were on either side, and it was clear ahead. Our silence gave way to heaves of relief, and we resumed talking all the way to Rodney's house. While it was good to see a friend from Albany Park, I left feeling envy and distant. Rodney's hints about his active social life and his parents' beautiful Brentwood house challenged my fantasies. Was I fakin' it by indulging the dream that California would be my Eden? Would my dream be a blessing or a curse?

The doubts triggered by my visit with Rodney proved to be temporary. Oddly, that trip up the foggy hill into the city became a metaphor for me, clinching my determination to move to Los Angeles. I saw the fog as Chicago, a place that obscured my vision and offered me no way out. The clearing, of course, I saw as Los Angeles, where the future was wide open, with no barriers and nothing holding me back. The sharp dividing line between the opaque fog and the clarity of the road and mountains ahead told me there was no decision to make. I do not remember anything about that evening after we passed through the fog. But I did not need to. It was all about leaving the fog behind.

Chapter 28

NOT MY FINEST HOUR

Later that month, after we returned to Chicago, my parents drove me down to the University of Illinois for my junior year. The car was packed not only with my clothes and gadgets, but there was a box lined with dry ice and filled with kosher meat. When we arrived in the city, the first stop was at the Hillel, the community center for Jewish life on campus. We had rented out a corner of a large freezer in their kitchen to store the meat. The freezer was almost full with boxes and bags of beef, chicken, and lamb, all labeled with the names of their student owners. I put a few packages of the still-frozen meat in the freezer, and we drove to my new apartment on California Avenue.

If it were the Playboy Mansion, I would have been no more thrilled than I was with the apartment. The building was half a block from the quad and only a five minute walk to the Illini Union. A better location could not be found. Our apartment was on the first floor of a three-story building. It was a large three-bedroom furnished place, with a living room, dining room, kitchen, two bathrooms, screened-in porch, and a bedroom for each one of us. David and Alan, who lived there the previous year, had already claimed their bedrooms and mine was the one off the dining room. I didn't care a bit. I walked into my large bedroom, and saw perfection. My mother walked in and saw disaster. "Lou," she cried out, "get me hot water, soap and rubber gloves." My dad went to his car and pulled out a box of household cleaning supplies. I had no idea they brought them in the car. For the next two hours, my mom scrubbed the bedroom, adjoining bathroom and kitchen, vacuumed the floors, lined the dresser with paper, added a sheet of plywood under the mattress, and announced that the apartment was passable. I still saw perfection. We went to dinner, and they left to return to Chicago that night.

I settled into my perfect new apartment, and was soon on the usual hunt for a richer social life, which is a euphemism for wanting a steady girlfriend. Ben was dating a girl named Joanne Sajdak, who lived in the Florida Avenue Residences or colloquially called F.A.R. She introduced me to her friend, a freshman named Jane Walsh from McHenry, Illinois, who also lived at F.A.R. She was as cute as Leslie Caron in the movie *Gigi*, petite, smart, and a burst of positive energy. We went on many wonderful dates, talked endlessly about both trivia and matters of substance, like my classes in abnormal psychology and juvenile delinquency (two great date topics). Jane and I were quite compatible and felt comfortable together. It was the first time I was in a relationship that went beyond the awkward stage, and was able to avoid aimless palaver. We would often end the evening in my bedroom at the apartment on California Street, and we definitely felt a strong attraction to one another. Once, one of my roommates banged on my bedroom door and muttered something unpleasant, signaling his disapproval of whatever he thought was occurring, but we ignored his thumping. We never did go as far as I wanted, though I often fantasized that, if I pushed a bit, there might be more on the menu. But I never did. We dated for more than a month, and I planned on asking her to be my date for the annual Praetorians holiday party. And then it happened. I went to my mailbox, and there was an envelope from Jane. I opened it. Inside was a lovely card, extolling in print how special I was, along with her handwritten note of great affection for me.

I froze. *Wait a minute. This is going too fast. She is really falling for me. I have to do something. It is going to get out of hand.* These and similar thoughts took control of me. A coward's way is often to slink out the back door. And that is what I decided to do. I had to end it. But how? I couldn't be honest, as that might hurt her feelings. But what could I say? I then had a brilliant idea, and did not want to waste a moment. I hurried over to F.A.R., and, when I got there, I called up to her room on the phone in the reception area. She came down. We sat on one of the couches. "Jane, thank you for the beautiful card. It meant a lot to me. And that is why I need to talk with you," I started out. She looked at me with great earnestness. "I have developed strong feelings for you," I confessed. She said, "Me too." I continued, "And that is why we must break up." She looked at me with utter confusion. I avoided her eyes, as I said, "I am Jewish and you are Catholic, and, for that reason, our relationship could never end happily, and it is better that we put a stop to it now than later, before both of us get really hurt. I am really sorry, but that is what we have to do." She looked as if someone had just dumped a pile of dung on her, which is exactly what I had done. I said goodbye and left.

To say that I felt like a lowlife would be an understatement even to an Englishman. I could not handle the genuine feelings of a lovely young woman, and, instead of being honest with her and talking it through, I concocted a lie and hurt her. I thought of Hemingway, who, in *For Whom the Bell Tolls*, wrote "He was just a coward and that was the worst luck any man could have." That was me as I walked to my car. Not my finest moment.

One night, around a week later, the phone at the apartment rang. It was Jane. I thought I heard her say she was at Kams, and she had obviously been drinking. I could barely make out what she was saying due to a din in the background, her slurred words and the out-of-control thumping of my heart. She wanted me to meet her at Kams. I told her she should not have anything more to drink and should go back to her dorm, and that I couldn't come to Kams. I just left her there, feeling low and vulnerable. I was given another chance. And, once again, I lived the truth of Caesar, who said, "Cowards die many times before their death; the valiant never taste of death but once."

Chapter 29

TAKING MYSELF SERIOUSLY

By far, the most significant event that year was the worsening condition of my father. Despite a brief period when he seemed to stabilize, he was becoming increasingly weak. The cancer was active and was ravaging his body. I returned home several times that year to see him. During the December break, he looked fragile and was laboring. My father had always been a strong man. He was not big, 5'7" (although his discharge papers said 5'5½"), and weighed about 150 pounds. He had a full head of black, wavy hair, an aquiline nose, and a strong chin. He was a good-looking man. He did not exercise, but his job required muscle, and he was lean and taut. But when I saw him in December, for the first time, I saw a weakened man. He had endured his first year with the cancer without much loss of vigor, but he had now entered a downward spiral, and it was visible to all of us.

During my visit, the opening in his abdomen started to bleed. And it bled a lot. We needed to get him to the hospital to have it cauterized. He and I went down to his car, and he was pressing a towel against the bleeding opening. The towel was turning red. When we got to the car, I said, "Dad, let me drive." "No," he said, "I will drive, no problem." "Dad, you are in no condition to drive. Look at you. I will drive." He repeated, "I am going to drive. Now get in the car." I knew I had no choice but to sit helplessly in the passenger seat, while he drove the car, all the time continuing to press the towel against his abdomen, clearly in pain – and terrified. I wanted to cry but held myself in check. I realized that what he wanted most of all was to protect *me* from seeing him sickly and dependent. During this terrible moment, when all that mattered was attending to his medical emergency, his concern was for me. That realization made me want to cry even more. We got to the emergency room, they repaired the problem, and he drove home. But I would never forget seeing my father hunched over the steering wheel, driving with one hand on the wheel and the other pressing the ever-reddening towel to his bleeding stoma, worrying about how this would affect his son. I then knew, in my gut, what a father's role was, and vowed that if I ever had children, I knew who my role model would be.

That was the last time I saw him outside the hospital. My mother called in March 1968 to say that my father had been rushed to Forkosh Memorial Hospital and things did not look good. I took the next train to Chicago. I got to the hospital, and he was very frail. We talked about school and how he was feeling. I held his hand. His breathing was labored. Barb came in from Los Angeles and came straight to the hospital. He told her he wanted a good old fashion Chicago hot dog. She brought him one, but he had trouble keeping it down. I went back and forth from Harding Avenue to the hospital over the course of the next few days. I was there on March 13, and he was semi-conscious. He was 49 years old. One of the last things he said was to my sister: "I am not ready to go." He passed away that day with his family around him. I never got to tell him I loved him or how much he had done for me.

I would like to say that I took command. There were a myriad of details to attend to, preparing for the funeral, sitting Shiva, sending out notices, contacting people, preparing documentation, and countless administrative tasks. But I did not. I was like a dead leaf on the surface of a flowing stream, being carried along with the current. To this day, I have no idea who did all the work. I presume it was my mother. I was the child who lost his father. I remember sitting Shiva in the living room of our apartment. Chairs were added to line the walls, and people, many of whom I did not know, came to pay their respects.

I looked over and there was an elderly rabbi in a black robe. He was short, had a long white beard, rheumy eyes, a quiet dignity and a spark of holiness about him. He sat silently on a chair. My mother brought him over to me. Although I was the mourner and, according to Jewish law, was obligated to sit lower than all those who came, I got up to greet him. I could not just sit and force him to stand while I sat. He was Rabbi Small. I froze. This was the rabbi who signed the letter allowing me to have an apartment. What would he say? What could I say to him? He offered his condolences. I did not know it at the time, but Rabbi Small was one of the most distinguished Orthodox rabbis in Chicago at the time. Born in Russia, he studied with Rabbi Yisrael Meir ha-Kohen Kagan, popularly known as the Chofetz Chaim, one of the greatest and most influential rabbis in the world in the late 19th and early 20th centuries and later with his revered son-in-law, Rav Hirsch Leib Levenson. Rabbi Small was not only a towering religious figure within the orthodox community, but he worked tirelessly to promote keeping kosher, going so far as to personally check for sharpness the knives of the ritual slaughterers every other month. This was the holy man who offered me condolences. Then my mother said something to the rabbi that made me want to hide. If I had known of the piety and renown of Rabbi Small, I would have wanted to disappear forever. She said, "Rabbi, do you remember last year when you signed a letter allowing Cary to live in an apartment on campus so he could keep kosher?" "Yes, of course, I do," said Rabbi Small. He then continued, "I remember because it was the only time I was asked to sign such a letter. And it gave me great joy to do so." I was not disappearing fast enough. Then my mother added, "I want you to know that he did not want to eat kosher. Actually, he didn't care about being kosher. He just wanted to be able to live in a private apartment." Why was she doing this? Was there something about my father's passing and the solemn spirit of the room that made her want to confess?

The rabbi's face had a puzzled look, and he said, "But did he keep kosher?" "Sure, he did," said my mom, "when Cary says he will do something, he does it." The rabbi spoke slowly and clearly, "That is all I care about. Jewish law is not so much concerned with why someone does a mitzvah, but with whether they do it or not." He looked at me, and I tried to show respect by looking back at him, but it was painful. His eyes were blue, and they had a sad, opalescent, lustrous quality to them. He stroked his long beard, and said, "Cary, what we do is more important that why we do it. If you keep doing a mitzvah, eventually, the feeling will come. The mitzvah will change you. Would God like us to do good deeds *and* have the right intention? Of course. But God cares more about our actions than our reasons, as it is our actions that have the greatest impact on others and the world. In time, our actions will have a life-changing effect on ourselves. We can wait for good intentions, but we cannot wait for mitzvahs."

His words stunned me. They removed a heavy guilt that had been festering inside of me. I thought I had deceived a rabbi by hiding my true motivations. I now knew that he cared only about my actions. This realization was liberating. Motivations are often obscure or complex or even in conflict. They could be unknowable or self-interested or even shameful. I could leave them unexamined, as if they were some quaint historical relic for someone else to interpret at an unknown time. Was this a rationalization? A form of denial? Or a healthy way to judge my self-worth? Rabbi Small gave me a gift, telling me it did not matter. It was a lesson in Jewish wisdom that became my personal bible and freed me from messy introspections. Whether this was a cause or merely a reinforcement of my inclination to eschew self-examination, I will never know. But I left that Shiva with a rationale for avoiding messy internal soul-searching. There were times when I tried to honor my unconscious, but my penchant for avoidance remained obdurate.

I did assist my mother with one post-Shiva detail. My parents had virtually no savings. My father never made more than $100 a week, but he left a small life insurance policy provided by the Teamsters Union. And my mother had saved a few dollars from her work at Bankers. She did not know what to do with that money. She needed to supplement her income but also to ensure the preservation of her modest capital. There was only one person we would ever think going to for advice, and that was my great-uncle, Maurice Shapiro, the investor. He was the capitalist extraordinaire, the polar opposite of his brother, my grandfather, Louis Shapiro. He was to our family as Warren Buffett is to the world. He was the wise oracle who knew how to invest in the stock market, buy equities and bonds, and mitigate the risks. He had made a fortune. We went to his magnificent condominium on Lake Shore Drive, overlooking Lake Michigan. His face radiated warmth, astuteness, and a deep intelligence. His eyes danced with shards of light. His advice was not a tempered lecture on the broad principles of investing, and he wasted no time. He laid out a specific portfolio, selecting the exact equities and bonds to buy and prescribing the amount to invest in each position. We followed his advice to the letter, and it served my mother well for the rest of her life – the next forty-five years.

I took the Illinois Central railroad back to campus at the end of March, again lugging a large box of kosher meat packed with dry ice. In Champaign, I took a taxi to the Hillel to store the meat in the large freezer. As I lifted the large, heavy freezer door and the vapor from the frozen meats hit my face, I felt a shock. I was fatherless. A major change had occurred in my life. I was twenty years old, and I had lost my father. I did not make a conscious choice; it happened naturally. I began to take myself more seriously. I did not have the luxury of continuing as a free-spirited college student. I felt the weight of my family's hopes and aspirations. It was as if I had a singular purpose to take myself and work seriously and to make a success of my life. That was the path ahead of me, and I had no thought of deviating from it. I threw myself into my classwork and even enjoyed my psychology and sociology classes. Yes, I still went out on dates, often dismal dates with girls from Chicago who had no imagination and no fire, not because their fire had gone out but because it was never there. Yes, I still maneuvered them to the couch in my California Avenue apartment and tried – unsuccessfully – to satisfy my frustrated sexual drive. But I was more determined than before and vowed never to let my social life interfere with studying.

My grades had been ok in the first two years – mostly B's with a few A's and a couple of C's, but in my junior year I fully embraced what academic life had to offer. I was taking a number of criminology courses to fulfill my requirement for my sociology minor. While I never thought of a future in criminal law, these courses were fascinating to me because of the intersection between human behavior and society's attempts to control that behavior with laws and institutions. I toyed with the idea of becoming a forensic psychologist, combining a law degree with a Ph.D. in psychology, but the more psychology courses I took, the more this flirtation cooled. But I had fallen into the *rhythm* of studying. That semester, I finished with four A's and one B.

There was another way in which I changed. I measured time differently. I was only twenty, and, quite naturally, I had not given any thought to my mortality. Elie Wiesel said, "We still are looking for someone who knows the secret of immortality. Only God is immortal;

we are not." Sure, I understood this intellectually, but it takes age and experience for our souls to accept, if we ever do accept, the inevitability of death. The passing of my father made me count my life's years differently. The world is filled with different calendars. As I write this, depending on one's religion or culture, today may not be the year 2021. It is in the Western calendar, which begins with the birth of Jesus. The Hebrew year is 5782, measured from the beginning of creation in Genesis. The Islamic year is 1443, as the calendar begins when Muhammed and his followers travelled from Mecca to Medina. We count our personal years from the date we were born. We are constantly comparing, measuring, and evaluating from some reference point, which helps us appreciate where we have been and where we might be going. I fully expected, but really had no right to expect, to live as long as my father – forty-nine years. I was confident that I had another twenty-nine years. But, once I turned forty-nine, I viewed every additional year as a gift. I could no longer take for granted living longer. As the years between my father's age at death and my birth years widened, I became ever more grateful for the gift of life. To this day, I cherish my birthdays, not by counting the years since I was born, but the years I have been blessed to live in excess of my father's untimely death. Beginning in 1968, I had a new personal calendar.

Before the end of the semester, though, and only a month or so after the death of my father, I went home on spring break. I needed to make plans for the summer. My dad was no longer there to line up a job in Chicago for me, and I had no desire to go back to Screen Floc. The warm donuts drizzling with vanilla frosting were not that good, after all. This was spring 1968, almost a year after the June 1967 Six-Day War in Israel. I was neither a religious Jew nor a Zionist. But anyone with even a modicum of Jewish consciousness was deeply affected by the Six-Day War. I recall being on campus at the end of my second year in 1967, following the ominous events as they were unfolding. In real time, I personally felt the existential threat to Israel when the Arab countries escalated their threats against Israel. Each time Egyptian President Gamal Abdel Nasser bellowed that he would drown the Jews in the sea, I believed it. I followed the announcement of the Syrian-Egyptian military pact and then Jordan and Iraq's decision to join it with growing anxiety. I trembled when I heard that Nasser had ordered the UN Emergency Force to leave the Sinai Peninsula. I knew that war was imminent when I listened to news of the buildup of the Egyptian army in the Sinai. And, finally, I was stunned to hear that Nasser had sealed the Straits of Tiran, closing off Israeli shipping through that critical waterway. I knew that this was a *casus belli* for Israel. Israel launched a pre-emptive strike on June 5, 1968.

I and my Jewish friends followed each day of the war as if nothing else mattered. When it ended with Israel victorious on all three fronts – the Sinai, Golan Heights, and Jerusalem/West Bank – I, like most Jews, felt a new pride. It was as if a miracle had happened in my lifetime, one worthy of adding a new book to the bible. In many ways, I had a new consciousness. Prior to the war, I had been largely indifferent to the State of Israel. But the war and its aftermath planted the seeds of interest in me for this faraway country. I did nothing to fertilize the seeds, but they were there. So, in spring 1968, when I was trying to decide what I wanted to do that summer, I came across stories about American college kids going to Israel to work on kibbutzim. It sounded exotic. It was the escape I needed. I mentioned it to my mom. "What?!" she cried. "You want to go to Israel this summer? No way. Forget it." She was right. How could I go 6000 miles away and leave her, newly-widowed, alone in Chicago? What was I thinking? I was being selfish. I buried the idea.

After my father died, my mother realized she could not drive me to Champaign any longer, as they had done together so many times. She decided to give me his 1964 Chevy. She bought a 1965 Mustang, a black, two-door hardtop. It was a beautiful car, and, although it only had a four-cylinder engine, it accelerated faster than my hand reaching for my grandma's strudel. She loved that roadster (it had a hard top and unusable back seats, but it felt like a roadster to me), and I could not believe my good fortune in having a car of my own. Once again, I loaded up on kosher meat, but this time I drove, by myself, past the cornfields and soy bean silos, past those proud folks in Gibson City to my apartment in Champaign. It was one of the saddest road trips of my life.

Chapter 30

CAMP WINADU

In May, just a few weeks before the end of the semester, Alan Weintraub asked if I wanted to be a counselor at Camp Winadu, a Jewish camp for boys in the Berkshires near Tanglewood. It was situated on Lake Onota. He had been working there for many years, and had heard that the camp needed several more counselors for the summer. The camp focused on building character through sports and team work; it was kosher, but not particularly religious. Campers came mainly from the New York area. He told me that most of the families were rich, and the parents tipped the counselors generously. It sounded perfect. Though I had never been a camp counselor and my experience as a camper was less than stellar, I decided to try it. What was there to lose? I recruited Ben, to come as well.

I broke the news to my mom, who was not as opposed to the camp idea as she was to a whole summer in Israel. I would still be in the U.S., and would be gone for eight weeks rather than twelve. And I would make some money as well. Still, in retrospect, I cannot be proud of my decision. I thought only about what I wanted to do and not what she might have needed. I never once asked her how she was holding up, how she would spend the summer after I left, or how I could help. There was a part of me that wanted to be out of the apartment, away from Chicago and reminders of my father's passing. I never considered the fact that I was leaving my mother alone to deal with the economic and emotional detritus of my father's death.

For a ship to optimize its potential it needs both ballast and propulsion. The ballast, some heavy material, is placed at the bottom to provide stability and control. My father gave me that. His work ethic, devotion to family, and ability to control his emotions gave me security and balance. His example moored me with a sense of responsibility and self-reliance. No one was going to move me forward other than me.

But a boat with only ballast will not go anywhere. It will be anchored just fine, but it will be stuck. The boat needs an energy source to thrust it through all kinds of waters. My mother was my propulsion system. She provided the love, support, energy, and ambition that gave me the drive to move forward. A mother's love is a given for many, and, when it is felt, it is a gift that is present each day. It was for me.

There is a powerful story that captures the depth of this love. It is about a brilliant rabbinic scholar who was a hunchback. Because of his heralded knowledge of Torah and his acclaimed wisdom, the community considered him a treasured catch for any woman. Indeed, it was arranged for him to marry an extraordinarily beautiful woman. But when she saw him, she was horrified by his deformity, and refused to marry him. When the young rabbi heard this news, he said to her family, "I will certainly cancel our wedding plans, as I do not wish to inflict pain on your daughter, but give me five minutes to talk with her." After he met with her for the five minutes, both the young rabbi and the woman told their families that the wedding would proceed. A student of the rabbi asked, "Rabbi, what did the two of you talk about during those five minutes?" The rabbi said, "I explained to her that forty days before we were conceived, there was an edict from heaven. It said, 'This man is destined to marry that woman, but one of them will be a hunchback.' The woman peered into my soul, and she heard me say, 'Oh no, please God, if one of us must be a hunchback, let it be me and let her be born without any deformity.' So, I was born the hunchback and she a beautiful woman. When she saw the mystical workings of heaven, she said we would be married."

It was that type of unselfish sacrifice that my mother communicated to me and to all members of our family. I knew that she was pleading with all her soul, "Please, God, if something terrible must happen to someone in our family, let it be me." With that kind of love and support, it was hard not to feel special and protected. I knew I had a lioness in my corner. She also had an unwavering confidence that I could succeed in whatever I wanted to do, and she communicated that belief to me. Was I a vessel for her own ambition, a way of healing her own disappointments in life? Perhaps, but I never doubted that it was her love for me and her desire that I achieve that were the springboards for her ardent support for whatever I decided to do, whether in my personal life or my career. She added one more critical feature to my own ship of life. In many ways, she was also the navigator. When she thought I was veering off course, she did not hesitate to nudge me back to center. She had her own idea of where I should be headed, but she did not impose her desires so much as guide my own ambitions with her gentle reminders and encouraging advice. With her OK, I was off to the East Coast for the summer of 1968.

Ben and I flew to NY and decided to spend a few days in the city. It was my first trip to New York, and, while I was dazzled by the lights, ever-present crowds, and the fast pace of everything, it held no allure for me. It was something to experience but not something I wanted to immerse myself in. I would be there for a few days and that would be enough. Los Angeles was where I wanted to be.

We did not have much money and had heard that the YMCA was clean and inexpensive. We settled on one located on 23rd Street and 7th Avenue, it was in a good location, and we thought it would be fine as a place to stay for a couple of nights. After we had arrived and checked in to our shared room, I looked around the reception area, the canteen, the hallways, and knew we were in the wrong place. The place gave off an unfamiliar, unsettling vibe. The Y was later immortalized by the Village People in their 1978 song "Y.M.C.A.," which, although not written to be a gay song, was later adopted by the gay community as their national anthem. Still, the line "you can hang out with all the boys" perfectly captured the ambiance of the place. We went to our room that night and closed the door. We heard a door open and loudly slam shut. Over and over again. I opened our door and looked across the hall. The guest in that room had tied a towel on the door, placed a container of Vaseline on the floor and repeatedly shut his door to signal his availability. For a sheltered Jewish boy of twenty whose only sexual experience was the encounter with Mary four years previously, this was an inauspicious start to what I had hoped would be an idyllic adventure.

We took the bus to Pittsfield, where a camp bus picked us up and deposited us at Winadu, one day before camp was scheduled to open. The setting was everything I had been led to believe. Luscious greenery, sparkling Lake Onota, up-to-date cabins, a magnificent dining hall, envious sports facilities, and enough acreage to feel liberated. Orientation for us counselors consisted of a tour of the facilities, a schedule of the activities, a list of campers for each bunk, and a map of Winadu. There was no training. Nothing on how to be a good counselor, what we should expect, or even do's and don'ts. It made me nervous, having had no experience at being a counselor.

Chapter 30: Camp Winadu

I met my campers and those parents who dropped them off. Several of the parents discreetly handed me a couple of twenty-dollar bills, and I even got a fifty; they told me to keep an eye on their sons. I gathered in a few hundred dollars and hadn't done anything yet. This was going to be a great summer.

Alan was counselor for a bunk of second graders, as he had been in prior years. Ben was given a bunk of third graders. Then I learned my fate. I was given a bunk of sixteen and seventeen year olds, who had grown up at the camp and were eager to be kingpins during their last year. This was the moment they had waited for since they were seven years old. Now they were masters of the camp. They knew all the ins and outs. They didn't just know the rules, they knew how to flout them. They came that year for one reason only – to be at the apex of the camp hierarchy. They were Winadu aristocracy, and they were going to rule the Winadu Tower of London. Nothing was going to get in their way. Certainly not a novice counselor from Chicago.

I stepped into the senior bunk more naive and ignorant than when I entered kindergarten. There were twelve campers in the large wooden cabin, with seven bunks lined up on one side and six on the other. My bunk was the first one upon opening the door. I was the titular boss of the cabin, and it was my job to enforce discipline, ensure that "my" campers arrived at mess on time, went to their activities, and went home in one piece.

The boys, for the most part, were amiable. There was Hank, who was bigger than me, and his bunk was next to mine. He was a clear leader who threw his weight around, literally and figuratively. He had an attitude that hung in the air like a Los Angeles smog attack. There was Alan, whose smirk reminded me of Eddie Haskell from Leave it to Beaver. I had a feeling he could be trouble. Then there was Steve, shy, skinny, almost fragile. His family owned a large chain of sporting goods stores in New York. He was someone I had to keep my eye on to make sure he was not trampled over by the others. I was only three or four years older than these highly experienced campers. We went to the dining hall for the first dinner, and I loved the food. It was delicious comfort food, and plentiful. "Lights out" for our bunk was 9:30. I had a challenge getting them to bed down, but I attributed it to the excitement of the first day and night. The morning bugle over the PA system was set for 6:30 am the next morning. That would be the first test of my maiden voyage as a camp counselor.

As promised, at 6:30 sharp the next morning, the PA system loudly played Reveille. I jolted awake. I looked around. No one else in my cabin moved. I stood up, clapped my hands and yelled, "Morning boys. Time to get up." No one stirred. "Hey, come on. Let's get up." A few started to stretch. Hank moaned, "Let us sleep." I went to each bunk, and gently nudged each boy to get them up. Most struggled to get out of bed, but they were devoid of energy or enthusiasm. The morning smell was ennui. I could handle that. But then I tasted defiance. A couple boys would not budge, including Hank. I faced a dilemma. I could try to reason with the holdouts, plead with them, appeal to their innate humanity to go easy on a new counselor, bribe them with the promise of a future benefit, or use brute strength. As I said, some of these "campers" were bigger than me. But I had been weight training at the Armory for two years and had some muscle on me. I decided that force would get it done and set an example. I stood beside Hank's bunk. "Hank, one more chance. Are you getting up?" All eyes in the bunk were on me, and Hank did not move a muscle. I put both hands on the metal edge of the bunk bed and, with all my strength, in one move, I turned it over until Hank was on the floor, and the bed was on top of him. The noises in the bunk ranged from gasps of surprise, to snickers, to outright guffaws. He got up in sullen silence, turned his bunk over, got dressed, and we all went for breakfast. It was an ignominious beginning. It was not, as Rick Blaine called out to Louis Renault, "the beginning of a beautiful friendship."

I thought things would take a turn for the better later that morning. I did not have to see my campers again until lunch, and I was going to be the baseball coach for a group of fifth graders. What could go wrong there? I went to the baseball diamond, met the other two coaches, and we decided to divide the boys into groups. I would take one group and hit them fly balls to catch. Now I was in my element. I had the boys run to the outfield, and I picked up a bat and hard ball. When I held the bat, I was back in Gompers Park, playing ball with my dad. There was one problem. My baseball days ended six or seven years before, and swinging a bat at a ball was not like riding a bike: it was a skill easily lost. I tossed the ball in the air just above the bat, and swung. I hit air. I did it again. Swish. Air. Again, and harder this time. I connected with molecules of nitrogen, oxygen, argon, and carbon dioxide, but not the ball. I started to perspire. This was getting embarrassing. I eventually traded places with another coach, and played catch with the boys. At least my muscles remembered how to catch a ball. I spent the next few weeks relearning how to hit a ball with a bat.

Eventually, my boys came to respect me, or at least agreed to a non-verbal truce. I had to impress them with my strength, and there was no end of arm wrestling, chest bumping, half nelsons, and even the occasional bunk flipping with a camper still asleep. I learned that I could motivate them better with random rewards, such as declaring some mornings as sleep-in time, stealing extra cookies and cakes from the dining room for an unplanned treat at night, going to a remote part of the camp for a campfire, and telling racy stories about college, most of which I had to invent. I had not yet read Machiavelli's *The Prince*, but I intuited that the intermittent, arbitrary reward worked best.

After four weeks, parents were allowed to visit. All my campers had visitors. I held my breath for fear I would be criticized for my earlier roughhousing. To my relief, there were no complaints, and I received over $1000 in mid-summer tips. The next four weeks flew by in a flurry of activity: a bus trip to Tanglewood to hear the Boston Pops, a day roaming the streets of Pittsfield, several counselors-only nights out to meet girl counselors at a nearby all-girls camp, and various end of camp festivities. I hung out with one girl in particular. She was tall, angular, and reasonably attractive. She was from Vermont and gave the impression that she came from money. She invited me to visit her at her home after camp let out. I demurred as I was anxious to get back home, and was not keen to embark on a long-distance relationship.

The best week at Camp Winadu was the last one. All my campers were in good spirits; we had reached an accommodation with one another. I knew the rhythm of the place and I couldn't wait for the final weeks' meals, which I had been told would make me want to come back next year. The food that week was spectacular, but I still saw the camp as a one-off experience. I had more fried chicken, potato pancakes, hot dogs, schnitzel, bug juice, and desserts than my twenty-year-old body could handle. And that was a lot. As the big men on campus, my campers put on a skit for the whole camp and roasted me with relish. Parents arrived on the last day to take their precious cargos home. I cleaned up in tips, taking in almost $2000 on that last day. Some of my campers were teary-eyed when they said goodbye. Even Hank gave me a bear hug, but I think that was less out of affection and more of a last chance to break my ribs.

I flew home to Chicago, hung out at home for a couple of weeks, and touched base with a few friends who were still around from my elementary school days. Most of my time was spent preparing for senior year. I signed up to take courses in history, sociology, psychology, and philosophy. I was experienced enough in my classes to know that the psychology and sociology courses were simply to fill out required hours for my major and minor. But the history and introduction to philosophy classes were the two that I was eagerly awaiting.

I had arranged for a new apartment, far south of campus, in a complex called the South First Street Apartments. The rent was relatively inexpensive, which is why I picked it, but it required me to drive each day several miles to the heart of the campus. The two-story red brick buildings were of recent vintage with non-descript interiors. To get there from the campus, I drove south on First Street, passed a series of university laboratories on the right, cornfields on the left, and then, about a mile later, turned right into the apartment complex. I would be sharing a two-bedroom apartment with Norman Kanter, a studious guy I met in Praetorians, and a non-Jewish roommate we had found through advertising. (I mention that he was not Jewish only because he insisted, as was his right, on a Christmas tree in December. It was the only time in my life I lived in an apartment with a Christmas tree.) We flipped coins, and I lucked out. I got the room sans roommate. I paid a bit more in rent, but as it turned out, based on an unexpected upswing in my social life, I would have gladly paid a hefty premium for that single room.

Chapter 31

WHO'S THAT GIRL?

Early one evening in late September or early October, I saw an ad in the *Daily Illini*, the student newspaper. It mentioned a lecture that night by the economics counselor from the Israeli Consulate's Chicago office, who was in Champaign for that one night. It caught my attention. To this day I do not know why. I was not particularly interested in Israel, and a talk on economics there was far from anything that would usually have pulled me away from my studies. I called Ben, who had even less of an interest in Israel than I, and talked him into going to the lecture. It was a weeknight, which required a bit of salesmanship on my part. What was drawing me to this lecture? It remains a mystery. But Ben came along to keep me company. I probably would not have gone alone. We got to the auditorium, and it was filling up fast. We walked down the aisle, eventually finding a row of empty seats, but instead of sitting down, we stood there looking out into the auditorium.

Then it happened. We both saw her at the same time. I was immediately fixated. She was in the center of the auditorium, fairly close to the front, standing and engaged in animated discussion with a boy on her left. Her back was to the stage, and she was looking toward the rear of the auditorium in my direction. She was smoking a cigarette. My eyes locked onto hers for just a second, and then I looked away, self-conscious, as if I had been caught in a forbidden act. She was young, perhaps seventeen or eighteen, but her age could not hide something I had never seen before. I don't know if it was her long black lustrous hair, which was the most alluring I had seen. Perhaps it was her short, powder-blue A-line dress that cut off at the middle of her thigh, showing so much sexy leg that my imagination was out of control. Or it might have been her eyes, blue, glowing with life, pulling me in as if I were the prey and she the hunter. Was it a raw sexual energy that overwhelmed me? As I think back on it now, I know it was the whole package. I was reminded of Marshall McLuhan and his distinction between hot and cold media. His hot media engaged all of one's senses completely, but the participant's role was minimal. This girl was hot media in every sense of McLuhan's usage. Every part of her, which was pulsating with emotion and radiating a wild, untamed sexuality that even Carmen would have envied, paled when compared to the power of her whole being. Whatever it was, I was anima possessed and could not move. As Jung might have put it, I was caught by this gamine phenomenon.

"I will sit on the aisle," I said to Ben. He too was looking at her. "Do you see those eyes?" he said. "They are the sexiest eyes I have ever seen. I will sit by the aisle." We were fighting over which of us would have the most direct line of sight to this mysterious woman. I finally pushed him into the row and claimed the end seat. I have no idea what the lecturer said that evening. My focus remained on this enigmatic woman. Every once in a while, she turned around and looked in my direction. I stared, but for only the briefest of moments, and then turned away. Was it because I was too shy? Or too inexperienced to know how to respond? Or was it self-protection out of fear of staring into the sun too long and going blind? Was I a faux Icarus, fearful of flying too close to the sun? Whatever it was, there was something in that room I felt unable to handle.

The lecture was over. And she was gone. She just disappeared. Vanished. If Ben had not been there, I would have thought it all a hallucination, a form of temporary insanity, the product of an overactive imagination and an underfed sexual craving. But he confirmed that she was not a mirage. She had been there. Then she was gone. Vanished. I thought to myself, "I am never going to see that girl again." But I could not forget her, and she remained a vision that occupied me during the day and haunted me at night. I left the auditorium haunted by one question: Who's that girl?

If there were an interloper that intervened at critical moments in my early life, it was the 1964 Chevy. About a month later, in October, my car needed servicing. Back then, we called it a tune-up. One afternoon, I drove to Sears Roebuck in downtown Champaign, dropped off the car, and was told to come back in a couple of hours. I carried a paperback book with me entitled *Symbolic Crusade: Status Politics And The American Temperance Movement*, by my sociology professor Joseph Gusfield. I needed to find a place to sit down and read the book while I waited for my car. I walked out and turned to the left. I passed a bookstore. I doubled back and stood facing the window display, just reading the books that were on display. I was about to walk away when a girl exited the store, turned to me, and, in the most innocent of ways, said, "Haven't I seen you somewhere before?" I was startled, scrunched up my face in a look of bewilderment (I did not realize it at the time, but I suffered from *prosopagnosia* or an inability to recognize faces), and said stupidly, "I don't know." She said, "Didn't you go to a lecture about Israel?" And then I knew. This was the mysterious girl who had disappeared so suddenly that night. "Yes." This time I gathered up the courage to ask, "would you like to get something to drink?" She said, "Sure," and so we went next door to a café and sat down at a table.

She told me her name. I was stunned the whole time we were talking. It was for about an hour. She burned with energy and intensity. She projected a persona that was part ingénue and part seductress. When she asked me questions about myself, her eyes locked with mine, and I felt I was alone in the universe with her. It was as if all that mattered to her at that moment was whatever I had said. She talked excitedly, and I was off balance the entire time. "Who is she?" I kept asking myself. She talked animatedly about having spent the previous summer, the summer of 1968, on a kibbutz in Israel with soldiers who were guarding it on the Lebanese border. She called them part of a Nahal unit, and I had no idea what she was talking about. Her best friend, Hannah, was a member of that unit. She picked peaches, cleaned fish, hitchhiked around the country with Hannah and other soldiers and friends. She showed me a photo of herself, crouching, holding a rifle, and wearing an IDF uniform. If ever a photo were destined for an army recruiting poster, this was it. Her sexuality could not stay within the colored photo; it hovered above the paper. "She must be Israeli and in the army," I said to myself, just to try that thought on for size to see if it fit. I was trying to make sense of what I was hearing. I could barely hold still. "Who is she?" I asked myself again. She had a strange accent. I could not place it. "Is she Israeli?" I asked myself with more conviction. I heard her say that she had just returned from the Israeli Consulate in Chicago where she signed up to be a paratrooper in the IDF. She was returning to Israel the next summer, but first she needed to learn a skill that would be helpful to the country. She might become a nurse. That was it. I told myself, "She *was* in the IDF as an ordinary soldier, but now wanted to be a paratrooper." She was petite, no more than 5'2", and could not have weighed more than 110 pounds, yet she was going to jump from planes

Chapter 31: Who's That Girl?

with an eighty-pound backpack and an Uzi machine gun. No wonder I thought she was extraordinary when I first spotted her.

I was even more confused about who she was when she answered these questions: "Do you go to school here? Where do you live?" "Oh," she said, "I am going to Parkland College, and I live at home, but not for long as I will be going back to Israel." She said it so clearly and confidently that there was no doubt. This was a girl who knew what she wanted. I was starting to get the picture. "So, you are an American?" I asked. "Oh yes, but not for long. I grew up in Evansville, Indiana, near the Kentucky border and graduated high school last June in Boca Raton, Florida," she gushed in that hard-to-place accent and suddenly the geography of her life was becoming a jumble to me. Israel, Champaign, Evansville, Boca Raton? Her list of where she had been the last year and why and where she was headed was losing me again. She continued, "I did not want to leave at the end of the summer and my parents knew it. They hired a lawyer to make sure I got on the plane home. Because I was under eighteen, they had control over me. But I am eighteen now, and I am going back." "Who is she?" repeated the echo of my internal voice. I was born and raised in Chicago and now I am studying in Champaign – it was simple. There was nothing simple about this girl. If she had seemed mysterious in the auditorium, she was now beyond my comprehension. Was I just too overwhelmed by how gorgeous she was, by her sexuality that drew me to her every word and gesture, by the sheer intensity of her eyes, by the way she enveloped me and wouldn't let me go, that I was getting lost again?

I was awakened from my confusion when she said she had to go. We walked outside. I panicked inside. I had to do something. I couldn't just let her disappear again. This was my second chance. *Don't blow it like you did with Devillo.* But what should I do? If I asked her out on a date, she would probably say "no," and I would be crushed. If I did nothing, she would walk away, and I would be devastated. I still have no idea where the strength came from, but I believe I quickly relived my shame at my inability to approach the enigmatic blonde in the rhetoric class. No, I resolved, I am not going to let that happen again. I choked out that I happened to have two tickets to see a play on Saturday night, and then squeaked out the words, "Would you like to go?" "Sure," she answered, almost reflexively. I was stunned. I could not believe my luck. I was going on a date with her. She started to walk away. "Hey, what is your phone number?" She gave it to me and walked away. I kept staring at her until she was out of sight. I wrote her information inside the cover of the book I was still holding, *Symbolic Crusade*. I still have that book. In pencil, I had written "Hallie Tager – 217-352-2770."

Chapter 32

A BLUR OF BLISS

After picking up my car at Sears, I had to do two things. First, I had a problem. I didn't have tickets to anything. I remembered a poster advertising a campus play by Samuel Beckett called *Waiting for Godot*. I knew nothing about Beckett or the play. I only knew that people were talking about it, and it was on the impressive end of the intellectual spectrum. I immediately went to the playhouse and got two tickets for that Saturday night. I was all set for an unforgettable evening.

Second, I could not contain the news of my miraculous meeting, and I had to tell Ben. I drove straight to his place and told him. "You mean you met the girl with the sexy eyes? And now you have a date with her?" he asked in disbelief. I was smug, and simply said, "You heard that right."

The rest of the week crawled by. I went to classes but could not concentrate. I came home from classes, but did nothing. I just wanted the evenings to pass so the mornings would come and go. I called her once just to confirm we were still on. My heart was pounding inside my chest when I called. What if she had changed her mind? What would we talk about on the phone? What if she didn't even remember me? Our call lasted forty minutes. I had never talked to anyone on the phone that long. The conversation was fluid and effortless. She kept asking me questions, and I gave long-winded answers. She cared what I thought about everything. I was in heaven.

I drove the Chevy to her house Saturday evening. I still remember the address: 1204 Belmeade Drive. In my three-and-a-half years in Champaign, I had never been to that area. It was several miles west of the campus, and it was filled with single family homes with large lawns and abundant trees. To me, the area was everything Albany Park was not: it spoke of money and comfort and university privilege. I parked and walked down the driveway to the front door. It was a neat, single-story house painted a pale green. I rang the bell, and Hallie came to the door. She was even more beautiful than I had remembered from just a few days before. I walked into a small hallway and turned to the right into a living room. The first thing I noticed was the overwhelming sensation of turquoise: wall-to-wall turquoise carpet, turquoise couches, and a lamp with a turquoise base on a turquoise corner table. Her mother, Ruth, was standing there, gracious and formal. She wore a dress with long sleeves and a hem cut to mid-calf. And she wore pearls. The only person I knew who wore pearls in their own house was June Cleaver in the TV show *Leave it to Beaver*. She welcomed me and asked me a few questions about where I was from and where we were going that night. I called her Mrs. Tager. I turned around and noticed on the wall a large oil painting of Queen Elizabeth II. Then I looked back at Mrs. Tager and noticed a resemblance. Hallie said, "That painting is of my mother when she was much younger. Doesn't she look like the Queen?" She did. Hallie's father was sitting in a chair near the fireplace on the opposite side of the room. The first thing I noticed was his large bald head, then that he was probing one of his ears with his finger. He was wearing a bow tie and sweater. (This was a departure from *Leave it to Beaver*: Ward Cleaver wore long neckties.) His face was buried in a book, and he did not look up. "Stephen, Hallie's date is here. Say hello," Mrs. Tager remonstrated. I walked over, and he finally looked up. "Oh, hi," he said. I shook his hand, as he sat and I stood. He went back to his reading. It became clear that I should call him Dr. Tager. And that was it. We were out of the house.

We drove to the playhouse, talking the whole way. Never once did I put on the radio. I cannot remember what we talked about, only that it was non-stop. We got to the playhouse and found our seats. I was excited to be taking her to see a play by a famous playwright. *Waiting for Godot* turned out to be waiting for something to happen. I recall that it was staged with two actors whose heads were protruding from a pile of sand. That is all we saw, except for a tree, barren but for a few leaves. The two heads talked nonsense, at least to me, as they waited for someone called Godot. He never came. A couple of other characters arrived, but their talk went nowhere either, and it was not clear why they were even there. The two talking heads spoke of suicide since there was nothing worth talking about. The play ended with the two sand protrusions still waiting for Godot, whoever that might be? God? A messenger of hope? Their egos? I was left with a sick feeling that there was no meaning to life, no purpose, and no direction. This was not perfect first date material.

We went to a small café and had some dessert. Of course, we had to talk about the play. I had a choice. I could put on a pseudo-intellectual hat and pretend that I found deep meaning in the play. It was by Samuel Beckett after all. Or, I could confess that I hated it from start to finish and was both bored and bewildered by it. I chose the latter. Hallie felt the same way. We shared our dislike of the play and gloated that we were among the few who saw that the emperor had no clothes. (The Nobel Committee for Literature was convinced that the emperor wore a diamond studded suit, as *Waiting for Godot* was a prominent part of the oeuvre that earned Beckett the Nobel Prize the following year. But what do they know?!)

I drove her home and walked her to the door. The lights in the house were turned off except for the corner lamp with the turquoise base. First date. End. Awkward moment. What do I do? Say goodnight and walk away? Shake her hand? Kiss her cheek? I went for broke and leaned in to kiss her on the lips. She closed her eyes and moved toward me. I kissed her. Her response was warm and inviting. We stood there kissing for five minutes and then said goodnight. I asked if I could call her. She said yes. I left feeling so light-headed that my car would have made it home even if it had run out of gas. I could have carried it on my back without noticing the weight.

The next month was a blur of bliss. I had something I had never had before. I had a girlfriend, whom I saw every morning and evening. And not just a girlfriend. She was beautiful, intoxicating, enamored with me, and she was mine. Did I go to classes? I may have been physically present, but I was not there. They were a temporal obstacle to the only thing I thought about – spending time with Hallie. We went out each night, sometimes to a movie, sometimes to a fast-food restaurant, but more often back to my apartment where, in the privacy of my single room, we talked and kissed and talked and kissed some more. When we were together, there was no outside world. We learned that we had both lost someone close within the same year and that they had died within two weeks of one another. For me, it was my father; for her, it was Clevie, her family's housekeeper in Evansville. Clevie was Hallie's surrogate parent, who gave her love, warmth, humor, and street wisdom about life. Clevie worked her fingers to the bone picking cotton in Texas; my father hauled heavy milk canisters. These deep and recent losses tied us closer together.

Chapter 32: A Blur Of Bliss

We settled into a quotidian routine that became the center of my world. I would drive her home each night, never earlier than 9:00 pm, but often later. After finishing my morning classes, I would rush to her home directly from campus, getting there around 11:00 am. She was still in bed. Her sister, Deborah, would let me in. Deborah was thirteen months older than Hallie, but could not have been more different. Hallie was petite and radiant compared to Deborah, who was tall, large-boned, and reserved, but had a delightful laugh that put me at ease. Hallie was striking; Deborah was pretty. Hallie's persona was effervescent, but Deborah's was mellow. Hallie drew boys to her like kids to ice cream trucks; Deborah was a one-guy woman. She snared a boyfriend, Steve Yulish, who was studying at Case Western Reserve in Cleveland, and she was fiercely loyal to him. I was thankful that Deborah liked me and was an active co-conspirator in making my late morning liaisons with Hallie possible. Dr. Tager was usually off to work at one of the area hospitals where he practiced as a radiologist, and Mrs. Tager was often about town on one of her peripatetic missions. With only Hallie and Deborah in the house, our meetings were easy. I quietly entered her bedroom. She was still asleep. I laid by her side and woke her up with a kiss. I had given her a kiss goodnight twelve hours earlier, and now I was the first person she saw in the morning. We would spend the next few hours together, usually parting around 2:00 pm, as I would go to class in a febrile state, and she did whatever she needed to do, and then I picked her up again around 7:00 pm. This routine went on for at least a month. I had never had a relationship like this. This is what I had been missing throughout my undergraduate days.

The non-fraternity fraternity I belonged to, Praetorians, had an annual holiday dinner dance. I had not gone the previous year. After breaking up with Jane, there was no one I wanted to take. But December 1968 was different. I had Hallie. I couldn't wait to invite her. I brought her home one night, and we were standing outside her front door. It was the beginning of December, we lingered outside in the cold air, and I kissed her a few times. Then between kisses, I asked her to the dance, thinking that my "ask" was a mere formality. Of course she would go with me. Her answer stunned me. "I can't." I stumbled as I asked, "What do you mean you can't? Are you going out of town?" She became serious and, with her eyes facing down, said "I'm engaged." "What do you mean, 'you're engaged?' How can you be engaged? Who is it?" She explained, "Do you remember the Israel lecture where I first saw you? Well, it's the guy I was with." My mind was not working. This cannot be happening. "What guy? That guy? How could that be? Who is he?" She said, "His name is Jordy Goodman, and he is a student here. And we are engaged." I could hardly get the words out, "How could you be engaged to him when you have been seeing me morning, noon, and night? When have you been seeing him? If you are engaged, why are you seeing me?" She was unable to answer. She didn't try. It was as if all the air had escaped from an inner tube and there was nothing left to let out. What had been a lifeline was now an anchor pulling me under. Without so much as a nod to my shattered pride and confusion, I weakly said, "Well, you have my phone number. Call me if something happens." I left and drove back to my apartment slowly, unable to make sense of what had just taken place.

Wait. I have to rewind. I got the chronology all wrong. After writing about the first encounter with Hallie based on my clear, certain memory, I found the book *Symbolic Crusade*, which I had been carrying when I ran into Hallie at the bookstore. On the first inside page, I had indeed recorded my meeting with her. I wrote her name. "Hallie Tager." I wrote her telephone number: "352-8081." It was a different number than the one I had remembered. And then I wrote "Fri night 12/3/1968." I went to a calendar. December 3, 1968 was not a Friday night. December 3 was a Tuesday, and the next Friday was December 6. The most reasonable interpretation is that I met her by the bookstore on December 3, and we planned our first date for the next Friday, December 6, 1968. December 3, 1968? December 6, 1968? Those dates cannot be right, I thought. I was sure I had first seen her in September or October, and that we started seeing each other sometime in early November. My memory could not have been that far off, could it? But I was holding the book with confirmation of the date of our first meeting.

I needed to probe further, to research the events in Champaign in the Fall of 1968. I needed to go back to square one, to reconstruct the timing. How would I have learned about the lecture by someone from the Israeli Consulate? Yes, perhaps there was an ad in the *Daily Illini*, the student newspaper that was not a daily, but was published Tuesday through Saturday of each week. Maybe their old editions were in a searchable archive on the internet, I thought. I was in luck. There was a terrific database going all the way back to 1874. I searched the archive for any reference to the lecture in September 1968. Nothing. I went to October 1968. Nothing. This cannot be. My memory could not be that far off. I searched the daily editions for the first half of November 1968, day by day. Again nothing. Then I found it. On Tuesday, November 19, 1968, in a small box, was an advertisement of a lecture sponsored by the Israeli Students Organization and the American Youth Zionist Foundation, to be held in the Law Auditorium on Thursday, November 21, 1968 at 8:00 pm. The lecturer was Yitzhak Leor, Consul for Press and Information for the Consulate General of Israel in Chicago. He was not an economics consul. The topic of his talk was: "The Middle East: Ripple and Reality."

I first saw Hallie at the lecture toward the end of November, just before Thanksgiving recess (November 28 – December 1), and I saw her again outside the bookstore on December 3, 1968. I went back to the *Daily Illini* archives. When was *Waiting for Godot* performed? There it was. Opening night at The Depot was Tuesday, December 3, 1968. Future performances were on December 5, 8, 10, 15 and 18. Ticket price: $1.50 each. My notation in the book confirmed our date for Friday, which was December 6. But *Waiting for Godot* was not being performed that night.

Instead it was *Happy Days*, also by Beckett. The play had two main actors and one, Winnie, was buried in a mound, waist-deep in the first act, and later up to her neck. Her husband, Willie, is hidden by the mound of dirt and, at times, is crawling around, seemingly trying to reach Winnie but to no avail. Poor Winnie is baking in the sun, and even an umbrella does not help. The play raises, but never even attempts to answer, issues of the meaning of life and who we are meant to be. We are left with the deadening feeling that Winnie is sinking into despair and there is no way out for her. Like *Waiting for Godot*, this play, the real one we saw on our first date, was depressing. It was anything but *Happy Days*. Why did I confuse the play we saw? Maybe because *Waiting for Godot* was the more famous of the Beckett plays, and both revolved around two principal actors who spoke in illusions, and both were existentially depressing.

Does any of this matter? Is it simply confirmation that our memories are at most an erratic and unreliable tool, a truth we know intellectually but ignore emotionally? Or is it much more than that? If my first date with Hallie was on December 6, and if I learned that she was engaged to Jordy shortly prior to the Praetorian dance in December 1968 (which had to be before the December 21 winter break), it meant that we had been dating fewer than two weeks, and perhaps no more than ten days, before she disclosed Jordy to me and said she had chosen him over me. Why then did ten days seem like a month or two in my recalling the events? The intensity of the experience can shape and distort our sense of time.

In retrospect, I could not fathom that the depth of my feelings or the extent to which I was caught in the grip of an emotional seizure could have occurred in only ten days. I think of myself as Mr. Rational, the ever reasonable man, who does not let his emotions play him like a driven leaf. With this clearly mistaken view of myself, my memory played out my initial séance with Hallie as occurring over months. There was no way I could accept that within a mere ten days my feelings for Hallie went from curiosity to ecstasy to obsession to devastation. Those things did not happen to me; they happened to Lenny Cantrow in *The Heartbreak Kid*, but not to Cary Lerman of Albany Park. But I can now confirm the truth of Rosemary Sullivan's insight that "romantic obsession is like a cataclysm breaking up the empty landscape. Like a strange, exotic plant, it grows in arid soil." Until Hallie, I populated a desiccated romantic soil. During those ten days with her, that dry, parched soil overflowed with wave after wave of passion, giving way to obsession and distorting my perception of time. No, ten days were too few to contain such a powerful experience.

Chapter 33

AN OFFER I CAN REFUSE

I alternated between depression and confusion. I was depressed because I had lost the only real, intense relationship I ever had with a woman. I missed her, and felt deeply that I would never recover from the loss. I was confused because I was unable to understand what had really happened. She definitely had strong, deep feelings for me, and while we were together – however long it had actually been – she had spent virtually every waking hour with me. How could she have simultaneously been involved in a similar relationship with another guy on campus? It did not fit.

Ironically, the only solace I had at this time was the process of applying to law school. I say ironically because for most people it is a very stressful process. But I had pared it down to a few schools. I had neither the money nor the desire to cast a wide net by applying to a score of institutions. I followed the well-worn advice to apply to the school where you most want to go, apply to a safe school, and apply to a reach. So, I applied to three. Where I wanted to go was easy. The UCLA School of Law had no competition. Even with Hallie dominating my thoughts, the alluring beautiful co-ed under the tree was still on my mind. I also applied to the law school at the University of Illinois, which I considered my safe choice. For a reach, I applied to the University of Pennsylvania School of Law.

As I sat at my desk thinking about the applications, my mind wandered to one other option, presented to me during a trip I'd made back home to Chicago a few months earlier. My mother was starting to date, and I met one of her steadies. He was sitting on the dining room couch/pullout sofa. Sitting is not quite the right word. He was too massive to sit. It was more like he was splayed all over the couch, all 400+ pounds of him. Every time he moved, I could hear the springs in the mattress groan and ping. I kept thinking, "I am not going to be able to sleep on that mattress again." Fittingly, his name was Tiny. Yes, he was called Tiny. What my beautiful mother was doing with Tiny, I could not fathom. Tiny was affable and liked to drop hints about his ties to the local mafia. "Kid, I hear from your mom that you want to go to law school," he said in a hushed tone as if he were giving away a state secret. "Good thinking," he said, "Where do you want to go?" I told him that UCLA Law School was my number one choice. "I got some friends who can help get you into the law school at the University of Chicago. They'd also help out with the expenses. Whaddaya think about *that*?" he said, as if it were an offer one could not refuse. "Who are these friends and why would they help me?" I asked in a bit of a challenging tone. "You don't need to know the friends. You don't ask those questions. They're always looking to help smart kids like you become lawyers. When you graduate, you'll already have a good paying job lined up. Whaddaya think about *that*?" Tiny asked, with the emphasis again on "that."

Rabbi Jonathan Sacks, of blessed memory, once notably said, "The most important distinction in life is between an opportunity to be seized and a temptation to be avoided." I have been blessed with a failsafe inner barometer, warning me away from temptations that seemed too easy or too good to be true. Some I shied away from because I took a long-term view and intuited that the choice before me posed unacceptable risks at an unknown time in an uncertain future. I don't know if I was born with the ability to make the distinction, or if perhaps I instinctively learned it from my father, who worked so hard for everything he had. Maybe it was from my mother who was fearful of change and cautious to a fault. My role models had all worked hard and had to work for everything they had. My compass may have come from a deeper place. I wanted to avoid owing anyone anything. I wanted to do it on my own and to have the luxury of choosing from options that I made possible. And the last thing I wanted was to be indebted to scoundrels. "Tiny," I said, "I'm going to UCLA Law School, if they will have me." And that was the end of the matter. Fortunately, my mom's move to Los Angeles the next summer was the end of Tiny as well. The sleep sofa, however, never recovered, and it didn't made the trip out West.

As I sat at my desk, scrutinizing a pamphlet awkwardly called "UCLA Announcement of the School of Law," I imagined myself in the photographs. I saw law students in white shirts and ties, reminiscent of the lawyers at Sears Roebuck, looking seriously at law books and typing weighty words into a typewriter. I read about the *Law Review*, described as "one of the most coveted honors available to exceptionally qualified students," and knew that I wanted to write for it. Most of all, I read about the courses. "Constitutional Law I" and "Constitutional Law II". I was going to learn about the separation of powers, the Interstate Commerce Clause, and the limits of the taxing authority. I was going to become expert in the First Amendment with its guarantees of free speech and freedom of religion and assembly. I was going to study the great jurists and their opinions. Then there was the contracts class. I would know how to make and possibly break a contract. Property. There was a full year's course on property rights, eminent domain, adverse possession, deeds, titles, and more. Look at all those courses on local government law, law and psychiatry, legal philosophy, and comparative law. There was even a course on copyright taught by the nationally-acclaimed Professor Mel Nimmer. Oh look, Professor Nimmer also teaches a seminar on the First Amendment. Commercial transactions? I would learn the legal framework for commercial dealings, including warranties, bills of lading, secured obligations, and remedies for violating the law on commercial transactions. This was my moveable feast, but, instead of Hemingway meeting the greatest artists living in Paris in the 1920s, I was fantasizing about my upcoming encounter with the best of the law. Who were Gertrude Stein, Ezra Pound, Salvador Dali, and James Joyce compared to Oliver Wendell Homes, Jr., Louis Brandeis, Roscoe Pound, and John Marshall? I read all thirty-two pages from cover to cover, again and again. The more I read, the more excited I became. A feeling of empowerment overcame me. And then I had a dream, a premonition: I was going to finish first in my class.

I was also determined to go to Los Angeles. After all, there was a woman waiting for me under a tree, and I had mentally planned out my whole life. Although I was a land lover, I fantasized about living in Santa Barbara, a wealthy enclave on the Pacific Coast only ninety miles north of Los Angeles. I would have a magnificent home on the water and sail a boat from Santa Barbara to LA, where I would have my office. This fantasy was not marred by my lack of any experience whatsoever on the water, let alone sailing, nor by the knowledge of how long it would take to sail from Santa Barbara to Los Angeles, nor by weather conditions, nor my aversion to winds and getting wet, nor by the fact that I had never been to Santa Barbara, nor by anything approaching reality. Yet, the dual dreams of being first in my class and sailing the blue waters of the Pacific Ocean made my last winter in Champaign tolerable, if only for a moment.

I could not help but think about Hallie. Simon and Garfunkel had released a new album, *Bookends*, and the song "Hazy Shade of Winter" hit me hard. I listened again and again to the lyrics:

> "Hang on to your hopes, my friend
> That's an easy thing to say
> But if your hopes should pass away
> Simply pretend that you can build them again."

Those words encapsulated my thoughts during the winter of 1969. I looked for comfort. Friends told me that I would find another Hallie, and that I just needed patience. Others told me that impermanence is a permanent feature of life, as if this were supposed to be reassuring. I read stories about breakups. I even read poetry, but John Keats was of no help:

> "Shed no tear – O, shed no tear!
> The flower will bloom another year.
> Weep no more – O, weep no more!
> Young buds sleep in the root's white core."

These were lovely words, but they did not lessen my despair. I had no confidence that I would be able to find someone else who would captivate me like Hallie. It had taken me twenty years to find her. And then there was a layer of betrayal that I tried to ignore, but could not. She was engaged to someone else while she pretended to be with me. My feelings and intentions were real. What about hers? Was I just something to try on for size while she was having her wedding dress fitted? Was she an actress, playing a role, without regard to my feelings? I had no good answers to any of these questions. Every answer scored a problem and not a solution.

I often went to the Illini Student Union for its reading room. It was a perfect retreat – comfortable chairs and sofas, bookshelves lined with books, deep carpets, and deadly quiet. It was the second week of February, about two months since I had seen Hallie. She had never called so I had assumed that she was still engaged or even married to Jordy. I was walking down the stairs from the reading room when I saw her. She was buying something from a counter. Her blouse tails were sticking out. She wore an open winter coat. Each of her large pockets was stuffed with Hershey's chocolate bars. She had gained fifteen pounds. Her hair was disheveled. She looked a mess, liked a spavined maid.

We looked at each other with a mixture of surprise and excitement. She also wore a look of embarrassment and unease, which I later learned was because of her disheveled appearance. Her lithe figure was showing signs of Rubenseque envy. We knew we had to talk. We went to the reading room and found a quiet corner to talk. I asked her what had happened. Back in December, she had told Jordy that she was seeing me and he made her choose. Him or me. She choose him, and now she regretted it. It seems he gave her a lot to regret. She thought he was a student at the university but, in fact, he had dropped out without telling her. She would drive him to his class, he would walk into the building and walk out the back. She wanted nothing to do with him. I was never sure if this were the real story or if he had broken up with her. All I could be sure of, which I confirmed much later, was that he was a jerk of the first order. Hallie's sudden availability, whether because Jordy was now the unchosen or she was the unchosen, posed a choice for me. Do I wrap myself in hurt and anger and wish her good luck with her life? Or, do I put the whole Jordy episode behind us and start anew? I have spent more time deciding what kind of donut to buy than I did over what to do about Hallie. I wasted no time in saying, rather than asking, "Let's go see a movie this weekend, and we can talk about what happened and other things."

Chapter 33: An Offer I Can Refuse

We went to see the movie *Charly*, starring Cliff Robertson, the next Saturday night, which was opening weekend. It seemed that everyone was talking about the film. It gave *Happy Days* a run for its money for worst date material. It centered on a mentally disabled man who desperately wants to be smarter. He is introduced to a scientist who was able to substantially increase the intelligence of mice through an operation. The scientist operated on Charly, who becomes a genius, establishes a relationship with a beautiful woman, and appears on the verge of leading the perfect life. The scientist learns that his laboratory mice have regressed to their pre-surgical state. This too will be Charly's fate. The movie closes as it opens, with Charly playing with children, his intellectual equal, in a playground. Depressing and dispiriting. I briefly wondered if the movie were a metaphor for my relationship with Hallie. I met her when my social life was a desert, she made my desert bloom for a short season, and she then withdrew all nourishment, turning a lush garden once again into a desert. If I restarted the relationship, would my life be locked into a Charly-like cycle? That was the risk, and I decided to take it without much of a thought.

Chapter 34

MEETING THE FAMILIES

We spent the rest of February and then spring together, day and night. Our relationship deepened emotionally and physically. We alternated between my bedroom and her bedroom, when her parents were away. There were times when we spent whole afternoons in bed, just lying there whispering in cloistered conspiracies, and, when I finally got up, I regretted having to go. When we weren't in bed, we engaged in an endless conversation. Hallie seemed to hang on every word I said, which worked as its own aphrodisiac. She would often say, "Let's have an intellectual conversation," by which she meant I should spew out ideas and she would listen and ask an occasional question. I didn't mind. What man could resist a woman whose centerfold would have curled the pages of *Playboy* magazine one moment and who would let him pontificate on the topic of his choice the next?

When Jules Renard said "on earth there is no heaven, but there are pieces of it," he was thinking of that spring I spent with Hallie. I was immersed in pieces of heaven each day. Hallie was not just hot in photos; she simmered in person. I am reminded of a scene in Woody Allen's *Midnight in Paris* where Gil Pender, a thwarted Hollywood script writer, is explaining the Picasso painting "La Baigneuse" (the Bather) to a group of pseudo-sophisticates. Gil explains that Picasso was painting his mistress and was "distracted by the fact she was a volcano in the sack." Picasso's mistress and Hallie had a lot in common. We spent much of the spring of 1969 in her bedroom or my bedroom or searching for a bedroom. We could not get enough of one another. Hallie erased Mary from my mind, and our moments together became my new sanctuary in time during my senior year.

I got to know Mrs. Tager well enough to call her Ruth. Not to her face, of course. I would say it to Hallie, but mostly I referred to her as "your mom." At their family dinners the table was set with precision, each utensil in just the right place and flowers in the center. She would take our plates from the dining room into the kitchen, add a serving of each dish, and return them to us in the dining room. There would be no leaning over to spoon from a common trough in the Tager household, and certainly no repeat of the ritual in my house where Barb and I would fight over who got the white meat in the Colonel's chicken bucket. Ruth made sure that each person got their fill, as defined by her exacting, measured standards, and no more.

Ruth was always on the go, hurrying from one organizational meeting to another, taking in an art show or dropping off food at the home of an ill friend. When she wasn't in motion about town, she was in the kitchen with the phone implanted in her ear, making plans, ordering the life of her family, or demanding attention to a grievance. Or, she was writing a weekly art column for the local newspaper. She was not a women to be trifled with. William Congreve could just as easily have penned, "Hell hath no fury like Ruth Tager scorned." But whatever she did, she did it with style and class. She always wore a lovely dress, pearls, earrings, makeup, and had her hair in place. She was elegant and the picture of decorum. If she were cooking, she would cover her outfit with a kitchen apron, but she kept her impeccable dress clothes underneath just in case she needed to be presentable at a moment's notice. She loved to exercise and walked everywhere. She appeared to like me, but she made it clear to Hallie that I was "just another poor boy from Chicago." I knew that she saw me as just one more stray dog, temporarily in Hallie's kennel. There were so many before me that she lost count, and she was sure there would be an equal number after me. There was no reason to invest much time and attention in this boy from Albany Park.

Dr. Tager eventually got up from his chair to speak with me. He was always in a shirt and bow tie. I recall once seeing his collection of bows ties, of which he was extremely proud, and was surprised to discover that they were all pre-tied by the manufacturer. Whereas Ruth was meticulous about her clothes, Dr. Tager couldn't care less so long as he had on a shirt and bow tie. I would often hear him bellow, "Ruth, where is my …" Just fill it in and you would be right. At the beginning of a conversation with him, I could never tell if he was serious or launching into a joke. It was usually the latter, and they were invariably long. They were not terribly funny jokes. Dr. Tager was a curious kind of doctor. He was not a fan of exercise, and he liked to retell the quip by Paul Terry that "when he got the urge to exercise, he would lie down until the urge went away."

As we get older, we all default to one or more episodes in our life that we remember fondly, imbuing it with meaning through stories. Dr. Tager did his undergraduate work at Cornell University on a full merit scholarship, but he could not get into a medical school in the United States because, as the family myth went, of tight quotas on Jews. He had to study in Europe. Dr. Tager went to Germany as an American in 1929 to study medicine, not knowing a word of German. He had to first master Latin and then German to succeed in medical school in Frankfurt and Berlin. He would often repeat stories of his days under the Nazis, who took control in January 1933, three years after his arrival. I could never be sure when he would start talking about Germany. It did not have to be relevant to the subject of the conversation. In fact, it was often totally out of place. But, once he began, it was like getting stuck in the groove of a record. A record groove starts on the periphery of a flat vinyl disk and ends near the center, as would Dr. Tager's memories of Germany. He would go on autopilot until the continuous groove was spent, and the listener was exhausted.

Dr. Tager's introverted and unusual persona hid a man of unusual depth and accomplishment. He played the classical piano daily, read philosophy and literature, studied religion, appreciated fine art, taught bible classes, translated German books into English, and had a resiliency that Napoleon would have offered as a model to his officers. Although not ritually religious, he loved Judaism and his fervor for Israel was undoubtedly the spark that ignited Hallie's passion for the country. Both he and Ruth were recognized leaders of the Jewish community, and they committed themselves to countless projects that served the needs of those less fortunate. If Ruth saw me as just another expendable suitor for Hallie, at this time, Dr. Tager barely saw me at all. I was not always sure he knew I was at the dining room table, even when I talked. I may have been insignificant to Ruth, but I was a vanishing act to Dr. Tager.

The Tagers had a wide circle of friends in Champaign, and many of them were associated with the University. Rubin Cohn, a law professor at the University Of Illinois School Of Law, made the greatest impression on me. This is not saying too much because he made a great impression on everyone he met. Rube, as he was called by his friends, could not have been better cast for the role of a distinguished professor of law. He was the very model of a modern major-general, or I mean, erudite sage. He had a ruddy complexion, white mane of hair perfectly combed, with bright, straight teeth. He walked with a bearing worthy of a procession of admirers following behind, even when he walked alone. But it was his voice that was unforgettable. No matter what he said, his sonorous tones made each word sound like a pronouncement from on high. He did not simply enunciate but used his mellifluous voice to almost hypnotize those within ear shot. It was not simply the packaging, but the substance of the man that was awe inspiring. He was an adviser to the Illinois state legislature on constitutional law, a recognized expert on administrative law, an author and lecturer, and a beloved leader in the Champaign Jewish community. And he was particularly fond of Hallie. Unlike others within the Tagers' circle, Rube always found time to talk to Hallie and to learn about her plans. Unlike her parents who would often compare her unfavorably to Rube's two children, Rube validated her self-worth. He used his best efforts to sell me on the University of Illinois law school, but my heart was beating to go to the West. Rube was majestic, and if he were an example of the genus of man that law schools produced, I was more than ready to get in the production line. Once he invited Hallie and me to his home for dinner. Above his fireplace was a beautiful, colored photograph showing Rube as the thoughtful, resplendent scholar he was. I thought of the painting of Ruth Tager, which was hanging in her living room. Now, I was seeing an equally impressive picture of Rube Cohn. I had never known anyone to have had their portrait professionally painted or taken, let alone prominently displayed in their home. Their world was far removed from Albany Park. We had snapshots of the family in modest frames displayed on table tops, but never a grand picture of lofty proportions for all visitors to admire. Was it the product of rightful pride or self- esteem on steroids? I was not sure. Nor did I aspire to have my likeness dominate a room in my home. Instead, I hoped that someday I would think myself worthy of such a portrait, whether or not I wanted it to adorn a wall.

Each day with Hallie taught me something new about her. I learned she was an excellent basketball player in high school, and she had campaigned to force the school to devote court time to girls. She was a professional gift wrapper. At fifteen, she had biked 1000 miles from Grand Rapids to Canada to Wisconsin to Chicago with a group of other teenagers. She had faced sexual harassment and potential sexual assault on many occasions, but always escaped unscathed. She knew how to reject unwanted advances with no more effort than a horse swatting a fly with its tail. Her hero was Helen Keller, and, in her honor, she not only learned how to hand sign but would experiment riding her bicycle with her eyes closed. She was a voracious reader and prized her modest, but impressive, collection of first editions. In Evansville, where the Tagers had a large custom-built home, she would mow the expansive lawn because she did not want her father to get a heart attack. What about that hard to place accent? She never learned to master the letter "R," making it impossible for people to guess her origins. But of all the surprises, I never expected that she would be a gourmet cook. Yet, that is what she told me she was when I was invited over for a special dinner in April.

Her parents were out of town for the weekend. She said her specialty was halibut with wild rice. On Saturday, she would make it for me for dinner. I arrived at 6:30 pm. She looked relaxed and beautiful. She wore a new dress, her hair was glimmering, and she could hardly contain her excitement. She was about to show off her theretofore hidden culinary talents. We went into the kitchen, and the table was nicely set for two. There was a chopped salad on each plate. The oven was on and the aroma notched up my appetite by two. Her sister, Deborah, was standing in the kitchen, wearing an apron. Hallie explained that Deborah had agreed to help serve and clean up. "What a considerate sister," I thought. The salad was delicious. Deborah cleared our plates. She brought the halibut out of the oven still sizzling on the tray, dripping with a magnificent sauce. She carefully placed two pieces of fish on a serving dish, layered with lettuce. She then added parsley, more sauce, and toasted slivered almonds. She brought it to the table. When she bent down, I could see the beads of sweat slowly working their way down the sides of her face. As Hallie and I helped ourselves, Deborah brought over the wild rice, and she actually served us. Dessert was a chocolate cake, brought out by Deborah on a tall glass cake server. I could not recall when I had such a magnificent meal. I once ate at a restaurant that listed its dishes unusually. One was chicken in brown sauce, *cooked to perfection*. Another was chicken in lemon sauce, *cooked to perfection*. Still another was chicken paprika – *cooked to perfection*. Every dish in the restaurant was cooked to perfection. I expect such hyperbole from a restaurant. But I must admit that every dish served to me that Saturday night *was* perfection, and I say it without exaggeration.

Hallie and I got up from the table and went into the living room. Deborah stayed behind to clean up in the kitchen. I complimented Hallie effusively on the dinner. She thanked me, gave me an Audrey Hepburn smile with closed lips, and said it was nothing. She looked so fresh and unfazed by the tour de force of a meal she had just made. Then, I thought of Deborah, moving quickly around the kitchen, adeptly placing the fish on the platter, proudly serving us, and wiping away small pools of perspiration. I had been had. "You didn't make the dinner, did you? It was your sister," I blurted out. Hallie's face scrunched just a bit, and she knew there was no point in pretending any longer. "Yes, she made it. But it was my idea. And I told her what to make," she offered by way of justification. It was a prime Hallie moment. Caught in a lie, she squirmed to avoid any blame or consequence. It was part of her charm. I learned that Hallie had a lot of hidden skills, but, at that time, cooking was not one of them.

I also learned other things about her that should have been obvious, but I naively ignored the signs in the earliest days of our relationship. We were together for all of March, April, and May. One evening she told me she had to see Bernie the next day. "Bernie? Who is Bernie?" She said he was someone she had met at a fraternity party before she met me. He was a student at U of I, he wanted to be a doctor, his family was from Springfield Illinois, and Hallie's mother liked him a lot. A real lot. Bernie Rubin was just the sort of guy that Mrs. Tager would have picked for Hallie. The problem was that Hallie thought he was boring, she was horrified at the thought of living in Springfield, so close to her parents in Champaign, and she disliked his mother. Mrs. Tager was unfazed. Her response was "What do you care about his mother? She could die."

My response was quite different. "His mother?" I asked. "When did you meet his mother?" "Oh," Hallie replied as a matter of fact, "when I went with him to visit Springfield." "What? When did you do that? Was that before or after you were engaged to Jordy, which was while you were going out with me last December?" I asked with exasperation. Who was this girl? I was never able to get a straight answer about Bernie. So, I asked, "Why are you meeting him tomorrow?" "So, I can break up with him," she answered as if it were the most normal thing to say. "Break up with him? Are you still going with him? Why do you need to break up with him, if you are not going with him?" I asked, feeling this was getting "curiouser and curiouser." "I am not really going with him, but he likes me a lot, says he can see being married to me some day. He calls me all the time, and we talk. He is a nice guy, and I need to tell him we are not a couple," Hallie's voice trails off. She met with him the next day. I was a bundle of nerves awaiting the outcome of the meeting. Hallie told me that Bernie was very upset to hear that they had no future together since he had so many plans for the two of them. And his mother would be upset also. Hallie was quite confident

Chapter 34: Meeting The Families

that the Bernie chapter in her life, or, if not a chapter, at least a verse, was over. I was not so sure, and I was right.

Later in the spring, Hallie confessed that she was going to meet Jordy. He had called her and wanted to explain his odd behavior. He said he loved her and thought about her all the time. This was the last thing I wanted to see happen. I was terrified that he would sweet talk her back into a relationship. I tried to talk her out of meeting him, but I had no success. She was going to see him the next Sunday on campus and just talk. I was a wreck all week. I couldn't concentrate or enjoy anything. I had visions of Hallie kissing him, holding him, telling him she now understood the pain in his life that led him to be so deceitful. And forgiving him. That Sunday, in anticipation of her appointment with Jordy, I was a mess. Depressed, fatigued, an emotional basket case. Unsure of myself, of her, of what I wanted out of life. I just sat in my apartment waiting for her call. She eventually called. False alarm. She had met with Jordy, and she had no feelings for him anymore. She told him they were over for good. My mood changed from morose to elation in two seconds. I was buoyant, positive, and confident. I could take on the world. I was Cyrano de Bergerac, deluded by the thought of Roxanne's love:

> *I – I am going to be a storm – a flame –*
> *I need to fight whole armies alone;*
> *I have ten hearts; I have a hundred arms;*
> *I feel too strong to war with mortals –*
> *BRING ME GIANTS!*

When we ventured out of my apartment or her house, we would go to a movie, an inexpensive restaurant, a bookstore. I learned more about her. She was an outrageous flirt. She could not help herself. In the presence of a new man, she was like an overexcited puppy. It could be a waiter, store clerk, salesman, or just someone waiting in line. Anyone. She was incapable of having a normal conversation with a male stranger. Her eyes, her wide smile, her head jerked back so that her lustrous black mane of hair swept the air and sprinkled her scent. She was instantly captivating. Even her laugh was an invitation to intimacy. It was wide and continuous, a combination of genuine joy mixed with no sound. It was infectious, drawing you in and making you want more. Her laugh was an innocent allure, offering you a chance to share a private connection. It was part of her charm. She fired out sexual bullets as if they were shot from an Uzi. But it was more than her physical presence. She was able to touch a person's inner being faster than a surgeon could make the first cut with the scalpel. She had an irresistible way of looking directly into one's eyes and asking the most personal, penetrating questions without seeming intrusive. The object of her attention was seduced and wanted to answer her, to engage with her. She had a natural ambiance that was not forced or artificial. It captivated any guy who came within her orbit. This was Hallie the flirt extraordinaire, bringing to mind Dolly Parton, who said "I love to flirt, and I've never met a man I didn't like." Hallie would deny she flirted. She would say that she was sincerely interested in people. And that was true. But she was an unrepentant flirt. She was a flirt for all seasons. That was a known. But would she stop at being flirtatious? That was an unknown.

How did I react to her open flirtations? Not well. I got jealous, angry, insecure. I would challenge her motives and accuse her of not caring, of behaving shamelessly, of embarrassing me. I would become sullen, withdrawn and inaccessible until she would do something that validated our relationship and assured me that I was the only one. I would then spring back to life like a Slinky.

I wanted her to meet my mother. This would be a first for me. I had never introduced my mom to a girl I had been dating. One reason was that I hadn't dated many girls, if any really. But a more compelling

Chapter 34: Meeting The Families

reason was that I did not share much of my social life with my parents. As an adolescent, they would typically ask me the secular version of the Four Questions when I said I was going out. And as with Passover, the responses were rote and known before the questions were asked. Question #1: "Where are you going?" I responded, "Nowhere special." Question #2: "Who you going with?" I answered, "No one special." Question #3: "When will you be home?" Customary answer, "Not sure." And, when I finally did get home, Question #4: "What did you do?" To which I said "Not much." Always those four questions in that order. And always the same answers. When I left for college, the pattern of mute responses to reasonable questions endured. So, the fact that I wanted my mom to meet Hallie was as significant as a caterpillar morphing into a butterfly. It was a transformational event.

In late spring, Hallie and I drove the Chevy to Albany Park. Although she was immediately taken in by my mom's warmth, Hallie asked why she yelled so much. "That is not yelling, she just has a loud voice. It was needed to be heard in her family," I reassured Hallie. Hallie and my mother hit it off right from the beginning. I later learned that my mother called my sister in Los Angeles and said, "Cary brought a girl home, and you will really like her." What did my mom like about Hallie? Perhaps it was her openness, spontaneity, and lack of any guile. But I think there was something deeper. I think she saw in Hallie a reflection of her own youth: a beautiful, vivacious ingénue who had made flirting a fine art.

In the fashion of the elites looking kindly down on the quaint natives, Hallie enthused about our apartment, "It is so warm and cozy. Uncluttered, unlike my home. And there is even a fire escape right outside your bedroom window. That is so romantic." Hallie slept in my bed right next to the fire escape, I slept in the foldout couch in the adjacent dining room, and, of course, my mother had her own bedroom on the far side of the apartment. That first night, after we had all gone to bed, I sneaked into the bedroom and climbed into bed with Hallie. The window to the fire escape was open and a light breeze, heavy with humidity, made its way in. Hallie was afraid my mom would awaken and find us in bed together and half-heartedly kept urging me to go back. I eventually did, but not until 3:00 am.

The next day, we went to downtown Chicago for a massive demonstration against the Vietnam War. We were appropriately dressed in jeans and blue work shirts. While we marched along with thousands of others, with banners and shouts, we were not really into the vigorous protest. We just wanted to sneak away and be alone with one another. We made our way back to Albany Park and back to my bedroom.

Before we returned to Champaign, Hallie wanted me to meet her cousins, the Liebermans. She called them at the last minute and said we would stop by to say hello. Natalie Lieberman was a first cousin to Hallie's mother, but, for some reason, Hallie referred to her as Aunt Natalie, a larger than life, emotionally vivacious, rapturous personality. Natalie was a giver, extending herself and her home to all those who came within her orbit. When she was determined, no force on earth could resist her. Natalie carried the Reyman gene of feminine irresistibility, a combination of beauty, magnetism, charm and emotional charge. Among the women in the generation following Natalie, Hallie inherited that incomparable gene. Natalie's husband, Howard, was an energetic, dedicated, highly-respected ophthalmologist, who sprouted a David Niven mustache and moved his trim torso with a quick assertiveness, allowing for no wasted energy. He was not simply an eye doctor. He was a surgeon who held several patents and perfected intraocular lens implant surgery when it was in its infancy. In 1969, he was the go-to doctor in Chicago for implant operations, performing 22 procedures a day three days a week and organizing his office and the operating room so that he concentrated on doing only what he alone could do. He would move from operating room to room with the precision of the command center for the Apollo space program. He became rich, very rich. He had so much money flowing into his office that he hired two money/investment managers who worked full time for him, keeping track of the cash flow and investments. These were the Liebermans that Hallie wanted me to meet before we returned to Champaign.

Hallie explained that the Liebermans lived at 1000 Sheridan Drive in Glencoe. "Glencoe!" I exclaimed. I had heard of the suburb but had never even been close to it. The North Shore suburbs along Lake Michigan were known for their exclusivity, affluence and beauty. The megawealthy suburbs of Winnetka, Wilmette, and Kenilworth bordered Lake Michigan and were the aspiration of every Horatio Alger. Unless your last name were Lieberman, Shapiro or Rottstin. They were closed off to Jews. Even I, a boy from Albany Park, who never ever dreamed of being able one day to live in those privately-guarded enclaves, knew of them. They lite up my radar screen in 1966 when a recent college graduate, Valerie Percy, was found stabbed to death in her bedroom. Her father, Charles Percy, was running for the U.S. Senate, and the newspapers ran non-stop coverage of the brutal killing and the inconclusive investigation. The newspaper stories opened a window onto the impenetrable North Shore suburbs that were so exclusive that a non-resident driving on their public streets was likely to be stopped for interrogation. What did the wealthy Jews do? They did what they always did in the U.S. When they were kept out of the well-heeled Manhattan law firms or the national accounting firms, they started their own. When they were barred from prestigious country clubs, they built their own. And when they could not move into Kenilworth and similar areas on the North side, they developed their own. It was called Glencoe.

My 1964 Chevy was an incongruous sight on a late Saturday afternoon, maneuvering the twisting bends of Sheridan Road and following the shoreline of Lake Michigan. We pulled up to 1000 Sheridan Road. The house was set back so far from the street that I could barely see it. We pulled into the driveway, and before me was a large Tudor style brick home with over 4000 square feet, majestically sitting on a half acre of prime real estate. My mouth was open when I stepped into the hallway. I had never been in a private home like this. I read about people who lived in such grandeur, but no one I knew did. Howie and Natalie greeted Hallie like she was one of their own children with an enthused warmth that I had not seen in Hallie's own house, but which reminded me of my family. Hallie settled into the house with an ease borne of familiarity and comfort. She felt like one of family. I was simply the latest in a string of Hallie's boyfriends, and, although I was treated by Natalie and Howie with grace and a welcoming spirit, I was the uncomfortable outsider. Their three adolescent children, Jack, Jim and Julie Ann, meandered in and out. Around 4:00 p.m., some friends of Natalie's stopped by unexpectedly with their teenage kids. I recall that I gawked at a white-lacquered grand piano that had once been the provenance of a well-known pianist and that now dominated the living room. Hallie told me it cost tens of thousands of dollars, multiples of what my father earned in a year. I marveled at a back yard that appeared larger than some parks.

My other vivid memory of that afternoon is what would have been an ordinary, forgetful moment under other circumstances. Howie spontaneously said to all of us, "Stay for dinner. We'll have a barbeque." I was familiar with barbeques -- hot dogs and hamburgers and maybe corn on the cob or a baked potato. But that is not what Howie meant. He pulled out of the freezer 15 large T-bone steaks. He defrosted, grilled and served them to a pack of hungry carnivores. They ate the steaks as if they were ordinary fare, nothing special. I have no memory of anything else they served, except that there was an abundance of everything. The banter at the table was light and upbeat, as if life were a roll from one effortless moment to another. I thought of the ease with which Jay Gatsby, Tom Buchanan and his wife, Daisy, carried their wealth, as a taken-for-granted appendage, no different than an arm or leg. For the Liebermans, it was part of the air they breathed. The recurring thoughts in my head were, "Who has this much money? How are they able to display it so casually, wearing it with the security and familiarity of a well-used slipper, confident it will always be there? Who keeps in their freezer 15 steaks, just in case unexpected guests appear on their doorstep? And who serves steaks to a random collection of people who happen to stop by on a Saturday?"

Driving back to my mother's apartment, Hallie and I spoke of the Liebermans' wealth, the warmth of their family, and what goals are worth what kind of sacrifice. I arrived back in Albany Park starkly conscious of the vast gulf between my neighborhood and Glencoe, but I was fortified with the thought that, with hard work and perseverance, I could live a very comfortable life several notches above Albany Park. My California dream still included visions of my Uncle Marty's success, but, at that time, I did not see a path that might lead to the level of wealth of the Liebermans. Rather than discourage me, it gave me a perspective. I did not have to dedicate myself to maximizing material success to enjoy a meaningful life. The fact that I might never climb to the apex of Mount Everest did not mean I should resent its grandeur, or curse those who made the assent or diminish the achievement of other challenges. I left Glencoe with my eyes wide open to previously unknown possibilities and with my dreams intact.

Cary Grant once said, "Everyone wants to be Cary Grant. Even I want to be Cary Grant." We are not our personas. The more time I spent with Hallie the more I understood that, beneath her vivacious extroverted persona was a deep well of insecurity, doubt, anxiety, and fragility. She needed constant assurance and validation that she was a person of substance, of worth and intelligence. She related that her parents would assure her with the words, "Don't worry. Many smart successful men marry stupid women, just look at Rube Cohn," as they thought he had married a woman of ordinary intelligence. When she had trouble learning a concept in school, usually something having to do with math, Dr. Tager would yell at her and call her stupid. If she wrote a poem, her mother would denigrate it by telling her what Emily Dickinson was writing at her age. If she got a good grade, she would be told about someone else's child who was getting all A's. She had an emotional intelligence that, if capable of being measured like an IQ, would have made her a genius. But she couldn't control this gift; rather, at times it controlled her. Her emotions would drive her into deep despair, and I found I had to center her through hours and hours of talk and assurance. It was draining at times, and it was certainly not an easy relationship, but it was an intimate one, and I was ready for it.

It would take me a long time to realize how dependent I was on her attention and her moods. Emotionally, I was the yoyo, and I bounced up and down on the string that was in Hallie's hands. And she was an expert at playing the emotional strings. My moods would depend on her moods. My sense of security would wax and wane depending on her emotional state or her external wanderings. In so many ways, I did not have the personality, maturity, strength, or psychological understanding to know how to handle this wild filly of a woman. My failings were not without consequence. It would take decades to come even close to understanding her. Until then, a personal trail of tears would follow.

While we spent late spring together, we were on parallel tracks, wondering if and how they would cross. I was accepted into UCLA Law School, and I immediately accepted. In June, I was going to Los Angeles, finally realizing my dream. Nothing was going to keep me from heading west. Hallie was going to Israel for the summer, or at least that was one plan. She also hinted that she might move forward and join the IDF as she said she was going to do when I first met her. She didn't have any definite plans about what she would do during the summer once she got there, but she was going to stay with her cousins, Morty and

Ruth Reyman, who made Aliyah after the Six Day War. They lived in Jerusalem. She gave me a post office box in Jerusalem so I could write to her. We knew we would keep in touch and somehow find a way to be together, if not during the summer, than in the fall, but only if she were not in the IDF. It was all very fluid.

I finished college that June but did not go to the graduation. I was anxious to start my new life in LA, and I knew the ceremony was going to be enormous and impersonal. Besides, my mother was not going to make the trip to Champaign alone. I thought of my father and how proud he would have been that I was the first person in his family to graduate from college. I drove back to Chicago to start the process of packing up for Los Angeles. My mother was preparing to make the same move, completing the Chicago exodus for my immediate family. I packed up the Chevy in preparation for the cross-country trip. I was delighted to have a passenger with me. And not any ordinary passenger. My grandfather had offered to take the trip with me, and I took him up on it. He flew in from Los Angeles, and we set off for California in my trusty 1964 Chevy. My mom had gone ahead by plane, and hired someone to drive her Mustang across country. I don't remember too much of the road trip, except that I had a wonderful time. We stopped at the Grand Canyon, the Painted Desert and the Petrified Forest National Park. He took photos of me along the way. He later presented me with an acrylic painting of me sitting on a log in the Petrified Forest, with my long black hair blowing carefree in the wind. I was totally relaxed and mellow. That was all about to change.

Chapter 35

IT NEVER RAINS IN SOUTHERN CALIFORNIA

My mother arrived in Los Angeles shortly before I did. Her company had an affiliate in Los Angeles called Certified Life and Casualty Company, and she arranged for a transfer. She rented an apartment on Newcastle Avenue in Encino, California, in the San Fernando Valley. It was a one bedroom and den. It was also everything a Chicago boy could dream of. It had a swimming pool and each apartment had a balcony that opened onto the pool area. The landscaping was lush and green. Bright flowers and Palm trees were integral parts of the complex, and it gave me a feeling of Shangri-la.

My application for housing on campus was approved. I would be living in a graduate student dorm called Mira Hershey Hall, only a ten-minute walk from the law school. But first I was spending the summer on Newcastle Avenue, sleeping on a bed in the den. My Uncle Marty got me a job working at a transportation company called Jet Air Freight near Los Angeles Airport. Each day, I would drive ten miles, traveling down two freeways, going east on the Ventura Freeway and then south on the San Diego Freeway, past the Santa Monica Freeway to LAX, the international airport. I was learning to navigate the concrete pathways that defined Los Angeles. They were the lifelines to surviving in the city. I took to them with the fervor of a proselyte. My job was to fill up the trucks with gas and change the oil when needed. I worked in a large garage that was shaped like an airplane hangar and enjoyed the physical labor and earning decent money for someone with no skills.

The first month of the summer, June 1969, was routine. I went to work, came home, had dinner and wrote a letter to Hallie in Israel, sending it to the post office address she had given me. I understood she was traveling around the country, and I had no way to send mail to her directly. I wrote virtually every day, telling her about my job, my new life, and mostly how much I missed her and wanted her to come to Los Angeles as soon as possible. I may have received one or two letters from her, but no more. She was hitchhiking alone around the country and said she had met up with a cousin of hers called Israel as she was returning to Jerusalem. That was a new name to me. I had no idea what she was thinking or feeling, or what she intended to do.

On weekends, I would go to Westwood Village, the college town just south of UCLA, for a movie or snack. The sidewalk was filled with college-aged students, and many of them looked like the muses who inspired the Beach Boys to write the song "California Girls" in 1965. Other than a curious glance, they held no interest for me. My frame of mind was more in tune with Leonard Cohen, when he wrote "I'm not looking for another as I wander in my time ..." I was biding my time, waiting to learn what Hallie was going to do – stay in Israel as a soldier, return to Champaign, or come to Los Angeles. I was going to be a lawyer. Lawyers advocate. They persuade. And my letters had a purpose – to advocate for her to come to Los Angeles. I had no idea if she was getting the letters, reading the letters, or being moved by the letters. All I knew was that I was deeply moved by writing them, and I continued each day.

At the beginning of July I got a collect call from New York. It was Hallie. She had landed in New York and was staying the night at her Uncle Eli's house in the New York area. My questions were so numerous that they tripped over each other, coming at her with rapidity. "Are you back for good? What happened? What did you do in Israel? Who were you with? Who is this cousin named Israel? Are you going back? What about the IDF? What are your plans? Can you come to Los Angeles? How soon? Have you talked to your folks? Will they let you come to LA?" I remember only two things from the conversation. This guy called Israel was not a cousin after all. He was a boy she met when completing her hitchhiking adventures. But he was only a friend, she assured me. I had heard that one before. But he was there, and she and I were here, so I had the advantage. We finished the conversation with her expressed determination to come to LA right away, but first she had to let her parents know.

The next day was July 3 and she called again. And again it was a collect call. Her parents wanted her to fly to Champaign, but she told them she was going straight to Los Angeles. They were less than thrilled, but they reluctantly agreed. Time took a holiday, and it seemed like a week before the next day dawned. It was July 4, and she would be coming to LA that day. Barb and Neal had bought a tract home in Northridge, three bedrooms, family room and room for a swimming pool. This was California luxury, beyond the reach of most people in Albany Park. They invited the family over for a barbeque, and, since Hallie's plane was not getting in until 4:30 pm, I went to their home. My mom, Uncle Marty and Aunt Phyllis, my cousins Chuck and Rick, my grandfather and his wife Charlotte, and friends of my sister were all there. They all knew that I was going to leave the party to pick up my "girlfriend" from the airport and that she was arriving from a recent trip to Israel. They peppered me with questions about her, and I was feeling very uncomfortable. I answered in monosyllables and mostly sat by myself in the corner, staring at my bar mitzvah watch, waiting for the hour to leave. Time traveled in the slow lane.

I left the party for LAX. I had been in Los Angeles for less than a month, but it was enough time for me to be affected by the West Coast culture. It was probably a mistake, but I wore a new look. I put on stylish bell-bottom jeans, a flowered shirt, and, most conspicuously, I wore a long, colorful, paisley silk scarf around my neck, held in place by a golden ring. My hair was even longer than when I left Champaign. In those days you were able to walk right up to the gate to meet arriving passengers. Hallie waked off and was the same incomparable beauty as when I last saw her, except she was more bronze from the Israeli sun. Her hair was long and shimmering, and glittered as the sun hit it. She wore a dress cut so short that, even in Los Angeles, men took notice. When she smiled, she was radiant, and I melted. We kissed and hugged. Then she did a double take and asked why I was decked out as I was. I tried to explain that this was California, not Kansas, but she was not buying it. It was the last time I donned the scarf motif.

We drove straight back to the party in Northridge. I never thought twice about whether Hallie might be exhausted or reticent about meeting my family so soon after arriving in LA. During the ride, I tried mightily to understand what she had done in Israel and what her plans were, but I could not decipher either. I was just thrilled she was in LA, and that I was about to introduce her to my family. At least she had previously met my mother, so that was one fewer newbie to get to know. Being her effervescent self, Hallie worked the room, being sure to talk with everyone. She paid special attention to Marty, whom she thought looked like a movie star, and Neal, whom she said must have learned charm from Fred Astaire. One month in Israel had done nothing to diminish her allure. Cole Porter must have known someone like Hallie when he wrote the line, "You've got that charm, that subtle charm that makes young farmers desert the farm." Yes, she's "got that thing."

When the barbeque was over, there remained an unanswered question. Where was Hallie going to stay? She knew no one in LA, except for me. She had little money, only modest savings from her odd jobs. It was obvious to me that she should stay at my mom's apartment, but I had not broached the subject with either of them. I took my mom aside and asked her. She had a quizzical look on her face, as if asking me if I were kidding. She did not think it was a good idea. But I persisted, and she said yes. We did not touch the issue of how long of a stay it might be. I did not know. Hallie had nowhere to go, and she must have assumed she could stay at my mother's apartment. In retrospect, we were two young kids with a lot of chutzpah, not thinking twice about imposing ourselves on others.

At the apartment, the awkward question of where everyone would sleep finally arrived. There were only two beds – my mother's king-sized bed in her bedroom and the foldout couch on which I slept in the den. Surprise is too mild a word to describe my reaction when my mom offered Hallie one side of her bed, and Hallie accepted. Perhaps my mother was taking a cue from the military strategist Sun Tzu and decided, to paraphrase his advice, "to keep your friends close and your possible daughter-in-law closer." My girlfriend, newly-arrived from Israel, was sleeping with my mother. I am confident that Freud never confronted such a situation.

I talked Hallie into staying for the rest of the summer. She did not need much convincing since she had no other plans. She had decided to defer, but not abandon, her plans to move to Israel in favor of getting a college education in the United States. She eventually found an all-girls, two-year school called Harcum Junior College on the Mainline, just outside of Philadelphia. She was going to start there in September.

I continued working at Jet Air Freight, and Hallie began to search for a job. She learned that Sears Roebuck in the West Valley was looking for a salesperson. She interviewed and was offered the position on the spot. I always said that Hallie was the best salesperson imaginable. She projected an easy friendliness that made one feel special and invited into her world. She had a unique ability to zero in on whomever she was with to make him feel like he and he alone existed. When she talked about something and emphasized its advantages, she did so with such conviction that her view became your view. You were within her matrix and saw it just as she did. She could sell meat to a vegan. He might not eat it, but he would walk out the store with it, having paid retail and not fully comprehending what had just happened.

She had to take a long bus ride down Ventura Boulevard to the department store. After her first day of work, she came home to describe a traumatic incident. She was waiting for the bus and was concerned she was going to be late and make a bad first impression. A nice looking middle-aged man pulled up in his car and asked her if she wanted a ride. Quite naively, she jumped into the car. She was likely in an Israeli state of mind, having just left a country where hitchhiking was a way of life for soldiers and civilian youth, offering mobility at no cost and with no risk. Not so in Los Angeles, as she learned that morning. After getting in the car, she had an uneasy feeling. About halfway to work, he put his hand on her thigh. She froze and clutched the door handle, ready to bolt if he did anything else. When they reached her destination, he said he looked forward to seeing her the next day, and would give her another ride. She jumped out and ran to the store.

There was no way she was going back to the bus stop. I could not drive her as our hours did not mesh. Once again, my mother came to the rescue. She gave Hallie her car for the summer so she could go to work unmolested. My mother arranged for a friend of hers to take her to and from Certified Life each day. My mother's sacrifices were remarkable. She lost her bed, her car, and her privacy so that I could have my girlfriend with me in Los Angeles. It is only in retrospect that I have come to understand just how much support she gave me that summer. I had brought a strange woman, whom she had met only once, into our house, and it fell on my mother to endure major disruptions to her life, at the very time she was making a new life for herself in Los Angeles. I had the temerity to expect her to fall in line with my every request and solve every personal problem for me. That she did so, and without complaint, is a testament to her character.

The summer was humming along brilliantly when a speed bump appeared. One day, Hallie told me with more feigned disinterest than distress that Bernie was in Los Angeles. Bernie? I had thought we had gotten rid of Bernie in Champaign. What was he doing in LA? "He is just a friend, and he is visiting Los Angeles with a friend. He wants to meet up. Nothing wrong with that," she insisted. I was beside myself. No man is just friends with Hallie, just like no alcoholic is just friends with Mr. Jack Daniels. I could not talk her out of it, so I spent an anxious Sunday afternoon awaiting her return from meeting with her "friend" Bernie. I was a nervous wreck. She got back around 5:00 pm and enthused about a wonderful afternoon, sitting on the grass just talking. The time, for her, had flown by, and they covered much ground about what had happened to each of them during the last few months, and what their plans were and … "So, what did he want?" I interrupted her. "Oh, I told him I was going to attend Harcum Junior College in September. He loved the idea, and he wants to visit me during college breaks. He is really nice and easy to talk to." "What?!" I blurted out. "He is going to visit you in Philadelphia?" "Sure," she said casually, as if there could be no possible objection from me. "He still wants to marry me, but I told him no, and that I was dating you. He accepted it and is willing to be just friends, knowing full well that you and I are dating. He was really accepting of that." I swallowed hard, but it did not stop the acid reflux from coming into my throat. I knew Hallie well enough by now that I had to accept defeat. I could not put chains on her. That would not work. It would probably backfire. I had no choice but to accept who she was, although it was more of a capitulation than an open tolerance. She was a magnet for guys, and she had no ability, let alone intention, to shut that down.

At the end of the summer, Hallie, my mom, and I were walking one evening in Westwood. Hallie was scheduled to leave in a couple of days for Champaign and then on to Philadelphia. UCLA students were returning from summer vacation. It was crowded. I had never seen so many scantily clad co-eds in one place, gaily sauntering along, licking ice cream cones, holding hands with guys, laughing in response to nothing. Hallie grabbed my hand and held it more tightly than ever. Whether it was a squeeze borne of insecurity, jealousy, or possessiveness, I will never know. My mom blurted out, loud enough that Hallie could clearly hear, "Cary, look at all these attractive girls with darling figures. You are going to have fun." What was she thinking? Why would she say that, and why in front of Hallie? That night, I paid dearly for my mother's comment. I saw, for the first time, Hallie's quick and strong reaction when she contemplated that her relationship with me could face some competition. Hallie alternated between fury and insecurity. My response alternated between defensiveness and sullenness. She never forgot it.

I took Hallie to the airport to see her off. Our plan, if you can call it that, was to speak on the phone often and for her to return to LA for the Thanksgiving weekend. It sounds cheesy, but as we were standing outside the gate waiting for her to board the plane, the airport loudspeakers played a song. It was *Leaving on a Jet Plane* by Peter, Paul & Mary, and it had just been released as a single that year. It became our personal anthem, and I cannot count the number of times it reverberated in my head as I thought of our separations.

    Hallie left on a jet plane, and I left in my Chevy. I had other challenges before me. I needed to move into the graduate dorm, buy my law books, get settled, and prepare for orientation day at UCLA School of Law. As the start of law school approached, the serenity I had at the beginning of the summer started to wilt. I began to panic, understanding how Adam must have felt when, upon being ousted from the Garden of Eden, he realized that he was naked. Adam at least had Eve. With Hallie in Philadelphia, I felt alone and very uncertain of what lay ahead.

Chapter 36

THE DORM IS MY SHELTER

Mira Hershey Hall was a dream setup for me. I could park my Chevy next door in what was called Parking Lot 2. The law school was a short walk away. The dorm was heralded as co-ed, but in a semi-controlled way. Each floor was divided in half, one part for men and the other for women. The doors separating the male and female wings were open, making the whole floor accessible. The unwritten rule was that we were not to intrude upon the other side, but no one paid any attention to it. My roommate was Steve McMurtry, a first-year medical student. He was tall, blond, outgoing, and confident. He carried himself as if medical school was his right, and that right included access to as many women as possible. Our room was small, with single beds against each wall and a three-foot passageway from the door between the two beds to the desks at the back of the room. There was little room to maneuver, and I knew right away that I would not spend much time here studying. As it turned out, Steve did not spend any time studying in the room – or, so far as I could tell, anywhere else for that matter.

Most of the guys in the dorm were in their first year of law school, medical school, dental school, or the graduate English department. During the first days, I became friends with a number of them, including a first-year law student named Rick Romero. Rick was a diminutive, good-looking guy with slick black hair, a ready laugh, and a mustache in the shape of a modified horseshoe, with the tips extending all the way down to the bottom of his chin. He was taken with a country rock band called Poco, and their music spilled out of his room into the hallway as if he were the anointed DJ for the dorm. He had an outgoing, friendly nature and was instant good friend material. He also wore a brown suede jacket with fringes on the arms and front pockets, making me envious for the first time of another person's clothes. It would be more than forty years before I bought a similar coat – a long-delayed quench of my coveting that jacket.

Only a few feet away from my room was the door to the women's section. I became quick friends with Claire Pike, a graduate student in English. She was petite, with a bountiful side profile, and was cute, and outgoing. She was friendly and could flash a smile that suggested more intrigue than a glance by Ilsa Lund to Rick Blaine. It was not clear if she was more interested in securing a doctorate in English or a husband with a professional degree. Then there was Anita Ostroff, a graduate student in public health. Anita and I hit it off immediately. She was smart, driven, and a bit crazed, with anxieties and insecurities that defined her. She would have caused Freud to commit himself to a hospital. She had the ability to abruptly change directions multiple times while talking, so that many thoughts were only segments of consciousness. I am sure that an MRI of her brain would have shown the neural pathways as a scramble, trying hopelessly to find the end of a thought. She could never get lost in a crowd, spoke her mind, had no use for fools, and took life seriously. There was never a dull moment in her company. Her claim to fame, which she emphasized at every opportunity, was her involvement in the Free Speech Movement at the University of California, Berkeley, where she had done her undergraduate work. Her passion for Berkeley was exceeded only by her zeal for medical students. She thought that MD meant "Miracle Doctor." Anita was a deeply caring person who took an interest in me, and we became life-long fast friends.

Dave Edwards, a medical student, was studious and, according to the girls in the dorm, good looking and very eligible. He sported a short, evenly trimmed mustache that gave off vibes of the actor William Powell. Louellen was also in the dorm. She majored in finding the most eligible medical student around, and she quickly found Dave. Another fixture was Harmon Schwartz, a serious medical student. Linda Ledeen was also on our floor. She had an elusive, pre-Raphaelite quality about her. She did not walk the ground so much as float above it. Many of the guys followed her around like a puppy. She seemed to know what she wanted, but, whatever it was, it was hidden. Ultimately, six strangers met that first year at Mira Hershey Hall. They would quickly form three couples – Dave and Louellen, Harmon and Linda, and Rick and Claire – and then celebrate at three weddings. Three marriages from one floor in one dorm – for them, Mira Hershey Hall was a preview of the much later production of *The Bachelor* and *The Bachelorette*.

The first order of business was to buy my law books at the UCLA Student Union. The school year was divided into quarters and not semesters, so there was a fall, winter, and spring quarter. The upside of this schedule was that I was able to enroll in more courses than on the semester system. The decided downside was that finals were upon me before I could even get used to my seat in the classroom. My first quarter courses were contracts, criminal law, torts, legal research and writing, and "Law, Lawyers and Social change." I bought my books at the Student Union. I do not know what weighed me down more, the sheer heft of the books or the cost. I recall vividly being shocked at the prices of the law books. When I now look at the stickers on the books and find that they cost between $15.00 and $17.50, I am puzzled. Five books plus the paperback supplements that I also had to buy probably set me back $100. Why wasn't that a bargain? Back in 1969, the minimum wage was $1.60 per hour, which meant it would require over ten hours of work to earn enough for just one book, or sixty-two-and-a-half hours of work (or one-and-a-half weeks) to earn enough for all of the books for just one quarter of classes. While I earned more than the minimum wage that summer, the cost of the books translated into a lot of diesel that I pumped into the trucks.

Chapter 37

ORIENTATION DAY

I approached orientation day with a mixture of great anticipation and anxiety. My 1969 law school class had 300 students, divided alphabetically into four sections of seventy-five students each. All of our first year classes would be with the same section. I was in section three with all the other students whose last names started with K through P. I sat on a bench outside one of the classrooms waiting for the doors to open for our orientation session. Sitting next to me was Forrest Mosten, whom everyone called Woody. He would become my best friend in law school and a life-long treasure. We went into a room that was designed as a shallow amphitheater, with half-circle rows of continuous raised flat surfaces for taking notes in lieu of desks. Each row was a step higher than the next. The first row was on the level of the professor and the last row fought for oxygenated air. I gravitated toward the back, and Woody sat next to me. My stomach was in knots, not knowing what was next.

Eventually, Assistant Professor Michael Tigar sauntered in. It was not a walk. It was a deliberate, long-paced stroll to the center of the podium. He was tall and gangly, with dirty blonde hair that hung over the top off his ears and uneven bangs that kept falling into his eyes. He threw several books onto the table in front of him, then he passed around a seating chart and asked us each to put our name in the appropriate square for our seat. He looked out over the class for what seemed like an eternity. His voice sounded in cadences as if he were in a play and had a large audience to enrapture. He succeeded.

"Ladies and gentlemen, you are in law school. If you thought you came here to learn law, you should leave now. I am not going to teach you the law. No one here is going to teach you the law. You cannot be *taught* the law. The law is fluid, changing, open to interpretation, and I cannot tell you what the law will be tomorrow or the next day. You will never *master* the law. The study of law is a Sisyphean task. And I cannot tell you whose law it is. The law is not seen as the same in every region of this country, by every judge, by every class, by every litigant. The law? Whose law and when? No, you are not here to learn the law. You are here to learn to become lawyers." He paced back and forth along the lengthy rise on which he stood. His stride was practiced as if each were measured in rhythm with his words. As he continued to talk, I thought of Abraham Lincoln, Clarence Darrow, Louis Nizer, and Max Steuer, pacing before a jury, giving closing arguments that would save their clients' lives.

Professor Tigar continued, "If we and you are successful, you will learn to *think* like a lawyer. You will abandon your shallow, layman's way of thinking, you will keep your emotions under control, you will never come to the end of your analysis, you will search constantly for more and better answers, you will never stop when you think you have the right answer because you will question yourself again and again and again. Each supposed answer will be followed by, "What if?" You will test each position as if you were a scientist in a laboratory, but, instead of the search for a provable and repeatable hypothesis, your task will be

Chapter 37: Orientation Day

to fashion an argument worthy of respect and as impenetrable to attack as possible. You will struggle to arm your position with the best public-policy positions possible while at the same time realizing that there are always competing interests and positions. Your mind will never rest and your zeal to advocate for your client will never cease. That is what we will try to teach you in the next three years. Look around this room. Not all of you will be able to do this. Some of you are lazy, some are incapable and some will tire of the constant challenges, pushing, and pressure. Look to your left. Look to your right. Think of yourself. At the end of three years, one of you will not be here."

Silence. Then an uncomfortable murmur. Some half-hearted laughter. I did not laugh. I looked around. I felt a pit in my stomach. Would I be one of those who would fail? I thought I would be learning the law. I did not sign up for someone to retool my way of thinking. I did not seek three years of pressure and constant testing of my worth. This was not looking good.

Professor Tigar interrupted my insecure musings. He said, "And how do we teach you? Don't think for a moment that we are going to lecture to you. We are not going to spoon-feed you anything. You are going to have to work for every morsel of insight that lights up in your head. You will have to decide what the best answer is in the moment, based on the facts in front of you and the law behind you or the facts behind you and the law as you passionately believe it should be. And we will never tell you if you are on the right path; we will only ask you to consider other paths." What is he talking about? I was having a hard time understanding where he was coming from and what law school was going to be. I was intimidated, and the more thoughts that swirled in my head, the more I succumbed to the despairing feeling I should have chosen foundry work after all.

He paced again. Stopped. He looked down at the seating chart that had made its way back to him. "Mr. Parker," he bellowed, "have you ever heard of Ernesto Miranda?"

I heard feet scraping, people's faces were looking around the room, trying to find a Mr. Parker.

A voice answered, "No, Sir." And then it happened. I was about to witness my first lesson in the Socratic method that would be the one constant in law school. My stomach lurched.

Professor Tigar began, "Ernesto is walking along the street one day, minding his own business. The police, based on circumstantial evidence, arrest him and bring him into to the station for questioning. They are pretty sure he is the culprit in the rape and kidnapping of an eighteen-year girl. After two hours of intense questioning in a windowless room, Ernesto confesses and signs a statement that he committed the rape. He is tried, convicted and sentenced to twenty to thirty years in prison. Mr. Parker, do you have a problem with the conviction?"

"I don't think so."

"Was this truly a voluntary confession?"

"Sounds that way."

"Why does it sound that way?"

"I didn't hear anything that sounds like he was beaten or threatened or coerced."

"What does coerced mean to you?"

"Forced or intimidated."

"Is there any intimidation being by yourself in a police station, questioned for hours by police detectives trained in interrogation, when those police believe you are the guilty party, being denied a lawyer and not told what the consequences of a confession might be?"

"I guess so."

"You guess so? I don't want you to guess so. What do you think?"

"Yes, it sounds bad."

Professor Tigar then said, "In 1966, in a case captioned *Miranda v. Arizona*, 384 U.S. 436 (1966), the United States Supreme Court found that Ernesto was deprived of his Fifth Amendment right not to incriminate himself and his Sixth Amendment right to a lawyer. The court required in every case in which a person suspected of a crime is in police custody, before being questioned, he must be advised of his right to remain silent, anything he says may be used against him and he has the right to consult with a lawyer and if he cannot afford it, the state will pay for that lawyer. Mr. Parker, what do you think of that?"

"Sounds good."

"Is that all you have to say? Do you see any problems with it?"

Parker shifted in his chair, silent, and Professor Tigar looked at the seating chart before calling out, "Mr. Klein, do you see any problems with the court's decision?"

The student bravely responded, "Uh, not really. It will cost the state money for a lawyer but so what. It means more jobs for us."

The class laughs. Professor Tigar stares at us. He is not amused. "Mr. Lawlor, any problems with the court's decision?"

Lawlor identifies himself, "It can mean that some criminals go free."

"Good, and the dissenting opinions in the case had that problem as well."

It went on like this for thirty minutes. Professor Tigar would cite the names of cases, with their exact volume and page number and date from memory. It was a feat of memorization I will never forget. Must I be that good? I wondered. As Professor Tigar called on one classmate after another, I held my breath. I kept looking at the clock. Please let this session be over before he calls on me. Please. My mind was a blank. If he called on me, I would have nothing to say.

I later learned that Professor Tigar had been editor in chief of the *California Law Review* at the University of California, Berkeley School of Law and had been hired as a Supreme Court law clerk by the liberal

Justice William Brennan. But he was fired the week he started because of complaints by newspaper columnists and J. Edgar Hoover over Tigar's activist background as a university student. He would go on to a career as a criminal defense attorney, representing political activists and controversial causes and teaching at various law schools. In 1999, the California Attorneys for Criminal Justice placed him at number three – behind Clarence Darrow and Thurgood Marshall – in their Lawyer of the Century ranking. No wonder I saw him as a legal titan when he was but a twenty-eight-year old Assistant Professor trying to usher in an air of reality to a troop of nervous legal infants.

Professor Tigar was not finished with us, not yet. He paced back and forth once again. "Do you think you will win your cases by logic? Compelling argument? By the force of your great analytical abilities? By your smile? If so, think again." He stopped pacing and looked straight at us. "You will win your cases with stories. Justice Oliver Wendell Holmes said, 'The life of the law has not been logic: it has been experience.' Do not forget that. It is by drawing on the life experiences of ordinary people, showing their compelling emotional stories, and placing your audience within those stories that you will win." He continued, "Stories are your key to success not only because of their ability to reveal an emotional truth or teach an important lesson or to get your judge or jury to identify with you and your client, but because the same story can teach many lessons, depending on your purpose." He then told us a Zen story I never forgot.

"A general was tired of war. He retreated to a monastery to learn the one skill he lacked – archery. For ten years, he spoke not a word. He worked to perfect his archery skills. Each day, after a hearty breakfast, he would spend hours in the forest practicing by shooting an arrow at a bull's eye he had hung on a tree. He did nothing but hone his skill. After ten years, he became so good that he never missed. Each shot, no matter how far he was from his target, was a perfect bull's-eye. The abbot of the monastery told the general it was time for him to leave. The general protested that he needed more time to become even better at archery. But the abbot said, "No, it is time for you to go to the outside world and teach others the skill you have mastered." So, the general left the monastery. He walked through forests and over streams, climbed rocks and traipsed prairies until he came to a small village. He looked around. He saw a tree with a bull's-eye and right in the center was an arrow. He walked some more. He saw another tree with a bull's-eye and, lo and behold, there was an arrow in the center. He looked some more and saw even more bull's-eyes with arrows in the center. Over a hundred trees were the same. There is a master archer in the village, one even greater than me, he said to himself. The inner peace he had developed at the monastery after ten years evaporated. He must meet this archer. He spoke to the elders of the village. He told them that the archer who shot all these arrows into the center of the bull's-eyes must meet him by the river in one hour. The general went to the river and waited. A young girl came over and said, "Are you waiting for someone?" "Go away," said the general, "I am waiting for someone." The girl said that she came to the river because she was told someone was waiting for her there. The general said, "I am waiting for the master archer who was able to put an arrow in the bull's-eye of hundreds of targets." "Well, that's me," said the young girl. The general grew angry, puffed out his chest and bellowed, "If you are the archer, tell me how you got a perfect shot with every single arrow." The young girl answered, "That's easy. I took my arrow and shot it at a tree. Wherever it landed, I then drew a bull's eye around it."

Professor Tigar smiled, "Stories are like that. They can be woven around many different points of view. You are not just a lawyer; you are a storyteller. As you unfold your story, build the story around the bull's-eye you want people to see. Now go, and become real lawyers." He walked out of the room.

Then, it was over. I felt overwhelmed, scared, doubtful. My armpits were wet. I was a wreck, and he hadn't even called on me. I left the classroom in awe of what I had just witnessed. Professor Tigar had complete mastery of cases, of the facts of those cases, of the arguments and counter-arguments, of the majority and minority opinions, of the history and the effects of the decisions. As I witnessed the performance of this legal don, I shrank inside. I kept asking myself, "What am I doing here?"

I was breathless. That was not a class. It was not an orientation. It was a performance. He was dazzling. Through his storytelling, I was willing to follow the path he laid out, wherever it would take me. In fewer than fifty minutes, he had woven together the law, court decisions, and stories in a way that both inspired and dispirited me. I wanted to be the kind of lawyer he had just put on display. But I was convinced that would never be me.

I went back to the dorm and the first thing I did was call Hallie. I recounted my session with Professor Tigar and told her there was no way I was going to get through law school, and I should just admit it was a bad idea and cut my losses. She gave me a pep talk and reminded me that I hadn't even attended one real class yet. Who quits before the race starts? I knew she was right. I went downstairs to the cafeteria for dinner and then claimed a comfortable seat in the corner lounge near my room. I had to do work before the first day of classes. It looked easy. I only had ten pages of reading in contracts and eight in torts for tomorrow. Seemed pretty light to me.

Chapter 38

WHAT WAS I MISSING?

The corner lounge and chair would become my property for the next year. I opened the contracts case book to read the ten assigned pages. I quickly learned that not all pages are created equal. One page in the case book was like ten pages of a regular textbook. I had to read dense court opinions, consisting of detailed factual scenarios and majority and minority opinions. Then there were questions and supplementary material added by the author. It was tough sledding. I would read one case, and it was decided in favor of the plaintiff. The next case, presenting almost identical facts, would be decided in favor of the defendant. Which one was right? What was I missing?

Class the next day was just as challenging as the session with Professor Tigar. I had read all the material, but in class I could not remember the facts, how the matter was decided, what the court's reasoning was, or virtually anything. It was as if I had never read the cases. My torts class was taught by Professor Gary Schwartz, whose maiden teaching voyage was my class. He was thin, with black hair and large glasses that constantly slipped down his nose. He had a high-pitched voice that would rise a few decibels higher when he emphasized a point. What was most distinctive about him, however, was his intellect. He mind raced faster than he could get the words out of his mouth, and, since he spoke quite fast, that meant that his mind was faster than the speed of light. I could detect spittle in the corner of his mouth as he tried to get out five thoughts at once.

First it was Professor Tigar. Now it was Professor Schwartz. They were both brilliant. Other students in the class seemed to get it. They responded to questions intelligently and asked serious and probative questions. Mr. Minter, always sitting in the first row of each class, was the first to volunteer and the last to talk in class. He was on top of everything, whereas I had just one goal, and that was to keep my head down and not be called upon. I recalled the observation variously attributed to Mark Twain or Abraham Lincoln, but probably never uttered by either of them: "It is better to remain silent and be thought a fool than to speak and remove all doubt." That became my golden rule.

In my contracts class, Professor Leon Letwin, sporting a bushy walrus mustache and a loud voice, called out, "Mr. Lerman, did you read *Hawkins v. McGee*? *Me, did he really call on me?* I could not get a sound out of my mouth. Finally, I squeaked, "Yes." All eyes turned to me. "What are the facts of the case?"

The fact, what are the facts, I asked myself. My mind was blank. *Look at the book. You wrote notes in the margin.* "Oh, the facts. A guy by the name of Hawkins had scars on the palm of his hand caused by a burn. Years later, he went to a doctor by the name of McGee who said he could fix the hand. McGee said he could give Hawkins a 100 percent perfect hand. But the operation was not a success, and Hawkins sued."

Letwin nodded, but it was not over yet. "What did he sue for?"

"Money?"

"Yes, money. But what *legal right* did he claim was violated?"

"Oh, contract," I answered.

"What contract? I didn't hear anything about a contract, Mr. Lerman?"

"The doctor's promise to give Hawkins a perfect hand was a contract."

"A contract must have three things. What are they?"

I was hesitant. "A promise and an acceptance of a promise?"

"Anyone else know the three things needed for a contract?"

Minter did. He raised his hand and calmly told the room, "Offer, acceptance, and consideration."

"Right," agreed Letwin. "Now, Mr. Lerman, what was the offer, acceptance, and consideration?"

At this point I was not feeling very well. I was perspiring, and the pounding of my heart was louder than my voice as I choked out, "The doctor offered to fix the hand, Hawkins accepted, and the consideration is the money paid for the operation?"

"There is nothing in the opinion about Hawkins paying for the operation, Mr. Lerman."

Minter raised his hand again. Was there anything he didn't know? He explained: "The consideration was Hawkins undergoing the surgery."

"Right. Mr. Lerman, what did the court say the damages should be?"

I remembered this one, after a hurried glance at my notes. "The damages are the difference in value between a perfect hand and the hand he had before the operation."

"Right, but does that make sense? Why? Why not the pain and suffering he went through during the operation? Why not the additional scarring on his hand?"

"I'm not sure, but that is what he was promised."

The class ended, and I left feeling like I was a wounded soldier on the battlefield, but without a comrade to pick me up. I still didn't fully comprehend *Hawkins v McGee* or why the damages were what the court said. It would be much later that I understood that, for a contract lawsuit, the plaintiff gets his expectancy damages. It is what he would have had if the contract had been performed as promised. He was entitled to damages, as measured by the difference in the value of a hand as promised (a perfect hand) and the hand he had before the surgery (a defective hand). It might be hard to put a dollar figure on each of these conditions of the hand or the difference in value between them, and that would be another challenge for the court. But I did not understand all that from the give-and-take in class. The same was true in each of my other classes.

After two weeks of class, I knew only one thing for certain: I had no idea what was going on in any of my classes. I wasn't learning any law, I was exposed to court opinions that were all over the map, decided differently depending on slight changes in facts, or the temperament of the judge, or the mores of the time, or any one of a number of other factors. I was called upon only a couple of times, and I was able to avoid looking like a complete idiot.

Again I called Hallie to tell her I was going to drop out. I relayed that I had no idea what was going on in class. It was all so confusing. I prepared meticulously, doing the required reading, and thought I understood it until I went to class and then it all became foggy again. I was not cut out for this. She mostly laughed, but I wanted to curl up somewhere. She knew I could master the cases and that I would eventually get on top of it. I did not have that confidence. But I knew there was no way I was going to tell my mother that I was dropping out of law school because it was too difficult. I had to keep calm and carry on, as the British would say.

Having Hallie 3000 miles away was a blessing in disguise. I was not distracted by a social life. Yes, I became friends with people in the dorm and at the law school, and I did take some Saturday nights off, but most

Chapter 38: What Was I Missing?

of my time outside of the classroom was devoted to studying in my corner-lounge refuge. A few of us claimed it by eminent domain as an oasis for studying. Rick Romero, Dave Edwards, Harmon Schwartz, and Anita Ostroff (when she wasn't scouting out would-be doctors in the medical library) would study there along with me. They too were serious about academics, so it was easy to concentrate and not be distracted. Often, it would be empty. I started to study in a different way. I would read each assignment ahead of class, as required, but I no longer expected that the class would clear up my confusion. So, after each class, I would write out a summary of each case, the facts, and the holding, then I would incorporate anything from my class notes that seemed remotely comprehensible. In this way, I was gradually learning *after* class and not falling further and further behind because of my confusion. I did not move onto the readings for the next day until I had done all I could do to understand what we had just covered in class. It seemed to work.

I took breaks from my studies by practicing the guitar. I did not have a guitar of my own, and was only capable of strumming a couple of chords. But Claire Pike, who would regularly visit me in my room, let me borrow hers from time to time. Hallie flew out for Thanksgiving. We were sitting on one of the beds in my room when Claire came in carrying her guitar. She sat on the other bed opposite us and starting strumming and singing. She was looking directly into my eyes as she slowly sang a love song. I could feel the temperature in the room rise, and I could sense darts shooting out from Hallie's eyes. When Claire left, Hallie was on my case. "Who is she?" "Oh, she is getting a Ph.D. in English, and she is very nice. Very smart too. She is from New York," I replied. Hallie, displaying a jealously I had not seen since the walk in Westwood Village, said sharply, "I don't want her hanging around your room. She is out to get you." "No she isn't," I assured her, "She is dating my friend Rick Romero, who lives down the hall." Hallie said,

"I don't care who she is dating, she wants you." I thought this was nonsense and thought no more about it.

I had no intention of straying from Hallie and devoted myself to my law books, but my roommate, Steve, spent far more time with ladies than he did looking through medical instruments. He dated so many different women that I could not keep track of them. But one finally stuck. Her name was Cleta, which I always thought was an odd and potentially embarrassing name. Who would name their daughter Cleta? Cleta was tall and thin, had long, soft, light-brown hair and, frankly, was beautiful.

One Saturday night, I stayed in the lounge to study, and Steve and Cleta went out. I went to bed around 11:00 pm. I was just about to fall asleep when the door opened and two people, obviously drunk, stumbled into the room. I heard Steve say "It's OK, he's sleeping." Cleta mildly protested, "We should go someplace else." Steve pulled her onto his bed, only two feet from me, and told her there was no other place to go. I had turned to face the wall and made neither a move nor a sound. Big mistake. I heard them fumble with their clothes, undo their zippers, drop their shoes, then start kissing and moaning. Before I could let them know that I was still awake, it was obvious that they were deep into love making. I heard every sound and could feel (or almost feel) their movements. What should I do? Who would be more embarrassed if I said something or turned around? I wasn't sure. I would be for sure. Probably Cleta. Steve? No, he would not be. Definitely not Steve. I took the coward's way out and remained silent, praying it would all be over soon. It seemed like an eternity, but was probably only an hour; they quietly got up, dressed and were out of the room. Did this really happen? I wanted it to be a horrible dream, but it wasn't. I felt cheapened and soiled. Did he think so little of me that he could make love to a girl only a couple of feet away from me, as if I were a wooden prop? Did I think so little of myself that I was too embarrassed to make myself known? Or was I simply trying to make the best of an awkward situation and not make things worse than they were? I was never able to answer any of these questions. Perhaps the answer lurked in the vow I then took. If ever in a similar situation, one where I was viscerally uncomfortable with what was happening in my presence, I would not stay mute. I would speak out.

Hallie returned to Los Angeles that Christmas break with a present for me. It was a guitar so I would not have to borrow one from Claire. Clever girl, that Hallie. The holiday visit was a much-needed one, as we had drifted apart in the weeks after Thanksgiving, and we needed to connect again. When I dropped her off at the airport for her return to Philadelphia, it was gut-wrenching. The impact of her leaving was always so immediate. Her presence emitted so much fire that, when she departed, it was as if hot embers had suddenly turned to cold ashes. I have no memory of driving from the airport. I was an automaton.

After Hallie left, I went into full time study mode with a new intensity. I did not leave the corner lounge. My first law school finals were coming up. Because several of my classes, including contracts and torts, were two-quarter classes, I had only two finals – one in criminal law and the other in "Law, Lawyers and Social Change." When the grades were posted with anonymous letters in lieu of names, I pulled out a sheet with my number and was surprised and pleased that I got one H (which stood for Honors and was the equivalent to an A) and one HP (for High Pass – a B). I no longer felt like a dummy, but I did not think I was a highflier either. It was more like I was treading water, still very much unsure of this thing called law. But I was getting much more comfortable in the California legal waters.

Chapter 39

THE DRAFT AND THE DENTIST

In addition to keeping my head above water in law school and trying to keep my relationship with Hallie afloat, I had a third, potentially more challenging issue. And that was the Vietnam War. I was not particularly involved in anti-Vietnam protests. There was little activity at the University of Illinois by the time I left for Los Angeles. But events heated up in the Fall of 1969. There were demonstrations on the UCLA campus that turned violent. I recall crowds of students overturning enormous metal garbage bins, the kind that serviced large apartment buildings, and lighting them on fire. Students occupied buildings and called for strikes, and professors spoke up in their favor. The law school was neither silent nor actively protesting. Classes continued for the most part, but speakers did come to talk about the war.

Like most of my generation, I was against the war. I saw it as inflicting tremendous suffering on thousands of defenseless people in an unwinnable effort for no good reason. I agreed with those who argued that the prevailing domino theory was wrong. The Johnson and Nixon administrations argued that the loss of Vietnam to the Communists would lead to the loss of all of Indo-China, which would lead to a loss of mainland Asia, which would lead to a loss of Japan and the Philippines, which would directly threaten the security of the United States. In retrospect, both the pro- and anti-war factions got it wrong. The anti-war group failed to appreciate the evil that the North Vietnamese government would unleash on the South – it would lead to the imposition of a brutal, totalitarian regime, the slaughter of thousands of civilians, and a humanitarian crisis as thousands of refugees sought to escape tyranny and death in treacherous small boats. The pro-war camp misdiagnosed the war entirely. The North Vietnamese and their supporters in the South were fighting more for their national identity than they were for Communism. The Americans were simply the latest in a series of foreigners who had invaded their country, following the Chinese and the French.

The subtleties of the region, the history, and the demographics were all lost on me, as they were on most of those protesting. We just wanted it to stop. The radio airwaves were dominated by anti-war songs, and it was impossible not to be moved by them. Bob Dylan's "Blowin' in the Wind," from 1963, was played non-stop in 1969. Peter Paul & Mary sang "If I Had A Hammer," "The Cruel War," "The Great Mandala," and "Where Have All the Flowers Gone?" to sell-out crowds. Phil Ochs, a folk singer with an edge, wrote and sang "I Ain't Marching Anymore" and "Draft Dodger Rag." I had all these albums, and I played them again and again. The tunes varied from beautiful to haunting to catchy, and the lyrics were easy to understand and repeat. My fellow students and I did not simply listen to these songs, we imbued them. I sang them to and from classes.

Chapter 39: The Draft And The Dentist

However, while I wanted nothing to do with the Vietnam War, Uncle Sam thought differently. He wanted me. We had a draft. During the war, the military drafted 2,200,000 soldiers. As an undergraduate college student, I had an exemption, but once I graduated, I was fodder for the draft. I knew I could get a deferment as a law student, but only if I committed to joining the army as a lawyer for three years after graduation. I was not willing to do that.

Then a way out seemed possible. In May 1969, President Nixon announced his intention to ask to Congress to authorize a national lottery whereby those eligible for the draft would be selected randomly. From September to November 1969, I fretted about what to do. The lottery was not yet a reality. I had heard, though I was not sure, that I could apply for a hardship exemption by obtaining a medical opinion that it would cause my mother great emotional distress since my father had recently died, and I was the only son. I spoke to my mother about this. She was not thrilled about the idea, but would have acquiesced. But I did not have to go this route because Congress passed the lottery in November, and Nixon signed the law into effect on November 26, 1969. I was sure I had my passport out of the rice paddies.

The lottery was set for December 1, 1969. Every man aged between nineteen and twenty-six was eligible. If called, they would be inducted in 1970. A total of 1,891,661 men were included in the "order of call to military service." That included a Cary Bruce Lerman born on January 26 in Chicago. I had my fingers crossed. The Selective Service System took 366 days of the year (including February 29) and printed them on 366 slips of paper. Each slip was put into an opaque plastic capsule. The capsules were loaded into a shoebox and shaken to mix them thoroughly. The capsules were put into a deep glass jar, taken one at a time from the jar, and opened. Congressman Alexander Pirnie of New York drew the first ball. He chose September 14, which was given lottery number 1. All eligible men of draft age with that birthdate got number 1. They were certain to be called to service and right away.

January 26, my birthday, received lottery number 92. My goose was cooked (as my ancestors might have said in the Pale of Settlement, but only if they spoke Swedish, since one theory is that the expression originated with King Eric XIV of Sweden in the fifteenth century). We now know that everyone with numbers 1 to 195 was drafted in 1970. The Selective Service System called up about thirty numbers each month, and I would have been gone by July. The lottery was a dead end for me. How about the plea for a mother-in-distress? Further research convinced me it would not work. I needed a new strategy.

It was then that I learned that my old dentist, Dr. Feinberg, had done me a favor with his neglect of my oral health. My teeth were all out of alignment. My two eye teeth had no intention of being straight, and decided to face one another a long time ago. My other teeth were so crowded that they attacked each other for space. Thank you, Dr. Feinberg, for not advising us to have my teeth straightened when I was younger. We learned that, if I were under a doctor's care, I could get a medical deferment. Orthodontic work qualified. I located Dr. Julian Singer, an orthodontist in Westwood who had a reputation not only for being an excellent dentist, but also for being able to write persuasive letters to the draft board.

I went to see him. He looked into my mouth, pronounced me as in serious and immediate need for intensive dental care, and declared that he was the only person who could tackle this greatest of orthodontic challenges. All I needed to do was have four perfectly healthy teeth pulled to make more room for the others, wear braces for several years, see him once a month, and pay $2000 (equivalent to $14,000 today). I had a choice – do I spend a couple of years with Dr. Singer or with Ho Chi Minh and his minions? Not much of a choice at all. Dr. Singer got me my 1Y temporary medical deferment. I was now good to stay.

Chapter 40

YOU DON'T NEED A WEATHERMAN

Hallie and I started off 1970 with regular lengthy and very expensive long-distance calls. Our calls became less frequent, and I felt a growing distance, like being on one boat and seeing my companion boat drifting away, without understanding the currents. She had mentioned some guy called Bob Vanderlin, but in Hallie-speak I could not tell if he was a platonic friend or something more.

I spent my time studying and going on the occasional social outing with friends from the dorm. We often went out in groups, with no special parings, expect for Rick and Claire, Dave and Louellen, and Harmon and Linda. For my part, I thought Claire was quite cute, sexy and bright, and she did flirt with me, but I had Hallie and, besides, Rick had become a good friend. Leonard Cohen's line "I'm not looking for another," was still my mantra. During the spring, Rick told me he had a family emergency that required him to be away for almost two weeks, and he asked me to look after Claire. On a Saturday night, after Rick left, Dave, the medical student, asked if I wanted to go to a movie with him, Louellen, and Claire. I went. Dave had a convertible so, after the movie, we drove around enjoying the open air. Dave was in front with Louellen, and I was in the back with Claire. He parked on Mulholland Drive overlooking the Valley. The lights flickering throughout the Valley glowed like dots of light on black velvet. Dave passed around a joint, something I smoked only occasionally (just enough to keep my credentials as a member of my generation). It was a bit chilly, and Claire and I got under a blanket in the back. It became very quiet up front. The next thing I recall, Claire and I were kissing. Whether it went further than that, I am not sure. Perhaps I do not want to remember. Dave drove back to the dorm, and Claire held my hand. I sat there, frozen, feeling like the miscreant I was. My thoughts alternated between Hallie and Rick. I was a jerk all around. Back at the dorm, Claire gave me a come hither look that invited me into her room, but I declined and went alone into mine. No, I did not go into my room. I slinked into it.

I never mentioned the incident to Rick (and I did not tell Hallie about it for several years) nor did I offer encouragement to Claire, and she and I never spoke about that night. In retrospect, I have to thank my inner compass. I may not have known what I was doing, but I did know where I should not be going. Rick and Claire got married the summer right after our first year of law school. Not only were Hallie and I invited to the wedding, but I was part of the wedding party. As I walked down the aisle in a tuxedo arm in arm with a girl who had been Claire's roommate at the dorm, I knew I did not deserve the honor.

While my social life was fraught, my academic life was moving along just fine. I got two H's and one HP. I did not have a final in my other two courses, as they spanned two quarters and their finals would be in the spring quarter. Professor Schwartz, my torts teacher, called me in to his office. My first response was to wonder what I had done wrong. He told me that he wanted to meet the student who got the highest grade in his class. "What?" I sputtered out, "I got the highest grade?" "You did, and it was not even close," he said. I learned a lot from him, but when I measured my knowledge and analytical abilities against his, as he rattled off difficult concepts at warp speed during class, I felt like we were not even in the same race. Professor Schwartz had been number one in his graduating class at Harvard Law School, he had clerked for Judge J. Skelly Wright of the D.C. Circuit, one of the most sought-after clerkships in the country. Professor Schwartz later became one of the greatest scholars of personal injury law in the nation. He died tragically at the age of sixty-one of a brain tumor.

For me, Professor Schwartz was not simply an unparalleled thinker, brilliant lawyer, and erudite teacher. He was a mentor. That first talk in his office did more to build my self-confidence as a potential lawyer than a library of self-help books ever could. Like Mrs. Marble, Mr. Dix, and Mr. Cosmos, he instilled in me a belief that I had something special to offer and had confidence in my ability to be a really strong analytical thinker and legal diagnostician. And he gave me direction. I was no longer all over the map, enthused with every fascinating course that appeared. Over the next two years of law school, I took every course he taught – urban government, transportation law, housing law – and his fervor for these subjects propelled me, by the time of my graduation, seriously to consider transportation law. Ultimately, I did not find sufficient satisfaction in being a transportation lawyer to make it a career, but his example of how a lawyer must analyze the depths of a legal problem, by peeling each layer of a legal onion until one reached the core, leaving no onion skin unexamined, became the only acceptable way of tackling a legal issue for me. And he did something else. He had an ability to explain complex legal issues in simple terms, making them accessible to his audience. I tried to emulate both skills – top analytics with simple, but never simplistic, explanations. Professor Schwartz mastered it, and, in this respect, I am still his student.

I moved through the spring quarter more confident in my academic abilities, not losing a bit of my enthusiasm for the law. My University of Illinois roommate, David Resnick, visited me in Los Angeles with his fiancée, Nancy. I took them on a tour of the law school, and we ended in the law library. The library was an impressive space, with many private study areas and resources. It was dominated by a fifty-foot-long, nine-foot-high mural (the largest at UCLA) on the first floor, which had been unveiled in September 1969, not long after I arrived. It was called "Back in the Day" by muralist Douglas Riseborough, and depicted the social and civil rights issues in the 1960's. But I did not show David and Nancy the great learning spaces, the seemingly unlimited book stacks, or even the mural. No, I wanted them to see Shepherd's Citations, a set of reference books that made it possible to follow the subsequent history of every published court opinion, as it was adopted, followed, cited, distinguished, rejected, or overruled by other courts. The books contained a series of columns with numbers. That was all. No text, no photos, nothing of interest to anyone other than the law practitioner who wanted to know the legal genealogy of a particular court decision. Yet that is what I wanted to show them. I gushed and enthused over these reference books as if I were explaining to them the secret of the Rosetta Stone. To me, these were not simply books with numbers. They were nothing less than the key to uncovering the destiny of the law, a detailed map to unlock the thinking of the judges who decided the cases and the lawyers who argued them. It was the legal equivalent of breaking the Enigma Code, and gave access to the law in process. "Can you believe this actually exists? I use it all the time," I whispered (as we were in a library) with the wonder of a child who has just learned how to blow colorful bubbles. "Uh, very nice," they said and turned their attention to the mural. But, at that moment,

I saw more revealed mystery in the numerical columns in Shepherd's than in the painting dominating the library.

I had also become good friends with a number of classmates, mostly those within my section. Skip Miller, who was one of my only friends who came to law school married, was also from Chicago, and we became fast friends. Even back then, Skip had a bit of a swagger to him, by which he signaled he would be someone to contend with. And he was. Larry May was serious, straight-laced, and a straight shooter. Sincerity defined him. If you wanted solid advice, Larry was the guy. Howard Knee was, at times, a jokester, but he took his studies seriously. Want to learn something and enjoy yourself at the same time? Take Howard to lunch. Steve Mittleman was our resident hippie. His hair was down to his shoulders, and he carried himself with an air of "I couldn't care less." Want weed, or something stronger? Steve was there. Want to skip class and just hang out? Steve never said no. There was the irrepressible Jim Phalster. He was a big, loud, and boisterous redhead, who let the world know that he was not to be trifled with. He alternated between belly laugh and expletive explosion. His sobriquet was the Big Mexican, but it belied a fierce intellect. He was one heck of a smart Jewish dude from Mexico. Linda Mok wore three-inch heels so that she could stretch her height to 5'0". She wore her hair in a bun that was so large I used to wonder how she could hold up her head. Had she unfurled her hair, it would have reached her knees. She too was married and had a son she called HB. That was not a nickname. It was his name. And there was Allen Lebow, who was as smart as anyone, sincere, and calm. He had that Paul Newman cool. He moved around as if he did not have a care in the world, without sacrificing focus or seriousness. Allen was genuine in every interaction. He was best-friend material; you knew you could trust him with any confidence. Tragically, he died in the airplane crash of PSA Flight 182 in 1978, only six years after graduating from law school. His death was a huge loss for me, his family and friends, and the entire legal community in Los Angeles.

Then there was Woody Mosten, whom I had met on orientation day. Our backgrounds were similar, both from working class families with parents who never went to college. Woody differed from me in one important respect. He was not only idealistic; he was intent on putting his idealism into practice. He worked at the International Student Center, had a great sensitivity to the plight of others, and strived to make their lives better. Woody was not just an idea-generator; he was an innovator and an implementer. There is an exchange in *Through the Looking Glass,* which always reminded me of Woody:

Alice laughed. 'There's no use trying' she said: 'one can't believe impossible things.'

'I daresay you haven't had much practice,' said the Queen. 'When I was your age, I always did it for half-an-hour a day. Why, sometimes I've believed as many as six impossible things before breakfast.'

Woody was constantly envisioning changes that people, including me, would warn him were impossible. He subscribed to the quote, attributed variously, that "the difficult takes a little time; the impossible takes longer." His upbeat, never-say-no attitude was infectious. Lawyers are trained in tradition and, by nature, are risk-averse. Woody was the opposite, the antidote to staid conceit. Even in law school, his focus was on how to provide legal services to populations that were desperately in need of legal representation but could not afford it. He even wrote a paper entitled "Legal Services for University Students," in a seminar on the Internal Law of Academic Institutions. After graduating, he dedicated himself to legal access issues. He was one of the original founders of the nation's first legal clinic, Jacoby & Meyers, and he pioneered family mediation, the unbundling of legal services, collaborative law, the idea of the lawyer as peacemaker, an international competition for students in client counselling, as well as other innovative concepts and programs, and he authored many books on these topics. He became a life-long friend akin to a brother and confidant.

I finished the spring quarter with three H's and one HP, giving me a total of 6 H's and 3 HP's for the first year. In keeping with the egalitarian climate of the times, UCLA did not publish class rankings, so I had no idea where those grades put me in relation to others. We didn't exchange grades with one another so I had no idea how my friends were doing. I assumed, but it was only a rough guess, that I was in the top quarter of the class, which I considered a darn good place to be considering I had had thoughts of quitting after Professor Michael Tigar's Emmy-award winning performance.

As I had been immersed in my studies, Hallie too had been in her own separate world at Harcum College, and we had drifted further apart, so I was ecstatic when she agreed to come to LA for the summer. She was not sure what she would do in the fall – go back to Harcum, go to school in LA, return to Israel (an option she continued to emphasize), or some other choice – but at least we would now have a chance to put our relationship back together. She had always been interested in photography, and she enrolled in several courses at UCLA for the summer, including a photography studio course with the prized photographer, Robert Heinecken. Her talent as a photographer so impressed Heinecken that he asked her to become his protégé and work directly with him. She declined because she did not believe in her own talent. She refused to live with me (her father would have had an aneurysm if she had), and instead rented a room at a fraternity near UCLA, changing locations every few weeks.

I still had to figure out where *I* was going to live the next term. My good friend Ben Blakeman was graduating from the University of Illinois, and he applied to and was accepted by UCLA Law School. He was not concerned about the draft. His lottery number was 330. He was golden. We decided to room together the next school year, and we rented a two-bedroom apartment on Bundy Drive. He was arriving at the beginning of summer, and we moved into the apartment at the end of June. Housing was decided.

The only remaining challenge was what to do with myself over the summer. It was beyond difficult for a first-year law student to get a paying summer job in the legal field. Law firms were hiring those who had finished their second year of law school but not first year students. After finishing the second year, a law student had sufficient skills to research and write an intelligent memorandum, but a law firm's principal purpose of hiring second year students was to audition them for permanent law positions after graduation. I did not want to go back to manual labor at the transportation company, as I wanted to earn more money and to use my meager new-found legal abilities. Then, lightning struck. The Veterans Administration contacted the placement office at the law school. They wanted to hire twenty law students for the summer to help them clear up a backlog of veterans' applications for educational benefits. They were paying more than triple what I was earning the previous summer, and were willing to take us after just one year of study. I was one of the first to grab this opportunity. I had my summer job. I was going to be an "adjudicator" at the VA.

Chapter 41

PINK SLIPS

The summer at the Veterans Administration proved unforgettable. The Veterans Administration was housed in the Federal Building on Wilshire Boulevard, no more than a ten-minute drive from my apartment on Bundy. The building had just been completed in 1969 and was a testament to stability and no-nonsense. It was the tallest building around – seventeen stories – on twenty-eight acres of asphalt parking spaces. While it was styled as "corporate Late Modernism," it was really a rectangular tribute to plain and simple. The building accommodated over 2000 workers, most of whom were Federal employees working at the FBI, Passport Office, U.S. Weather Bureau, congressional staff and a senator's staff offices, and, as the largest tenant in the building, the Veterans Administration.

Our army of twenty law students descended on the VA, not as the bureaucrats the VA thought it had hired, but as legal eagles determined to play an influential role in administering justice. The first week was training. We learned about the program, the policy factors we needed to consider, the VA's approach to evaluating an application, how to fill out forms (most important), and where to go for assistance. Veterans who applied for benefits were allocated a fixed amount of money for an academic or vocational program and the school and the program had to be accredited by the VA. We were given desks, files, and told to go at it. We had a lot of questions. Why did the forms omit certain information that we thought essential? How were we to know how much the veteran had already received in benefits? What if the program looked suspicious to us? Was the service record relevant? What if attendance records looked shoddy? Why were the letters to veterans phrased the way they were? What would happen if an institution went out of business in the middle of the year? What would happen if the veteran withdrew from the program before matriculating? How can we be sure the veteran was really going to class?

By the third week, having mastered the basics, we asked to see the legislation that established the programs and delegated authority to the VA. We analyzed it, and concluded that the VA was not complying with all the requirements. Never mind that they had been doing it the same way for decades. We, newly minted students with one year of legal studies under our belts, knew better. We brought our concerns to our immediate supervisor, Margaret Fillerup. She summarily dismissed us, adding insult to our indignity that the bureaucrats were not complying with the legislation. The statute giving the VA powers was vague in many respects. There had to be regulations that spelled out in detail how the program was supposed to work, what the eligibility requirements were, what the VA was to do if the requirements were not met. We learned that a series of regulations had been adopted pursuant to the Administrative Procedure Act requirements. But where were they? The first weekend, several of us went to the law school library and found the regulations, which had been published in the Congressional Register. We made copies and distributed them to our fellow classmates and workers. We concluded that, in several important respects, the VA was not in compliance with its own regulations. This was serious. We needed to elevate our complaints within the VA. We went to our supervisor's supervisor. Once again, we did not get a full or fair hearing of our learned conclusions. We escalated further. We law students were not going to be denied. We went to the head of the VA in the Western Region, who had a sumptuous corner office in our building. All twenty of us showed up to present irrefutable evidence of VA incompetence, irregularity, and bureaucratic arrogance. We were dismissed out of hand. Dejected, we went back to our desks. Outrageous, unfair, arbitrary, and dismissive.

The next morning, we arrived to find an envelope on each of our desks containing a pink slip of paper. Our services were no longer required; we were fired and were told to clean out our desks by the end of the week. All of us. We were stunned. How could they do this? We went to the first floor to confer on next steps. Our number one concern quickly shifted from bureaucratic misfeasance to saving our jobs. We needed the positions – and the money. Sure principle was important, but so was the job. "Hey," someone said, "doesn't Senator Alan Cranston have an office in this building? And doesn't he serve on a committee having something to do with veterans?" We immediately had our strategy. Part contrition, part power. So, our group approached a higher power still, and headed up to Senator Cranston's office. To our amazement, he was there. His office was plush with high piled carpets, walls lined with photographs of the senator in various poses with other politicians and dignitaries and a hushed tone more in keeping with the solemnity of a mortuary than a political beehive. There was a receptionist, an aide and the senator's office. His office door was open, and we could see him at his desk, talking on the phone. It was clear that the presence of an agitated crowd of twenty law students about to lose their summer livelihood was a singular event for this office. We explained to the receptionist and aide what had happened and that we needed to speak to the senator urgently. I saw him look up from his phone call, put down the receiver and motion us to enter his office. Senator Cranston was sixty-six years old and was the junior senator from California, having been elected to the Senate in 1968 and taken his seat in 1969, only the year before. He was in top physical shape, being known as a sprinter in track and field competition in races for senior citizens. He was tall, lanky, and almost entirely bald. He had finely chiseled facial features, and he sported a wide, toothy smile that was both practiced and comforting.

"What can I do for you," he asked with an abridged smile on his face. (Did he already know of our firing?) Rather than acting like Sampson barging in to bring down the VA's pillars, we explained in reasoned, measured tones who we were, why we were hired by the VA and the problems we had encountered. We asked the senator to intervene on our behalf by asking the VA to recall the pink slips. We let him know that our top priority was to eliminate the backlog. We would save our advocacy for another time and place. After getting our assurance that, if we returned, we would keep our heads down and do our jobs, he said he would see what he could do. When we arrived at work the next morning, an envelope was on each of our desks. The pink slips had been rescinded. We had our jobs back. We let out a collective sigh of relief. I learned a few important lessons. To effect change, to be sure, it is best to work within the system, but, even more importantly, it is critical to think through all potential outcomes before you act. And never, never act rashly as a lawyer.

Hallie and I saw each other every day, after I finished my nine-to-five shift at the VA, and she came back from her photography classes. She stayed with me at the Bundy apartment most weekends. We needed the summer of 1970. She told me about her last months at Harcum, and I asked her about this guy Bob. "Oh," she said, "I could never marry him. He wants to be a school teacher. I cannot see myself married to a school teacher. But the final straw was when he talked to her about Yasser Arafat and the PLO, saying that they had a point of view that had to be respected. No, they are terrorists, killing innocent Jews, and they are not to be respected. I knew it was over when he said that." I should have been comforted, but it was the opposite. "Were you dating him? Why would you ever contemplate the idea of marrying him? What was going on?" I never did get a response from her. But, in all fairness, I still hadn't told her about my evening in the back seat of a convertible with Claire. Jordy, Bernie, and now Bob. Was there a pattern?

Knowing how difficult separations were for our relationship and not wanting to risk what we had, Hallie decided to stay in Los Angeles, but only after being assured that we were a couple. She enrolled at Santa Monica Junior College and moved into a private co-ed dormitory called La Mancha on the edge of the UCLA Campus. It was a luxury dorm with individual suites, configured with a common living room surrounded by three bedrooms. By the end of the summer, we were committed to each other.

Chapter 42

FINDING WISDOM IN UNEXPECTED PLACES

That fall, I returned to law school no longer fearful of failure. I applied to be a member of the *Law Review*, the premier academic journal where scholarly articles by professors and not-so-scholarly articles by law students were published. I became a "note and comment editor," which meant that I would review and edit submissions for publications. I was clearly moving up in the law student hierarchy. While many students had no desire to write for the *Law Review*, preferring other activities, I considered it a prestigious position that would expose me to more law professors both at UCLA and at other universities in a collaborative academic setting.

I had become very accustomed to the rhythms of my classes and the great secret truth, which was largely hidden from me during the first year. It seems obvious now but, as a first year student, it never was: the law is not black and white. There are no absolute truths, no unchangeable markers, no right answers. There are positions, policies, and principles, which can be argued, modified, and advocated, to achieve a desired result. There were indeed lofty principles which, at a high level, told us how the legal chess board had to be arranged and what had to be respected to avoid chaos, but the number of moves was limited only by the good will and ingenuity of the players. Contemporary values, economic conditions, access to the courts, quality of advocacy, among other factors, were pressure points shaping the ever-changing body of law. Knowing this was a relief. It freed me from a slavish search for the great unified theory of the law. It may someday be found in physics, but I now knew not to waste my time or my emotions trying to find it hidden in the law.

There is a country music song with the lyric, "I was lookin' for love in all the wrong places." The same can be true in seeking wisdom. We can read the great works of the most influential philosophers, but come away with headaches, confusion, and nothing useful. Pirkei Avot, the Ethics of Our Fathers, teaches "Who is wise? The one who learns from every person." (Avot 4:1) If we are open, we can learn the greatest lessons in the most unlikely of places from the most unlikely of people. That happened to me during my second year, when I took two taxation courses. Why, I do not know. I had no interest in becoming a tax lawyer, but I probably thought that a lawyer should know something about tax to avoid looking dumb at a party. Professor Ralph Rice, a veteran teacher, taught the crowded class. He was earnest, clear, and knowledgeable, and he constantly stressed the ethics of tax planning and being a tax practitioner. He was sixty-one years old, an established fixture at UCLA Law School and was no competition for the young Turks then being hired. He was no Michael Tigar. Tax is a dry topic, and Professor Rice was not able to dress it up as anything but dry.

Chapter 42: Finding Wisdom In Unexpected Places

During one class, Professor Rice stopped talking about tax codes and exceptions to rules and exceptions to the exceptions, except if you add in this consideration, and so on. He sat on the edge of a long table in front. He put his notes down. He looked out at us. "I am going to tell you the one thing you must remember from this class. You are going to forget almost everything you learn about tax once the final exam is over. But there is one thing you must never, ever forget. It is the most important life lesson you will ever get." Everyone picked up their pens and had them poised in mid-air to make sure they wrote down every word they were about to hear. It was sure to be on the final. Professor Rice said, "Whatever you do in life, remember this: *Don't be a pig.*" That was it. Four words. Many in class laughed, thinking it was a joke. I took it in. I understood exactly what he was saying. In this tax class, a professor not known for profundities had just given us a piece of advice that could not be measured in money. It became a principle by which I have lived my life. I have since studied the colossal philosophers of the past, those searching for meaning in life, erecting great ethical codes, advising on the nature of mankind, offering solutions to the most challenging conundrums, but none of them has given me the gift that Professor Rice did with his four words, *"Don't be a pig."* I knew he was not talking about taxes; he was talking about a way of life. To this day, I am grateful for signing up for Professor Rice's tax class. He was right; I do not remember one bit of the tax he taught. But I did learn something infinitely more valuable. I also learned that the search for wisdom begins with humility. I had thought that Professor Rice was a competent teacher, but I never expected that the greatest lesson of law school would come from him. I was humbled by learning that I was looking for wisdom in all the wrong places.

As part of my role on the *Law Review*, I was required to write an article – a "note" – and I had to pick a topic. There were many cutting-edge legal controversies. The constitutional right to an abortion was percolating among the Federal courts, ultimately culminating in the 1973 decision in *Roe v. Wade*. There were legal challenges to the Voting Rights Act of 1965, a landmark piece of legislation that prohibited racial discrimination in voting and that was designed to remove barriers to voting for the African American community. Free speech issues were front and center as campus protests against the Vietnam War escalated on campuses. Ronald Reagan was elected Governor of California in 1967, and his strong stance against the Free Speech Movement at Berkeley raised a plethora of legal issues. In 1969, the trial of the Chicago Seven, who were arrested for conspiracy and crossing state lines with the intent to cause a riot riveted the nation. Professor Tigar, then barely out of law school, was one of the attorneys for the defendants, and he wrote the pre-trial motions. In 1967, Governor Reagan signed into law the Lanterman-Petris-Short Act, which basically ended the involuntary commitment of the mentally ill in hospitals, putting on the streets thousands of people who had no ability to cope with life. This legislation raised critical issues concerning the right of society to impose protected custody on the vulnerable versus the right of the individual not to be coerced by the state.

The legal issues available to a law student seeking a critical topic worthy of an educated audience and a prestigious *Law Review* article were abundant. The problem wasn't to find an issue, but which one to choose. And what did I choose? Ad valorem financing of law enforcement services in Los Angeles County. If this were a movie, the action would stop. Freeze frame. Bright, young, inquisitive law student searching at ground zero for the most important and challenging legal issues of the time picks as his *Law Review* topic, drum roll: "ad valorem financing?" Can't be. Let's rerun the film and change the script. But I cannot do that. That was my topic. Why did I choose it? Professor Schwartz suggested it, it fit in nicely with my new-found interest in urban law, and, unsurprisingly, no one had written on the topic before. I spent countless hours researching and drafting an article that was marked for obscurity before the first draft. Eventually, it was published under the title "Ad Valorem Financing of Law Enforcement Services: An Equitable Solution to an Inequitable Condition." My mother ordered several copies of my article, which she never read, so she could hand them out to her friends, who would also never read it. Hallie got a few copies so she could send them to her parents, who would never read it, but they did share it with their friends who also did not read it. To this day, I have never found anyone who read my article. I wonder if Professor Rube Cohn read it. I once had trouble falling asleep and found the perfect, non-medicinal cure. I started to read my article. Worked like a charm.

Chapter 43

A PERFECT DIAMOND

Hallie and I had now spent two summers together and, for the last year, we had seen each other almost every day. Then Hallie popped the question.

"What are our plans?"

I was flummoxed. "What do you mean, plans?" I asked.

Hallie replied, "You know, what are our plans?"

I guess I knew what she meant all along, but there was one possible escape route if she had something else in mind. "Well, we are very serious about one another."

"Yes," she said, "but what about marriage?"

"Oh, that plan," I answered. "Well, if things keep going like they are now, yes, someday, but not now."

"Of course not now, but are you serious about us getting married someday?"

A long, uncomfortable pause.

I blurted out, "Yes, someday." Did I just say that? I couldn't take it back. I didn't want to take it back, but I still wish I hadn't said it. I was trembling inside. Sometimes one word can pack more wallop than the Gettysburg Address. This time, that word was "yes."

The question of marriage kept cropping up that fall. We even stopped at a jewelry store in Westwood Village to look at rings. Call it window shopping with a twist. At Crescent Jewelers, she tried on a dozen rings, just to see how they would look on her finger. She liked the look. Was I humoring her or was this my ever so gradual glide into the deep end of the pool? I don't know if I were being pushed or pulled, but I know I was approaching a day of reckoning. Hallie was going back to Champaign for Christmas vacation and subtlety was not foremost on her mind when she stated emphatically that she wanted to be wearing a ring by then. Or else.

In the first week of December, I went to Crescent and bought a diamond ring. To appreciate the magnificent ring I bought, I need to mention that a diamond is rated by the four C's: carat (weight), color, clarity (how free from inclusions it is), and cut. The larger the diamond, the more difficult to find one with the color, clarity, and cut that mark an exceptional diamond. Not so much with smaller ones. If the diamond is so small that some might refer to it as a chip, it is easier to find a perfect diamond, one with spectacular color and clarity. The diamond in the ring I bought was a perfect diamond. I should have purchased a magnifying glass with it so the recipient would be certain it was a diamond. As a percentage of my assets, the diamond ring represented almost everything I owned in the world. I put it in my pocket, not sure when or even if I would give it to Hallie. Each day I trembled with the thought that I would have to make a decision and soon.

As the day approached when Hallie would be going home for the holidays, I became immobile. I was like Jacob Horner in *The End of The Road* by John Barth, who sat on a bench in Penn Central Station,

Chapter 43: A Perfect Diamond

unable to move or decide. He just sat. Frozen. His doctor told him he had to act. It didn't matter what he did, but he had to do something. I felt like Jacob Horner. I was in equipoise. I was frightened to take that unprecedented step and get engaged. I was also scared about the prospect of *not* giving Hallie a ring and losing her altogether, as she had threatened. I remained in that untenable equilibrium right up to when I drove Hallie to LAX for her flight home. I knew I had to act, but I wanted to delay the moment of decision as much as I could; even so, I knew a decision was imminent, and I was shaking. We parked in one of the parking structures, and I turned off the key. She looked at me and said, "We do not have much time. Well?" I knew what she meant, but all I could do was mouth some nonsense. Then she trotted out the nuclear option. "Well, if we do not get engaged now, I am going to get engaged to Bernie. He wants to marry me, and he said that, when I come back to Champaign, if I am not engaged to you, he will give me a ring." I was speechless. Stuck. But I had to do something or Hallie would be engaged to my nemesis Bernie when she returned from the trip. I couldn't let that happen. I finally said, "But why is it so important to get engaged now? You are only twenty years old." Hallie looked straight into my eyes and said, "I am not talking about it. Enough talk. It is time for you to do something." I felt like Freddie being dressed down by Eliza Doolittle who was telling him in no uncertain terms, "Don't talk of stars burning above. If you're in love, show me! Tell me no dreams filled with desire. If you're on fire, show me." Eschewing poetry, Hallie was telling me to put up or shut up.

Ever the frightened lawyer-in-training, I said, "OK, we can get engaged now, but I have three conditions: first, I do have a ring, but you cannot wear it in front of anyone we know until we agree; second, you cannot tell anyone we are engaged; and third, we do not set a date for a wedding." Hallie nodded her head and agreed. I took out the ring I had purchased, showed it to her and put it on her finger. "This is a perfect diamond. It may look small, and it may be small, but the size does not matter so long as it is perfect," I offered. Hallie beamed and kissed me. We were engaged. When we departed at the gate, I choked up and drove home in silence. I now realize that, if I had in mind the wisdom of G.K. Chesterton, I would not have put myself into such a paralyzed state of anxiety in the parking lot at LAX. He wrote that there "is a way of testing a man's love: one can always tell the real love from the slight by the fact that the latter weakens at the moment of success; the former is quadrupled." I was at the moment of success – I had the girl and she wanted to marry me, not Bernie or anyone else – and I wanted to make sure I did not lose her. I gave her the ring because my love had quadrupled.

Hallie came back to LA two weeks later, still wearing the ring. I could not help asking about Bernie. "Did you see him in Champaign?"

Hallie blushed just a bit,

"Yes, and I showed him the ring."

"What was his response?"

"He looked at it and then blurted out, 'I would have gotten you a much bigger diamond. You can hardly see it.'"

"And what did you say?"

"I told him it was a *perfect* diamond."

And it was. And that was the end of my perturbation about Bernie.

I should have known it would happen, but all three of our conditions became suggestions and the suggestions were ignored. Her mother saw the ring, so Hallie told her. And they discussed a wedding during the summer after my graduation. I had not told anyone, not even my mother. We went to her place that weekend, and Hallie was wearing the ring. We were sitting around a table and Hallie had put her left hand, palm down, on the table. The ring was indeed small, but it was still visible. My mother was talking, and she stopped in mid-sentence, "What is THAT? Oh, my God, is that an engagement ring?" She guessed it, and, within ten minutes, all of Los Angeles knew.

Chapter 44

A SUMMER IN BEVERLY HILLS

Toward the end of my second year, I received a surprise offer. I was asked to be editor-in-chief of the *Law Review* during my third year. This was an honored and prestigious position. It was the pinnacle of success for a law student. A mark of great distinction. To say I was shocked would be an understatement. I thought of myself as a quiet, diligent worker who wrote a middling piece for the review. I did not think I was cut out to be editor-in-chief. That meant leadership, responsibility, decision-making, managing a staff, having a vision for the review, long hours, hard work. The more I considered the position, the more I shrank, convincing myself that I was unqualified and unworthy. I would rescue them from the folly of their own decision. I would decline. And so I said no, and walked away. I did not realize it at the time, but my decision marked a tendency that I have had to fight against my whole life. My first reaction to a challenge is avoidance, feeling incompetent and unworthy. I have had to learn to overcome an ingrained imposter syndrome, and to force myself to accept the challenge. My regrets are never from the challenges I met head on, but from the opportunities I walked away from for all the wrong reasons.

But I continued getting strong grades that second year. I finished with seven H's and four HP's, but, again, I had no idea where that put me in the class. The school still refused to issue rankings, wanting to avoid anything that smacked of elitism or encouraged competition among the law students.

Ben and I decided to get separate places for the next year, my last one in law school. We got on well, but we weren't ideal roommates. Although he was a first-year law student and should have been studying in the library, Ben seemed always to be around. And he was distracting. He did not care about studying and was more interested in promoting his social life, as he had been at the University of Illinois. New girls came in and out of the apartment with a rapidity usually associated with job applicants. Besides, during the weekends, when Hallie would stay at the apartment, I craved a privacy that was simply not there. I lucked out when a classmate, Linda Mok, offered to rent to me a studio apartment above her garage. It was in a quiet, single-family residential neighborhood just south of the campus, only a five-minute drive from school. I took one look at it and grabbed it. It was only about 400 square feet, but it had everything I needed. There was a bathroom, a kitchen area, and even a small closet. The garage was detached from the house and set back at the rear of the property line. Quiet and private.

In the spring of 1971, I decided to seek one of the plum summer jobs that was available to law students. The law school's job placement office primed us for the competition to land high-paying summer associate jobs with prestigious law firms. Not only would we earn an unheard-of salary and gain practical experience, but it offered the potential for a full-time position after graduation. What did I have going for me?

Decent first-year grades and a position as a note and comment editor on the *Law Review*. Because we did not have class rankings, I had to rely on the interviewers to compare my grades with those of other applicants. I applied to over fifteen firms, and only three of them thought my resume was interesting enough to warrant an interview at their offices. Two of the firms, though, were behemoths in downtown Los Angeles, each having hundreds of lawyers. They were the pillars of the established legal community, whose partners were members of restrictive clubs, such as the California Club; became presidents of bar associations; peopled the "who's who" columns in the *Los Angeles Times*; had graduated from Harvard and Yale Law Schools; lived in Hancock Park, Pasadena, and San Marino; retired from the practice of law to become judges; and regularly attended church. I had come a long way from the days when I would deliver packages to the outside counsel at Sears Roebuck and dream about being able to go beyond the reception area. Finally, it was going to happen.

I owned one suit, a blue polyester-blend with a square pattern. I thought it looked great. I had half-day interviews at both O'Melveny & Myers and Gibson, Dunn & Crutcher. We talked about my classes (my love of urban law), my law review article (a work in progress), my future desires (uncertain and open), whether I was married (hell, no; despite being engaged, I shuddered at the thought I might be married), whether I was religious (not sure what that means, but probably no), interests (reading, musicals, Hallie), and most memorable experience as an undergrad (Kams). I did not get an offer from either firm. Was it my suit, the lack of class rankings, the interviews, my braces? Or did this Jewish boy from Albany Park just not fit in? I could not shake the feeling that it was the last one.

Fortunately, I received an offer from a small (fewer than ten lawyers) firm in Beverly Hills. They practiced securities law, real estate, estate planning, commercial transactions, and just about anything their clients needed. The two named partners were polar opposites. One was chubby, subdued, warm, and friendly. His principal practice was in real estate. He wore his suit as if it were a tent, but without a shape, and his tie was perpetually stained. I could tell instantly he would be OK to work with.

The other partner was about thirty years old, lean, with perfectly coiffured hair and blue-rimmed eyeglasses that dangled from his neck on a chain. His bespoke suits were always crisp and clean. He dressed the part of a Hollywood model, and he knew it. He paid such close attention to his appearance that he would have made Narcissus blush. He was a study in motion, darting around the office like he was trying to snuff out small fires. When I interviewed for the job, he took me to lunch at an exclusive Beverly Hills restaurant, but what I remember most was his prized yellow Corvette convertible sports car, which was immaculately polished. After lunch, when he retrieved his car from the valet, he examined the paintwork more carefully than a structural engineer inspecting a nuclear plant's cooling tower for hairline fractures. Back at the office, he shouted commands at the staff as if he were a distracted major general. No doubt he would be a challenging boss. Their offices were on Wilshire Boulevard, in the heart of Beverly Hills, a decided plus. The salary was not on a par with the big firms, but it was an ample, bona fide offer, and, besides, it was the only one I had. I was grateful. One of my classmates, Jim, also received an offer from the firm, so I would have a colleague with me. All in all, it looked promising.

It proved to be no more than a place to earn money. Now, that was important to me, as I had no other source of income. But I had also hoped to grow in the law and to be exposed to what the real-world practice of law was all about. And I was open to the potential for a permanent job offer after I graduated. I spent most of the time by myself in the conference room, which doubled as a law library. I received assignments that were far afield of anything I was familiar with, such as corporate securities law, liens, and family trusts. Most disappointing of all was the absence of a mentor. I was given no guidance or direction. I wrote one research memo after another and received no feedback. My work went into a black hole that defied the laws of physics. Even a black hole emits Hawking radiation. I would give the partners a memo, but nothing ever came out of their legal black boxes. Each day, I would pack a lunch and eat by myself in a strip of a park on Santa Monica Boulevard. Jim never seemed to be around. I became good friends with a park bench and the pigeons that called it home.

The only upside was that I got a ringside seat to witness the ersatz-movie-star partner yell, bully, and humiliate his much younger and very attractive secretary. She would occasionally cry and run out of the office. The next morning there would be flowers or a gift box on her desk, and she would then sneak into his office, close the door, and presumably get a proper apology. The scenes were not pretty. It was an open secret that the sheets they shared were not just typing paper. The partner would re-establish proper office decorum only when his wife would make an unannounced visit. This Beverly Hills soap opera did little to entice me to join the private practice of law. And, certainly, this firm was not a job option for me after graduation. There was as much of a chance of me working at that firm than becoming a traveling salesman for a line of frozen gourmet beef Stroganoff dinners. I wondered, "Whatever happened to the prestigious, wood-paneled law firm where I would deliver mail when I worked at Sears Roebuck in Chicago?"

While I may have floundered in the summer of 1971, Hallie flourished. She applied and was accepted for the fall semester to Occidental College in Eagle Rock, not too far from Pasadena. It was a forty-minute drive from Westwood, but it was an outstanding private college and whatever inconvenience it threw our way was offset by the opportunity. We were about to spend our third summer together, our wedding had been set for August 1972, after graduation, and, while we were headed toward that place called familiarity, the passion I felt toward her had not diminished. She was still the vivacious, enthralling, and unpredictable woman I had meet in 1968. But in many ways she was *not* the same person; Hallie was in the process of developing her own interests and nurturing her intellect. She was no longer content to hear me pontificate on a subject of my choosing, and was now my equal when it came to talking about most issues. She was always head and shoulders above me when it came to art, and, with her new found interest in photography, she was racing ahead. We spent hours at Los Angeles museums, and she was my knowledgeable docent every time. We would move from piece to piece, and she would give me a brief biography of the artist, talk about his or her techniques, and add a story or two about the work or their life. I marveled at how much she knew, much of it imbibed from her mother's art columns and slide presentations, but also augmented by the art courses she was taking. I was an eager student.

Chapter 45

A STUDENT BECOMES AN ADVOCATE

UCLA Law School was one of the leaders in offering clinical courses. Medical schools are basically clinical programs with classes, which is why a person graduating with a medical degree knows something about treating a patient. Law schools were traditionally all about academics. Upon graduating, a newly-minted lawyer did not know the first thing about consulting with a client, advising her on her problem, or formulating and implementing a strategy. In the mid to late 1960s, legal educators started to respond to this lacuna in legal education, and UCLA Law School established the first clinical legal education program at a major US law school. We were encouraged to take a clinical class, and, for the most part, the students were eager to do so.

When I returned for my third and final year of law school, I signed up for the poverty law advocacy program, under the tutelage of Professor Paul Boland, a pioneer in clinical education. We would represent indigent clients in dependency court cases under the supervision of a licensed lawyer. Not only would this be invaluable experience, but I would get a sense of whether I wanted to practice in the area. Professor Boland was an exemplary teacher and a compassionate human being. He knew how to litigate but, even more importantly, he knew how to relate to clients and devise a strategy. He was a patient, guiding instructor. He later left teaching to become a judge, eventually rising to be an associate justice of the state Court of Appeal before his untimely death at the age of sixty-five in 2007.

Professor Boland brought me a case he called difficult and fraught with complex issues that would profoundly affect the lives of many people. Was I interested? You bet. I would represent a single father in a dependency court case. The county had taken his two daughters, aged nine and eleven, out of his house and put them with his sister, their aunt. The county wanted to make the arrangement permanent. The father loved his daughters and wanted them back. It sounded simple enough. I needed to meet with the father, and, since I would be his "lawyer," my job would be to make sure he got his daughters back.

The first step was to interview the father. Professor Boland's assistant scheduled an appointment for me. I had to decide what to wear. I wanted to look serious and professional. I put on my blue, polyester suit, with a shirt and tie. I was the very model of a modern, wannabe lawyer. I drove to Watts, in South-Central LA. The father lived in a blighted area consisting of bungalows and small clapboard houses. I found the right address, parked, and looked around. Many of the houses looked clean and well maintained. Some had flower pots and gardens. My client, however, lived in a run-down, dilapidated one-story house surrounded by a low chain-link fence. I knocked on the door, and a Black man in his late forties answered. I identified myself, and he invited me in. I walked immediately into what was the living room. It was dark, musty, and sparsely furnished. I sat on the couch, and my client sat across from me on a bed. I could see three pairs of eyes looking out at me from under the bed. There were beer cans and the occasional whiskey bottle on the floor. Crumpled newspapers were strewn about. That first impression never left me. I was depressed and wanted to get out of there.

To say there was a lack of instant connection between us would be an understatement. I was a White stranger who had been imposed on this man to help him with an intensely personal, painful, and potentially life-altering issue. Our backgrounds, life style, communication skills, and confidence in a dependency court system run by the government were as different as could be imagined. I had to earn his trust, but I had neither the life experience nor the clinical skills to do it.

I decided to leave an explanation of the legal technicalities he faced for later, and we just talked. He told me how much he loved and missed his girls. He never mistreated them, made sure they went to school, made bag lunches for them, and stayed out of trouble. He watched over them when they did their homework. Did he have a job? Not at the moment. He said something about not being well enough to work. I never did figure that one out. Where was their mother? She had died of an overdose three years previously, and he was doing his best to be both father and mother to them. So, what happened? His sister, the girls' aunt, told child protective services that they were not being looked after properly, and they were taken away. How did he support himself and the girls? He mentioned disability checks, and the odd job here and there. I could not get much more out of him. Where did the girls sleep? He showed me a bedroom with two beds. There were a few suggestions that it had once been the bedroom of two young girls, but not much. There were some drawings on the wall, trinkets on a side table, and colorful throw rugs, but that was it.

The education of most lawyers has an obvious lacuna, obvious, that is, only in hindsight. We are taught to analyze a problem from every possible angle, and there is a tendency to intellectualize, to become proficient at identifying legal issues. In this process of learning to be as analytical as possible, a lawyer can forget that there is a person for whom all this analysis is being done, someone whose life or fortune will be deeply affected by the decisions the lawyer makes. It is too easy to see the intellectual problem as the client, like a puzzle to be solved, and not the person. The poverty law advocacy program taught by Professor Boland was an antidote to this hidden trap. Drawing on the work of Professor Louis M. Brown, who established the first ever client counseling competition in 1969, we were taught to always ask the client what an acceptable outcome in the case would be for them. (In 2007, under the guidance of Woody Mosten, I would organize the first ever client counseling competition among law schools in Russia and then accompany the winning Russian team as assistant coach for the international competition in Australia.) I asked my client what he wanted me to do for him. He replied he always treated his daughters well, and he wanted them back home. "Anything short of that," I asked? "No," was his definite reply. As I got up to leave, the three pairs of eyes emerged from under the bed. They were the largest German shepherds I had ever seen. They did not appear aggressive, at least at that moment, but their presence immediately dominated the room. I left before any introductions.

I visited the case worker, who was not very forthcoming. She said that the children would be better housed, fed, clothed, supervised, and protected with the aunt. *Was the father violent?* No. *Had he ever abused the girls?* No. *Were they truant from school?* No. *Did he have a criminal record?* Nothing out of the ordinary. *Meaning?* He was arrested a few

Chapter 45: A Student Becomes An Advocate

times for public drunkenness, once for a brawl, and once for passing a bad check. *Was he an addict?* No.

She gave me the aunt's phone number and permission to visit her. I could see, but I could not talk to the girls. She did not want me to "interrogate" them. I agreed, and the next day I went to the aunt's apartment. The aunt lived in the Washington Heights neighborhood of Los Angeles, not far from downtown. I parked in front of an attractive, well-maintained, relatively new apartment building. Her apartment was as far removed from the father's house as Albany Park was from Beverly Hills. It was light, airy, beautifully furnished, and spoke of home. The two girls were on the couch. They were pretty, wore pigtails, and were clean and nicely dressed. They showed me their bedroom, which was picture perfect. It looked like a page from an interior design magazine. The aunt was about forty, nicely dressed, unmarried, lived alone (except for the girls), and worked for the city in an administrative job. She said she loved her nieces and wanted to give them the best possible home. She had nothing against her brother, but he could not provide for the girls as well as she could. She kept saying, "It is all about the girls."

I left depressed. As I drove back to the law school, my mind was Tevye the Milkman, but instead of a dialogue with God, it was with two parts of my nature. *What was my role here?* To represent my client, the father. Yes, that much I knew. *But what if the best thing for the girls is for them to remain with the aunt?* Not your job. *Do I still try my upmost to convince the administrative law judge at the upcoming hearing that there was no legal basis to deny the father full-time custody of his girls?* You better, as you are all the father has. He needs you in his corner. *Is economics alone a basis for denying a loving father his own children? Is poverty a crime?* No, the court cannot penalize him for being poor. *Should he lose his right to his kids simply because another relative can provide a better home?* That would not be fair to the father, your client. *But what about the kids? What would be fair for them?* The judge would decide. Not my place to judge. *What if I were so persuasive that the judge ordered the girls back to the father? How would I feel?* You should feel satisfied that you had done your job. *But what if...* I kept going back and forth. I knew what my role was, but I was not comfortable with it. I should have taken another tax class rather than poverty law advocacy, I told myself.

I spoke with Professor Boland about my conflicting thoughts. He understood, but he stressed that my loyalty had to be to my client. Then he gave me some wise advice. He said that while it was not my job to dissuade my client from pursuing his chosen course of action, there was nothing wrong, and indeed it was my obligation, to ensure he understood all the angles, all the consequences of his decisions. Professor Boland suggested I take a step back with my client and take as broad a perspective as possible about the entire situation and potential outcomes. That way, my client would be able to understand the full range of options available, both for himself and for his girls.

It was the day of the hearing. I looked as sharp as I could in my blue polyester suit. My client wore a nice pair of trousers and a button down white shirt, as instructed. The caseworker and the aunt testified first. I cross-examined them, but I have no memory of what was said. I then put my client on the stand, and he acquitted himself well enough, even if he would not have won any awards at a Rotary Club dinner. I then called the eleven-year old to the stand. I had prepared for this examination as diligently as I could. I had lain awake in bed at night, with my mind racing, then got up and jotted down additional questions for her. I was ready, and, in part, it went something like this:

> Lerman: How are you today? Nervous?
> Daughter: Yes
> Lerman: Well, don't be, as we are all friends here.
> *The daughter shuffles in her chair.*
> Lerman: Do you see your daddy?

Daughter: Yes

Lerman: Can you point him out for us?

The daughter points to my client.

Lerman: Does your daddy love you?

Daughter: Yes

Lerman: Does he want the best for you?

Daughter: Yes

Lerman: Does he tell you to go to school and study hard?

Daughter: Yes

Lerman: Does he make lunches for you and your sister to take to school?

Daughter: Yes

Lerman: Are they tasty?

Daughter: *Starting to open up and become talkative.* Oh yes, they are delicious. Sometimes he puts in cookies.

Lerman: Does he tell you to dress nicely for school?

Daughter: He does not like it if I wear dirty clothes. And he makes us wash our faces.

Lerman: Do you do fun things with him?

Daughter: Once he took us roller skating.

Lerman: And you liked that, didn't you?

Daughter: Yes, but then I fell down. He bought me an ice cream cone so I would feel better.

Lerman: And did you feel better?

Daughter: I forgot all about the fall. *She laughs.*

Lerman: Your Daddy does kind things like that often, isn't that right?

Daughter: Yes

Lerman: Is that one of the reasons why you love him?

Daughter: *Looking away.* Yes.

Lerman: When you go out to play, doesn't your daddy tell you to stay close to the house?

Daughter: Yes, all the time. He is strict.

Lerman: He makes sure you are in the house by the time it gets dark, right?

Daughter: Yes, and he yells at me if I am not back in time.

Lerman: You don't like it when he is that strict, do you?

Daughter: No, he should let me do what I want to do. I am big enough.

Lerman: But you know that he is looking out for you because he wants you to be safe?

Daughter: Yes.

Lerman: And you love your daddy, right?

Daughter: Yes

I continued in this vein, portraying him as a concerned and loving father, maybe a bit too protective at times, but only wanting the best for his girls. She started to cry. The room was strangled with emotion. The judge called a recess. I felt like a despicable person, trying desperately to maintain my palsied expression. It was so easy to manipulate an eleven-year old kid to say what I wanted her to say. I was putting into practice what I had learned in evidence class: let me phrase the question, and I will get the answer I want. But what was best for her? Her sister? The family? Where was the truth? *Was* there a truth, or only perspectives? I needed to do something.

I thought of doctors, some of whom enjoyed outstanding reputations, who treated the disease and not the patient. I did not want to be that sort of lawyer. I realized I did not represent a thorny legal problem. I represented a client who had a thorny legal problem, and his legal problem involved the life of others, little girls whom he loved. I needed to talk with him and right away. I took my client to a break out room to talk. I stepped outside the role of advocate and become a counselor. I asked my client to focus not only on what he wanted for himself, but also on what he thought was the best for his daughters. I stressed that he loved them, and they loved him, and no one could take that away. He said he had no hard feelings toward his sister as he knew she was a good person who loved her nieces, and she had made a good life for herself. He was moved by his sister's testimony, and he hated seeing his daughters being pulled apart. He wanted to cry when he saw his daughter cry. I asked him if there were any compromises. Then he said something that stunned me. All he wanted was to be able to see his daughters regularly. If they stayed with his sister, it would be OK, but he wanted to be able to see them and take them places. It took no more than a fifteen-minute meeting between me and the lawyer for Children's Protective Services to work out a deal. The girls would live with the aunt, but the father could see them whenever he wanted so long as he gave his sister notice, and the girls did not have something else planned. I left the hearing satisfied and redeemed. This hearing may have had an optimum outcome for all (I say "may" because I do not know what happened thereafter), but I had learned that I had a singular distaste for being an advocate for one party in the midst of an emotional firestorm. It was not for me.

I want to add another note about Professor Boland. Our relationship was close enough that both he and I would have been comfortable with me calling him Paul. Many other students did. I have always resisted informality when my relationship was one based primarily on roles. I had a close friend who would routinely refer to the senior rabbi at our synagogue by his first name, David. He wanted us to think he was personal friends with the rabbi, and that their relationship went far beyond that of rabbi and congregant. I knew they did not have such a friendship, and my friend was using the rabbi's first name only in a futile effort to increase our esteem for him. It did not work. But my objection went beyond the obvious artificiality of it all. I do not want to refer to my senior rabbi by his first name. The norm is to call most people by their given names, but there are very few people I can refer to as rabbi. I want to invite into my life people whom I *can* call rabbi. It is not only a sign of respect, but a recognition of a valuable, unique relationship. For that reason, I have always resisted calling my professors, doctors, judges, cantors, and rabbis by their first names. I have no need to flatten all relationships to a common denominator of familiarity. I want to honor those to whom honor is due and to recognize the different relationships in my life. That is why I called him Professor Boland until he became a Superior Court judge. Then he was Judge Boland. When he was elevated to the Court of Appeal, he became Justice Boland. He was never Paul.

Chapter 46

THE WILHELM WUNDT AFFAIR

Hallie had settled into Occidental College and had moved into an all-girls dormitory. Because it was seventeen miles away from UCLA and a forty-minute drive, we saw each other mostly on weekends. Occidental operated a shuttle bus to take their students to the UCLA library, which made it possible occasionally to see each other during the week, but she rarely took advantage of this to visit me. I would sometimes drive out to visit her during the week in my Chevy, but, since it took a big chunk of time from my schedule, it happened infrequently. Occidental had a strict rule against boys going into the girls' rooms. Boys could visit in the lounge, but were not permitted above the first floor. If caught, the girl student would be given a warning the first time. If caught a second time, it could mean expulsion. Hallie and I routinely flouted the rule, and she showed the skills of a Mossad agent in sneaking me into her room. She did not have a roommate to complain about a boy on the floor (or in the bed). The inevitable happened, and we got caught. She had one demerit against her. That did not deter us. Yes, we were foolish – but we were also young.

One evening, Hallie and I were talking in her dorm room when an alarm went off. There was a bomb alert, and everyone had to leave the dorm. The fire department was downstairs and would be checking each room. We could not take the risk that Hallie might get expelled, so I hid in a closet, behind her clothes. Hallie left, and I tried not to breathe. I could hear hall monitors opening and closing each door. The door to Hallie's room opened, and I heard someone enter. He or she paused just outside the closet door, just standing there, as if they sensed a presence. I started to perspire and noticed that I was starting to breathe through my mouth. Not a good sign. Finally, the person walked out the door and closed it. I could hear them scribble something on a piece of paper on the outside of the door. I kept still. About thirty minutes later I heard the all-clear sign over the PA system, followed by Hallie re-entering the room. I still did not move, concerned that a hall monitor might be in the immediate hallway. Finally, I heard the door close, and Hallie said, "Cary, are you there?" I emerged, feeling as if I had just escaped detection by the Stasi and had successfully made it over the Berlin Wall. I immediately raced down the inside steps, which led directly outside. My visits to the Occidental campus became much less frequent after that.

Occidental College was academically rigorous. Hallie declared a major in psychology, and I tried to help her as much as I could. She was exceedingly smart, but she had two gaps in her education. She never learned grammar and she was allergic to anything approaching science. When she was assigned to write a paper on one of the theories of Wilhelm Wundt, she was far from her comfort zone. Wundt was the father of experimental psychology and worked hard to gain respect for psychology as a science rather than a school of philosophy. He was the first to establish a laboratory for the study of psychology. His work involved a number of concepts, many of them very difficult, indeed beyond the ability of a layman to understand. Hallie had to read several of Wundt's original works, translated from the German, and comment on them. Her first draft was incomprehensible and a grammatical mess. We talked about the topic, and it was clear that she had no idea what Wundt was postulating. In order to help her, I had to read the Wundt papers, the last thing I wanted to do. She pleaded with me for help, and I knew that she needed it desperately.

Instead of being the magnanimous, ever-patient teacher, I became the resentful, hostile persecutor. I read the works, thought I had a vague sense of what they were about, and tried to edit Hallie's draft accordingly. That proved impossible. The paper needed a total rewrite, and I had neither the time nor patience for it. We battled. I would yell at her to read the pieces again, explain them to me, write the paper again, and she would cry with frustration that she had no idea what to do. I yelled some more. If I were going to have to write this damn paper, she was going to have to suffer for it. I am not proud of the way I behaved. The paper was due the next day. We worked through the night and finally finished shortly before the sun came up. I still had a hard time explaining what Wundt was all about, and the paper showed it. She turned it in and received a grade of D-. We would be able to laugh about the Wundt fiasco later, but at the time it was devastating. Both the process, in which I caused her to break down into an hysterical stew, and the product, which showed no understanding of the subject matter, were low points in a relationship that had otherwise been supportive and constructive. Needless to say, there would never be room in our lives for Wilhelm Wundt.

Later that school year, Hallie proceeded with wedding plans. The date was set for August 6, after my graduation and the California Bar exam. The city would be Champaign, where her parents lived. The venue would be the Illini Student Union. Not only was it one of the few appropriate venues, but it was where I accidentally saw Hallie the third time, after she broke up with Jordy. We even decided on a honeymoon spot. We would go to England, Scotland, and Wales, my first trip outside of the U.S., and we would do it on a shoestring, since we really had no money to put into a budget. We would backpack and stay in hostels whenever we could. We even romanticized about sleeping in a tent. I later learned that out of such romance disaster looms.

Chapter 47

KEEP ON MOVING FORWARD

In my final year at UCLA, I signed up for three non-law courses for the sheer fun of it. I took a classroom course in backpacking. The class was not going camping, but we learned about the right equipment, how to use it, and where to go. I became an expert in backpacks (check the welding and joints), hiking shoes (Vibram soles are a must), and quick-fix tents (you can't go wrong with a tube tent). So, while Hallie, her mom, and my mom were making wedding plans, I was thinking about how we were going to be traipsing around London. I also took a course in auto repairs, learning how to change the oil, give a tune-up, and make sure my 1964 Chevy would continue to hum along.

The third course was something out of the blue. Or, literally, into the blue: I took a course in sailing. I cannot fathom why. I had not sailed during the entire time I was in Los Angeles. I had not even stepped foot on a boat. I must have been grasping onto a slim reed attached to the Santa Barbara fantasy I had had when I applied to law school. Our sailing classes were in a boat house in Marina Del Rey, and we actually took turns, with the instructor in tow, sailing. After the training, the big day came. This was when we would be tested to determine if we earned a skipper's certificate. With one other student, I took a small sailboat into the inner bay, where we were observed by the instructor from another boat. We had to demonstrate that we could jib and tack, and, this was very important, turn the boat around. To tack required us to change direction by turning the bow (front) of the boat through the wind. To jib required us to change direction by bringing the stern (rear) of the boat through the wind.

We had no problem going forward. The boat cut through the water with grace and speed. This was a piece of cake. Then the instructor pulled close to us and shouted in a megaphone, "Turnabout." We tried but could not do it. The instructor shouted directions at us, but we simply could not execute the maneuver. We tried everything, the boat lurched and the mainsail started to tip over toward the water. Before we knew it, we had partially capsized, and we were up against the side of the boat with the edge that was on the lip of the water. We had no idea what to do. We were stuck and could not right the boat. My eyeglasses fell into the water and sank. I am sure that there is a fish somewhere in the Pacific Ocean that is swimming with my spectacles perched on its face, giving it a survival advantage over its mates. But I could not see a thing. The other student curled up into a ball with fright. The next thing I recall is a loud alarm, flashing lights, and the Coast Guard coming to our rescue. We got onto the Coast Guard boat and were taken to shore. They went back to secure the sail boat to prevent it from sinking. We later learned that the keel, a long, heavy fin on the bottom of the boat that is supposed to be deep in the water to provide stability and prevent capsizing, was never pushed down. Because the instructor thought himself partially responsible for not ensuring that the keel was in proper position, he gave us our skipper's certificates, which allowed us to rent sail boats and sail them within the marina. But I never used mine, and it was years before I was willing to get back on a sailboat. It was certainly the end, as The Mamas and the Papas would say, to Santa Barbara dreaming.

Chapter 48

DECISION TIME

The start of my last year of law school was decision time. I was in the process of thinking through my job prospects in September 1971, when I got a note from the dean of the law school, Murray Schwartz, telling me that the law school was recommending me to be a law clerk to Justice William Douglas of the U.S. Supreme Court. I went to see the dean. He explained that Justice Douglas hired his clerks exclusively from law schools within the Ninth Judicial Circuit, which included the states of California, Oregon, Nevada, Idaho, Arizona, Washington, Alaska, Hawaii, and Montana. Law schools within those states could nominate one or two students for the clerkship, but the decision would be made by a committee of former clerks who would meet in San Francisco. UCLA School of Law was nominating only me. Was I interested? I was completely taken by surprise. I had no idea that this was how Justice Douglas chose his clerks or even that I would be in the running. And now I was being told by the dean that I was the only one from UCLA being nominated. The law school was still not releasing class ranking, so I had no idea precisely where I was in the class hierarchy. I kept asking myself, "Why was I chosen?" But, of course, I was interested.

The prospect of being a law clerk in D.C. was appealing to both me and Hallie. We agreed that it would be best to live far from either family right after marriage to give us breathing room and space to adapt to married life on our own. There were two types of jobs for lawyers in D.C. One was with law firms and the other was with the government. I had no interest in the private practice of law, so I looked over the recruiting sheet in the placement office, and two caught my eye. One was to work in the Legislative Counsel's Office for the House of Representatives. Their job was to write the legislation that would be proposed in the House. The other was with the Department of Transportation, which fit precisely with my interests in urban government.

The head of the Office of Legislative Counsel came to the law school in early Fall, and I had a pleasant interview. He was tall, thin, and grey. Everything about him was grey – his hair, his complexion, his suit. But most of all, his personality. It was as bland, matter-of-fact, and, yes, grey, as could be. The position seemed interesting, although it was not clear what the career prospects were. Would I serve out my legal career in this Office? I got visons of never seeing the sun. I never received an offer from him, and, in retrospect, I have no regrets.

The Department of Transportation position sounded perfect. The interviewer explained to me that the Department had a new General Counsel, John W. Barnum. He was a former partner at Cravath, Swaine & Moore, the most prestigious white-shoe law firm in the country. Barnum had organized an Honors Attorneys Program, in which six recent law school graduates from around the country would be hired to work at the Department for one year. These new lawyers would spend four months in the General Counsel's Office and then four months in two of the Department's agencies, such as the Federal Aviation Administration, the National Transportation Safety Board, the National Highway Administration, or the Urban Mass Transportation Administrant. D.O.T., as it was called, was housed in a new building in Southeast D.C. Because the Coast Guard was also part of the Department, we would be able to use the Coast Guard's fully-equipped gym and rooftop running track. After one year, the Honors Attorney could pick which agency he wanted to work for, or he could leave D.O.T. for other horizons. For someone toying with the idea of transportation law, this sounded like a job description written just for me. It paid $13,300 per year, an enormous sum of money to me. The Supreme Court clerkship, was my top priority, and I kept the possibility of working at D.O.T. open as my backup plan.

I made arrangements for the Supreme Court clerk interview in San Francisco. It was set for October 1971. Hallie and I drove north in the dependable 1964 Chevy. We stopped at one of the new-age resorts in Big Sur. It was called Esalen. It emphasized encounter groups and alternative ways of expanding one's consciousness. The ultimate goal was to unleash one's personal potential. We stayed one night and were encouraged by tunic-wearing hosts and hostesses to spend part of the night in their magnificent outdoor hot tubs, large enough to accommodate a dozen people. We put on our bathing suits and followed the wooden walkway to one of the tubs, breathing in the sweet ocean air and the scent of the pine trees. Ahead of us was a wooden hot tub with steam rising and about ten men and women caressing the sides with outstretched arms. When we got closer, we saw that they were all naked. Hallie pulled me aside and said that there was no way she was getting into the tub with a bunch of naked strangers, even if she kept her bathing suit on. It was clear that Hallie and I were not going to be able to grow our personal potential on this trip. We nonchalantly walked past the tub and circled back to our room, dry as a bone and clear outliers in this uncomfortably people-friendly place. The experience so unnerved Hallie that I have never been able to get her to return to Big Sur, regardless of which of the many venues I proposed.

The Supreme Court clerk interview itself was at one of the best law firms in San Francisco. I wore, yes, my blue polyester suit, the only one I owned. The interview was in a large conference room with three lawyers who had once clerked for Justice Douglas. One was a practicing lawyer at the law firm, another was a professor of law and the third was dean of a law school. The interview was pleasant enough, but it was also perfunctory. They mentioned there was pressure on the Justice to hire a woman as a law clerk, and they had two clerk positions to fill. I left without a warm feeling, and I was convinced I would not get the position.

But Hallie and I made the most of the trip. We toured San Francisco, and drove to Marin County, just northeast of San Francisco Bay. It was home to some of the richest people in the country. We drove around, had lunch, and then spotted a clothing store. We decided to splurge on matching outfits. We bought identical burgundy sweaters, with turtleneck collars and subtle vertical ribbing. Then we bought complemental pants. I got bell-bottom pants with wide royal-blue and slightly narrower burgundy velour stripes. Hallie bought the same pants, except her burgundy stripes were larger than the royal-blue ones. Together we looked like well-heeled flower children. We stood in front of the mirrors in the store and just laughed. Perhaps if I had worn this outfit to the interview it would have gone better. It would at least have been livelier.

On November 12, 1971, I received a letter stating that I did not get the clerkship. They committee had given both clerkships to women. I never learned why I did not get the position. Was it because they, like me, had no idea of my class ranking? Or was it simply the year of the woman, and I never stood a chance? Was it my well-worn, undistinguished, suit? Was it because of my diffident nature? Or, was it because there were others more qualified?

I learned a great lesson about opportunities from my law school experiences. I now realize that I did not treat several opportunities presented to me with the respect that they and I deserved, going all the way back to high school. At Lane Tech, when I first learned about the honors track, I should have made waves to join that group. Would it have been a blessing or a curse if I had succeeded? I have no way of knowing. Then, in law school, I should have grabbed at the chance to be editor-in-chief of the law review. Not only would I have learned a lot about editing and writing, but also how to manage a staff of bright, ambitious law students, and how to lead. I would have challenged myself and grown in the process. Was my ill-advised decision a blessing or a curse? I will never know. And then there was the Justice Douglas clerkship. I had done the minimum: I went for an interview. In hindsight, I know I should have asked professors to write letters of recommendation, researched each of the three members of the committee to learn more about their interests and accomplishments, and asked if any of the UCLA faculty knew members of the committee. I should have written the committee a convincing letter about myself and why I would be an excellent choice for the clerkship. I should have asked the law school dean about my class ranking. I did none of it. But at least – at last – I had come to realize that I should never turn my back on an opportunity simply because I did not know the paths that would lie ahead. I learned the lesson taught by Andy Rooney, "Opportunities are never lost; someone will take the ones you miss." They always do.

I did not recognize these great opportunities, and so I failed to do everything in my power to make them work for me. There is a story that has always resonated within me about recognizing and seizing opportunities.

Mendel was caught in a flood. Everything around him was underwater. He was standing on the top of his roof, and the water was getting higher. He looked around and saw nothing, but water. He prayed to

God for help. Mendel saw a man in a rowboat. The man said, "Get in. I will save you." "No, thank you," Mendel said, "God will save me." As the water was getting even higher, Mendel saw a man on a raft who said "Get on. I will save you." Again, Mendel declined as he said he had prayed to God, and God would save him. Finally, Mendel looked up and saw a helicopter. The pilot threw down a rope, which landed on top of Mendel. "Grab the rope and I will pull you up," said the pilot. Mendel said "No, it is ok. God is coming." Before he knew it, the water rose above the whole house, and Mendel drowned. When he was before God, Mendel was angry. He said "I had faith in you, I prayed for you to save me, but you did not answer my prayers. Why?" God responded, "I sent you a rowboat, a raft, and a helicopter. What more did you want?"

Some believe this teaches us about how we fail to recognize God's beneficence. Others say it tells us to look at the world anew for there are miracles everywhere. Still others view it as a lesson that God does answer our prayers, albeit not directly. I see it as guiding us toward a basic truth: our lives are blessed with many opportunities, but we often fail to grasp them because we are blind to what is most obvious or we wait for something better, or we are fearful of making a choice, as there are always consequences. Albert Einstein observed that "In the midst of difficulty lies opportunity." Often the most difficult challenge is to realize there is an opportunity to be seized despite our anxieties.

Nevertheless, upon hearing that I did not obtain the clerkship, I immediately contacted the Department of Transportation to let them know that I was still interested in the job. I did not get a response until December 6, and when it came, it made my heart stop. I thought the job was a sure bet. I now learned they wanted me to fly to D.C. for a second interview and at my own expense. I was in the midst of my final exams and wrote them on December 17, 1971, immediately after my last exam. I explained that I did not have the money for a trip to D.C., but I stressed that I really wanted the positon and hoped that my lack of financial resources would not stand in the way. They arranged for a telephonic second interview and afterwards offered me a one-year position in the Honors Attorney Program. I accepted on the spot. We would be off to D.C.

Knowing we would be living in D.C. after the wedding, Hallie checked out schools in the area and was admitted to American University, where she would do her final undergraduate year. We made a bargain. We would stay in D.C. for one year and then return to LA to live. That was a huge concession by her. I agreed that we would not live in the San Fernando Valley, which was not much of a concession by me. Instead, we would live in the city.

This was not only a concession by Hallie, but a compromise with her dream. One consistency in her life was her love and devotion to Israel. She still talked about moving there some day. I was on a different tack than that. I was a US-trained lawyer who spoke no Hebrew and whose entire family was in the States. I had no intention of moving to Israel. I told her so. Hallie accepted this on some level, and would repeat throughout our marriage, "I chose a man over a country." But at the time we were planning our wedding, she had not given up on her dream, and she thought there was a chance that she could have her man and her country. Many women make the mistake of believing they can change a man. While they might be able to get him to pick up his clothes or wash the dishes or change his job, it is foolish for a woman to think she can make fundamental changes in a man's personality or outlook. Those type of changes have to come from him, and they will not happen unless he feels a deep discomfort with the way things are. Douglas Horton said that "change occurs in direct proportion to dissatisfaction, but dissatisfaction never changes." I was not dissatisfied in the least, and I had no reason to change my country, my language, my family, or my way of life.

During my last year of law school, my mom had made a dumb decision. I could have called it "ill-advised" or "unfortunate" or "regrettable," but "dumb" is the right word. She remarried. At the time, my mother was only forty-nine, still recently widowed (three-and-a-half years), attractive, self-supporting, active, and living a full life. Yet she hitched herself to Larry Goldman – a decent guy, but basically a loser. Materially, he had less than she did; intellectually, he could not keep up with her; socially, he was awkward (his one joke was to shake your hand, keep shaking it, and then ask, "are you pumping for milk?"); personality wise, he was dull and grey, and his hygiene left something to be desired. He had an aversion to washing his hair for fear it would fall out. Why did she do it? Companionship? Chauffer? Propinquity? Expense sharing? Substitute for a pet? My mother had a blind spot for men. They divorced seven years later, which meant she wasted many of her prime years with him.

Chapter 49

A SURPRISE AT GRADUATION

Time may be an absolute, especially when measured by a NASA Deep Space Atomic Clock, which is off by only one second in every ten million years. But time is not an absolute when measured by one's perceptions or experiences. Einstein told us that time virtually stops when we approach the speed of light. It is common to talk about time going fast or hardly moving at all. All of us have had the experience of seeing something in slow motion, even though we are not moving. How often do we ask, "Where did the time go?" without thinking of the meaning of the statement. Time hardly existed during the last and final quarter of my third year. I was no sooner starting my commercial transactions class with the famed, extraordinary teacher and communicator Professor William Warren, when I found myself packing up my garage apartment. I began studying for the July Bar exam in May 1972, and found myself inexplicably thinking about a different path.

I started to read a physiology textbook. I was fascinated by the anatomy and discussions of the different systems of the human body and how they interrelated. I poured over descriptions of the circulatory system and how it interacted with the muscular and nervous systems, and the impact of the skeletal system. Suddenly, I had an epiphany. I wanted to be a doctor. Forget that I was about to graduate from law school and that I had a job lined up in D.C. Forget that I was about to get married and would soon have a wife to support. Forget that I had not taken biology, physics, non-organic chemistry, organic chemistry, genetics, or statistics. Forget that I had not taken any lab courses. Forget that I had no practical experience in the health field, such as volunteer work in a hospital or clinic or doctor's office. Forget that it would take me two or three years of additional undergraduate education to complete these requirements. Forget all that. I spent my time finishing up my law course work, studying for the Bar, and reading medical texts.

As I look back on this episode of mini-mania, I see both a blessing and a curse. The blessing was that my immersion into medical texts was symptomatic of my growing thirst for knowledge. I wanted to know so much more than just the law. Toward the end of my third year of law school, I hungered to know more about the functioning of the human body, but I also wanted to delve into history, archeology, paleontology, biblical studies, cosmology, anthropology, the history of cryptology, and to read the finest biographies about the greatest people, to name a few. I did not realize it at the time, but what I really yearned to be was a polymath. Of course, it would have been easier for me to set foot on the moon or run a sub-four minute mile or design the next generation of computers or perform brain surgery than to be a true polymath. I settled for being a life-long learner.

My fledgling interest in medicine masked a painful truth. It was escapism, brought on by anxiety about the future. I was uncertain about everything. I was uncertain about my capabilities, my chances for

Chapter 49: A Surpirse At Graduation

success in the law. My insecurity made me turn momentarily to a new direction, where I would start over with the promise of success unhindered by the reality that I must now perform as a professional. There was comfort in being a student and not having to compete in the bruising world. I thought of being a permanent student, and I even coined a term to describe someone who never wanted to leave the university – a collegalika. My brief flirtation with another career offered me refuge from the stress of being tested where it counted. I would have to fight against taking this kind of easy route for years. One technique I have used is to role-play with myself by imagining a counter-factual future. How would I feel about myself if I abandoned the path I was on and took that alternative route? Would I feel like a quitter or an adventurer? Would it feel forced or right? Would I regret it or be content?

I finished my last year with strong grades, once again. And, as before, the law school did not reveal class rankings. At this point, I knew I was in the top 10 percent of the class because I was informed that I had earned admission to the Order of the Coif, which had a cutoff at the 10 percent mark. The graduation ceremony was at Royce Hall, a beautiful red-brick, stately building with a large auditorium. Three hundred students started in September 1969, and 264 were graduating. Professor Tigar's prediction of a one-in-three dropout rate never happened, but more than thirty-six had left because the 264 included a number of transfer students.

Hallie and my mom were there. My sister and Neal. My Uncle Marty and his wife, Phyllis, attended. I wore my only suit. My one memory of the ceremony is of the dean announcing the awards. He said that the last award was the Alumni Award for the person who finished first in the class. "And the Alumni Award was earned by Cary Lerman." I must have heard it, but I just sat there. It did not penetrate. Hallie nudged me and said, "That's you. Go on up." If the dean had said that Cary Lerman was selected as the next astronaut to go to the moon, I would not have been more unprepared. In a daze, I walked up to the stage to receive the award, a large bronze coin that had a simple inscription: "Cary Bruce Lerman, J.D. Academic Distinction School of Law 1972." I shook the dean's hand and sat down. It was all incomprehensible to me. Afterwards, we gathered in front of Royce Hall to talk about the ceremony. My mother looked at me and said, "Why didn't you tell me you were first in the class?" Why indeed. "I had no idea, that's why."

Of course, I was elated to learn of this distinction, and I soared in a state of disbelief for some time. But on another level I felt cheated. If I had any inkling of my class standing along the way, I would have had a different view of my own abilities. I might have made different choices. Others may have assessed me differently. I could have left the interviews for a 1971 summer job with one of the large law firms and for the Supreme Court clerkship with offers. Was my fate affected by the random decision not to release class rankings until graduation? We speak metaphorically about the pebble thrown into the pond, which produces ever expanding ripples, which, in turn, cause yet other effects. But what if the pebble is not thrown? The consequences can be every bit as real and significant as if it were. It is simply more difficult to appreciate. For want of a nail?

After graduation, Hallie went to Champaign, and I went to Hollywood. She was making final arrangements for the wedding. She and her mother made a trip to D.C. to find us a place to live. She called me from D.C. with great excitement. They had found a World War II garden apartment in a large complex called the Beverly Boulevard Apartments in Chevy Chase, Maryland, just over the D.C. line. It was a one-bedroom on the second floor, overlooking a forest of trees. Total size was about 600 square feet. There was parking right in front on the street, the rent was $114 per month including utilities, and from only a block away there was a bus that would take me to the Department of Transportation. It sounded perfect. Grab it, I said. The combination

Chapter 49: A Surpirse At Graduation

of the low rent and being on the second floor was the sell. The fact that it had no air conditioning never even dawned on me. Of course, I had no idea what summers were like in Washington, D.C.

I went to live in my grandfather's converted garage, where I studied for the July Bar exam. The garage was a perfect place to be cloistered for a month and a half. I took a Bar review class, studied, and then went back to class. That was my routine. When I finished the three-day exam, I packed my bags and loaded the Chevy with everything I would be taking to D.C. As I crossed the deserts again, this time heading east, I set three goals for myself, which I vowed to accomplish before I was thirty. I wanted to be fluent in French, earn a black belt in karate, and complete a marathon. This was a highly ambitious dream since, at the time, I had never taken a single French class (and I was badly handicapped when it came to learning new languages), I had never thrown a single karate punch or kick, and the farthest I had ever run was a 10K. And I had fewer than six years within which to accomplish these mighty challenges. Just like some rules are made to be broken, some goals are made never to be achieved. For some reason, the mere setting of an ambitious goal was exceedingly satisfying, even if I never realized it. I was able to live off the psychic pleasure of dreaming that I would make the dream a reality.

Chapter 50

THE WEDDING

In keeping with the hippie times, traditional white wedding dresses were out. Before she left LA, Hallie and my mom had gone looking for a wedding dress, and Hallie picked out a beautiful, pale canary yellow dress, floor-length with long sleeves and a high collar. She left the dress for alterations. She later got a call from the store that it had been robbed. The robbers had stolen every single wedding dress except for hers. This was a good omen.

I was not going to wear a suit (my dependable polyester suit was not an option) or a tuxedo. I went to a formal attire store in Hollywood, and, when I walked in, I spied the perfect shirt. It was a tuxedo shirt in that it had French cuffs requiring cufflinks and large ruffles in the front. Any resemblance to a traditional dress shirt ended there. It had large, bold flowers, in even bolder colors. It was an effusion of bright-yellow, red, medium-green, lime-green, and blue flowers. I stood no chance of being lost in a crowd with that shirt. I bought it right away. But I needed pants. I went to the Malibu Clothing store in Beverly Hills. I looked through the pants rack, shoving each one along, when a single pair stood out. Boy, did they stand out. They were lime green, and they matched perfectly with a color in the shirt. They were bell bottomed and had square-patched front pockets. Perfect. I could just imagine the look on Ruth Tager's face when she saw it. It would not be what she expected to show off to her friends. But then I imagined the look on my grandfather's face. I chuckled to myself. He would want them for himself, because they were the perfect dance costume. I bought them.

I stayed at Hallie's house when I arrived in Champaign. I admit it was not terribly romantic to be housed with your prospective in-laws and bride-to-be only days before the wedding. But I had nowhere else to stay, and I did not want to pay for a hotel. Ruth asked to see my wedding outfit. I tried it on and proudly walked out of a bedroom in full pulsating tones of color. She was aghast. I don't know if it was the brightly colored shirt of many flowers or the lime-green pants, but something did not sit right with her. Her gasp said everything. Perhaps knowing that there was no way she could talk me out of my hipster outfit, she focused on what was missing. "You are not going to wear a tie? You must have a tie!" she protested. How could I not accommodate such a modest request? I went shopping. I found the perfect tie. It was a large, blue velvet bow tie. It looked like it was made for my festival of colors shirt. It completed the outfit. I am sure it was not what Ruth had in mind, but she could say she had put the finishing touches on my wedding attire.

Hallie and I met with Rabbi Samuel Weingart, a reform rabbi in Champaign. Hallie emphasized that she wanted an egalitarian ceremony, with equal emphasis on the bride and groom. He understood and said that was his preference too. We each had a poem to read to one another. Mine was Sonnet 116 by Shakespeare, which was suggested to me by Ruth. Its core message resonated with me – the vow of marriage is a pledge of love not to allow adversities, which will invariably come, to tear two people apart. It read:

> Let me not to the marriage of true minds
> Admit impediments. Love is not love
> Which alters when it alteration finds,
> Or bends with the remover to remove:
> O no; it is an ever-fixed mark,
> That looks on tempests, and is never shaken;
> It is the star to every wandering bark,
> Whose worth's unknown, although his height be taken.
> Love's not Time's fool, though rosy lips and cheeks
> Within his bending sickle's compass come;
> Love alters not with his brief hours and weeks,
> But bears it out even to the edge of doom.
> If this be error and upon me proved,
> I never writ, nor no man ever loved.

Hallie's was a poem called *Far Off Whistles*, written by her newest crush, Julius Cohen. Jules Cohen and his brother, Saul, were Champaign-Urbana fixtures. They were both elder artistic statesmen, lifelong bachelors, musically gifted, and beloved by the community, which looked after them. Ever since she arrived in Champaign from LA, Hallie had been meeting with Julius at his nineteenth-century Victorian-styled home in Urbana, where they read poetry to one another and held hands. I could hardly protest, as Julius was eighty-four years old. The poem she would read to me was:

> I think no music thrills me through
> As certain far off whistles do,
> What dreams go voyaging the night

> *When steam-loosed beauty takes its flight*
> *O'er bounding meadow, naked plain,*
> *Moon-bathed field of shimmering grain,*
> *Little pools where star beams hide,*
> *Leaping streams and valleys wide,*
> *Silvery lakes and forests deep,*
> *Villages where poets sleep!*
> *I think no music thrills me through*
> *As certain far-off whistles do.*

It was a lovely poem, filled with beautiful images and a poet's romantic yearnings. But what did it have to do with me or our relationship or how Hallie felt about me? Yes, we were going to take a train trip through England, Scotland, and Wales on our honeymoon just after the wedding, but we had never been on a train together before, and had no memories of such trips. But if reading the poem gave solace to a gentle eighty-four-year old poet and pleasure to my bride, who was I to complain?

My mom; Barb and Neal; their baby son, Larry; Marty and Phyllis; and my grandfather and Charlotte arrived from Los Angeles. Family came down to Champaign from Chicago. My close friend, Ben, arrived after going home to Florida. He picked up a girl along the way and asked if he could bring her to the wedding. Ruth was apoplectic at the request because of the additional cost of the luncheon. She said he could bring her but she made him pay. It was yet another example of the grit and determination that guided almost everything Ruth did. She had a point about charging him for bringing, unannounced, a total stranger, but others might have been more gracious about it and absorbed the cost as part of the larger joyous occasion. Ted Neumann drove up from Paris Tennessee. Mike Gruskin, my friend from Praetorians, and his bride, Kathy, drove down from Chicago.

Chapter 50: The Wedding

The wedding ceremony was planned for 11:00 am, with a luncheon to follow. Ruth was adamant that there would be no alcohol. She said it was not needed for an afternoon affair, and, besides, she did not approve of people being tipsy. I think she did not want to spend the money, and she wanted to make sure people were kept under control. My mother was not happy about the abstinence. No joyous celebration was complete without wine and liquor, and a wedding without alcohol was like a flower without fragrance. But Ruth was putting on the show and got her way.

It could only happen in the movies, as they say, except it happened on the day of our wedding. It really did. It was 9:30 am and all was frantic in the Tager house as we were getting ready. The phone rang. Ruth answered it. She quickly hung up. "Who was it," we asked. Ruth said with a mixture of disgust and determination in her voice, "It was Jordy. He asked if he could speak with Hallie. I said, 'No, she is getting married today.' And I hung up." I could not believe it. The first time I saw Hallie she was with Jordy. And the last phone call before my marriage was from Jordy. "Will no one rid me of this turbulent jerk?" I thought. I did not know it then, but that was the last I would ever hear of Jordy.

Prior to the actual ceremony, we had to sign the marriage certificate. We also needed two witnesses. Ben Blakeman signed, using his formal, legal name, Jack Benjamin Blakeman. Kathy Gruskin signed. Under Orthodox Jewish law, women did not qualify to be witnesses. Therefore, one could argue that the marriage ceremony was not compliant with Jewish law. But we did not care. There was much about our wedding that threw tradition to the wind, anyway.

The ceremony was a hot affair in a courtyard in the Union. I mean literally hot. It was August in Champaign, and by 11:00 am, it was eighty-five degrees and humid, very humid. Students looked down on us from windows that bordered the courtyard. Julius' brother, Saul, played the piano as the guests took their seats. Saul was a spry eighty year old. Ruth hired a singer who reportedly had a beautiful voice to sing as we walked down the aisle, "reportedly" because she wanted to save money and did not rent a microphone. No one could hear him. He sang, or was told to sing, the song "If" by David Gates, with the following first verse:

> *If a picture paints a thousand words*
> *Then why can't I paint you?*
> *The words will never show*
> *The you I've come to know*

It was a beautiful song that captured the mystery that attracts one person to another and allows them to make a life-long commitment despite the inability to ever really know one another fully. I only wish I could have heard it.

Bucking tradition, Hallie and I walked out together, hand in hand. In retrospect, with years of life behind me and having hosted weddings for my two daughters, I regret that we denied Hallie's father and my mother the opportunity to walk their children down the aisle. There is a reason for traditions. They add meaning and continuity. They are an affirmation of the value of the past even as we live in the present and are about to embark into the future.

Hallie looked radiant. I could not imagine a more beautiful, glowing bride. She also looked like she was fifteen years old. To this day, Hallie blames me for making her walk too fast down the aisle, depriving her of one "brief, shining moment." She claims it was a gallop, but I maintain it was only a trot. We stood under a Cuppah, the wedding canopy, which was designed by a local artist. It crested with the Star of David formed on top from the intersection of the wooden beams, which could be seen from above, but only student interlopers were looking down.

Chapter 50: The Wedding

I read the sonnet, which Hallie did not understand. She read Julius' poem, which I puzzled over. The rabbi spoke about how woman was created from man's rib, and, therefore, she owed her life to him, and she must honor and obey him. So much for an egalitarian ceremony. Hallie was livid. The ceremony finished, I stomped on the glass, breaking it as tradition required, kissed my wife, and we were married. She was twenty-one, and I was twenty-four.

The luncheon was a tasteful occasion, but several things were missing, in addition to alcohol. Instead of a band, Ruth hired three musicians: a violinist, an accordionist, and a cellist. They were excellent, but rip-roaring simcha music was not their oeuvre. They looked like they were auditioning for the Glenn Miller Orchestra. But my grandfather, not in need of an invitation, exploded onto the dance floor with the moxie of a superstar, confident that the guests were eagerly awaiting his debut. Insofar as my grandfather was concerned, my wedding was but a stage set constructed for him. He and Charlotte dressed in home-made dancing costumes. He wore red pants with a matching red vest, a flowered red shirt, and white shoes. And he made sure his toupee was fitted correctly on his head, which may have been a first for him. He brought his own dance music and played it over a boom box. He even managed a costume change. He shed his red outfit and donned a *Fiddler on the Roof* costume, complete with fake mustache and goatee. He and Charlotte entertained us for at least thirty minutes with several folk dances to great applause. If we were giving an award to the person who enjoyed my wedding the most, it would go to my grandfather. To this day, after my memory of my wife in her resplendent yellow dress and her irresistible, captivating smile, my most vivid recollection is of my grandfather reveling in his dance performance. Liberace, with his irrepressible warmth and verve, never had as much fun as my grandfather. When he passed at the age of eighty-five, my grandfather was on a bus to a senior citizen's center to dance for them. He literally died with his dancing shoes on. And I am sure he had a smile on his face and was twiddling his thumbs as if he did not have a care in the world.

Also missing was the halvah. My father-in-law loved halvah, a favorite of mine. He was convinced – quite correctly – that a Jewish wedding party without halvah was like a chocolate sundae without the chocolate. He had ordered a magnificent halvah cake from Chicago. It never arrived. I missed the halvah but was touched not only that he ordered it, but that he was more upset than I was when it never arrived. I am convinced there must have been a rabbi at some point in history who declared that a Jewish wedding without halvah is null and void.

Hallie and I spent our wedding night at the Lincoln Inn in Urbana, and the next day we went to her house to pack up for our trip to D.C. Hallie and I often joked about different types of marital unions. There are mergers, in which the children of two very wealthy, prominent families combine. There are acquisitions, in which an impecunious spouse acquires a wealthy one. There are reorganizations, in which couples marry a second time in a do-over. There are spin offs, in which the couple decides to separate and go off on their own. My union with Hallie was a start-up, with very little capital but a lot of goodwill. Two days after the wedding, I loaded up my trusty 1964 Chevy, my father's pride, to embark on the next chapter of my life with my new bride. We were bound for the Beverly Boulevard Apartments in Maryland. Any doubts or butterflies I may have had were gone. I was standing behind the open trunk, about to close it, when Hallie's father came up to me. He handed me a generous check, which established our new capital position, although, with my considerable law school loans, we were still technically insolvent. And then, as I was about to embrace the future having made the most momentous decision of my life, he said, with humor in his eyes and a slight smile, "She's your problem now."

Postscript

Our minds do not think in a linear or logical fashion. Thoughts trigger other thoughts, skating across time, weaving in and out, darting in new directions without design or control, and skirting back and forth over horizons defined by non-contiguous years, sometimes only to circle back to the original thought. Often they spin around and out, leaving the initiating idea in a fog. So it is with memory. One memory bleeds into another, begging to be heard or recognized on its own terms, daring us not to let go. "But that memory doesn't belong there," I say, "let me come back to it another time." Sorry, it doesn't work that way. I recall only memory fragments. They unfold organically, without direction or aforethought. They are not defined by time. They may not all be true. They are just as I have written them here. And these memories change. Each time I recall a memory, just like working a piece of clay, it gets reshaped. It is altered or hardened.

This memoir, like any, was a product of memory, however imperfect. If "memory is the glue that binds your life together," as Kevin Horsley said, each time I recalled a memory, my life was glued together just a bit differently than before. As I think back on my early life, were the snippets of memory that pushed to the surface the ones that had the most significant impact on me? Or did they just happen to be associated with an emotional response? Were they reinforced through retelling? Did the stories I chose to tell mean that other experiences, repressed, lost or never recorded, were only transient, insignificant events? Unlikely. After all, these lost moments make up most of my life, and, while I cannot recall them, they undoubtedly had life-altering effects on me. It is trite, but I am the sum of my experiences and reactions to those experiences. So, by setting down those events that I can recall, I by no means imply that they are the only – or even the most significant – influences on my life. Dr. Edith Eger was clearly correct when she wrote that "our childhood memories are often fragments, brief moments or encounters, which together form the scrapbook of our life." But that scrapbook has more blank pages than recollections.

In thinking about the person I am today, I cannot help but seek to uncover which traits of character or personality can be traced back to a specific incident. I seek to find the thread that led inextricably from the event or the insight to make today's me. But I realize it is a fool's errand. It is the stuff of fantasy. The events that have shaped my life are multitudinous and interwoven. I cannot connect an event to a personal characteristic as if there were a simple cause and effect. It is unlike a knitted scarf that was made out of one continuous string of yarn, where it is possible to pull on one end and unravel the whole, revealing where it all began. My life is the weaving together of countless threads, each one reinforcing the other and blending so well together that the individual strands are invisible and the fabric is stronger. And those reinforcing strands make me who I am. There is no one strand, with a beginning and end. Even armed with that truth, I still search for origins.

Kurt Wolff was a German publisher who escaped Nazi Germany and eventually found his way to the U.S., where he founded Pantheon Books. When asked why he never published his own memoir, he responded,

"What one can write is not interesting, and what is interesting one cannot write." My effort should be judged with Wolff's observation in mind. If, in retelling moments that floated to the surface, I was not as judgmental or harsh on myself as I should have been, or as others who were part of that moment might have been, it is because no person is a villain in the retelling of their own life story. I may not be a hero, but my psyche is too well defended with my personal carapace for me to be a knave.

As I have revisited the key moments in my early life while writing this memoir, I could not help but struggle with the concepts of fate and destiny. Are we able to convert a curse into a blessing, or do the cosmic forces prevent us from mismanaging a blessing so as to morph it into a curse? The Jewish tradition is firmly rooted in the primacy of free will, a deeply-rooted concept. Baruch Spinoza was excommunicated by the Amsterdam Jewish community in 1656 for a number of heresies, but one of them was his denial of free will to make choices. The Jewish tradition frowns upon the Calvinist notion of pre-determinism. We can change our fate, and our lives are a constant struggle between our best and worst inclinations. We are in control of the decisions we make and the actions we take. Our prayers on the High Holidays become more fervent as the gates of Yom Kippur are about to close, for we know we have a limited time to change our fate for the next year. But we can, through our prayers and deeds, alter what would be our fate. Or so we would like to think.

Yet, we have Jewish folktales like this one, as told by Story Arts, Inc., which was later recast by W. Somerset Maugham in "The Appointment in Samarra:"

King Solomon's servant came breathlessly into the court, "Please! Let me borrow your fastest horse!" he said to the King. "I must be in a town ten miles south of here by nightfall!"

"Why?" asked King Solomon.

"Because," said his shuddering servant, "I just met Death in the garden! Death looked me in the face! I know for certain I'm to be taken and I don't want to be around when Death comes to claim me!"

"Very well," said King Solomon. "My fastest horse has hooves like wings. TAKE HIM." Then Solomon walked into the garden. He saw Death sitting there with a perplexed look on its face. "What's wrong?" asked King Solomon.

Death replied, "Tonight I'm supposed to claim the life of your servant whom I just now saw in your garden. But I'm supposed to claim him in a town ten miles south of here! Unless he had a horse with hooves like wings, I don't see how he could get there by nightfall . . ."

Was the poet Paul Eluard right when he said, "There is no such thing as chance, there is only destiny?" Or was Rebecca Newberger Goldstein closer to the truth when she wrote, "Our most powerful scientific theories – evolution in the biological sciences, quantum mechanics in the physical sciences – enshrine chance and contingency at their most fundamental explanatory levels. And when it comes to our accounts of human behavior – history, psychology, economics – then there is even less appearance of deterministic necessity." Destiny or free choice? Is it Albert Einstein's God who "does not play dice with the universe" or Max Born, the father of quantum mechanics, who believed that, "All is rushing about and vibrating in a wild dance," and everything is an unpredictable cosmic chance? Or is it neither destiny nor chance, with chance affected by a modicum of free choice? Is it something else?

Should I view it all another way? Perhaps Proverb 16:9 reveals the truth: "A man's heart makes plans, and God establishes their steps." This proverb became a Yiddish saying: "Man plans but God laughs." Was I destined to meet, marry and build a life with Hallie? Did God give me multiple ways to fall in line with His plan? Did He send me many ways to escape a flood as I stood on a roof? I seriously considered going to Israel in the summer of 1968. I now know that Hallie was there for the most eventful summer of her life. If I had gone that summer, would that have been when I first met her? Did God give me that chance, but I rebuffed Him? Then, in November 1968, did He give me another opportunity by dragging me to a lecture on a topic in which I had no interest? But did I foil that intention when I shrank from introducing myself to her in the auditorium? It is possible that God had a good laugh and was not done with me yet? Did He give me yet another chance when He made sure that I would drop off my car at Sears on December 3, 1968, and then rushed me along so that I would be standing outside that bookstore at just the right time? Did Hallie's decision to stay with Jordy temporarily set back the divine plan, only to have God try one last time when He made sure I would see her two months later in the Student Union? In enacting my role in this play of life, I may have given God a really good laugh. And now, almost fifty years after the events recorded in this memoir, I, a man "of no eccentric whim," still dream that someday I will have my Victorian gentleman's library. I think I hear God laughing again.